The Ethical Underpinnings of Climate Economics

Despite their obvious importance, the ethical implications of climate change are often neglected in economic evaluations of mitigation and adaptation policies. Economic climate models provide estimates of the value of mitigation benefits, provide understanding of the costs of reducing emissions, and develop tools for making policy choices under uncertainty. They have thus offered theoretical and empirical instruments for the design and implementation of a range of climate policies, but the ethical assumptions included in the calculations are usually left unarticulated.

This book, which brings together scholars from both economics and ethical theory, explores the interrelation between climate ethics and economics. Examining a wide range of topics including sustainability, conceptions of value, risk management and the monetization of harm, the book will explore the ethical limitations of economic analysis but will not assume that economic theory cannot accommodate the concerns raised. The aim in part is to identify ethical shortcomings of economic analysis and to propose solutions. Given the on-going role of economics in government thinking on mitigation, a constructive approach is vital if we are to deal adequately with climate change.

This volume will be of great interest to students and scholars of environmental ethics, economics, political science, political philosophy and the philosophy of economics.

Adrian Walsh is an Associate Professor at the School of Humanities, University of New England, Australia.

Säde Hormio is a PhD candidate and researcher in the *Climate Ethics and Economics* project at the Department of Political and Economic Studies, University of Helsinki.

Duncan Purves is a Faculty Fellow and Assistant Professor of Bioethics and Environmental Studies at New York University, USA.

Routledge Advances in Climate Change Research

International Climate Change Law and State Compliance
Alexander Zahar

Climate Change Adaptation and Food Supply Chain Management
Edited by Ari Paloviita and Marja Järvelä

Community Governance and Citizen-Driven Initiatives in Climate Change Mitigation
Edited by Jens Hoff and Quentin Gausset

The Two Degrees Dangerous Limit for Climate Change
Public understanding and decision making
Christopher Shaw

Ageing, Well-being and Climate Change in the Arctic
An interdisciplinary analysis
Edited by Päivi Naskali, Marjaana Seppänen, Shahnaj Begum

China Confronts Climate Change
A bottom-up perspective
Peter H. Koehn

Community Action and Climate Change
Jennifer Kent

Reimagining Climate Change
Edited by Paul Wapner and Hilal Elver

Climate Change and the Anthropos
Planet, people and places
Linda Connor

Systemic Crises of Global Climate Change
Intersections of race, class and gender
Edited by Phoebe Godfrey and Denise Torres

Urban Poverty and Climate Change
Life in the slums of Asia, Africa and Latin America
Edited by Manoj Roy, Sally Cawood, Michaela Hordijk and David Hulme

Strategies for Rapid Climate Mitigation
Wartime mobilisation as a model for action?
Laurence L. Delina

Ethical Underpinnings of Climate Economics
Edited by Adrian Walsh, Säde Hormio and Duncan Purves

The Ethical Underpinnings of Climate Economics

Edited by Adrian Walsh, Säde Hormio and Duncan Purves

LONDON AND NEW YORK

from Routledge

First published 2017
by Routledge

2 Park Square, Milton Park, Abingdon, Oxfordshire OX14 4RN
711 Third Avenue, New York, NY 10017

Routledge is an imprint of the Taylor & Francis Group, an informa business

First issued in paperback 2018

British Library Cataloguing-in-Publication Data
A catalogue record for this book is available from the British Library

Library of Congress Cataloging-in-Publication Data
Names: Walsh, Adrian J., editor. | Hormio, Sèade, editor. | Purves, Duncan, editor.
Title: The ethical underpinnings of climate economics / edited by Adrian Walsh, Sèade Hormio and Duncan Purves.
Description: Abingdon, Oxon ; Nwe York, NY : Routledge, [2017] |
Series: Routledge advances in climate change research
Identifiers: LCCN 2016016281 | ISBN 9781138122963 (hb) |
ISBN 9781315649153 (ebook)
Subjects: LCSH: Climatic changes–Social aspects. | Carbon offsetting. |
Emissions trading.
Classification: LCC QC903 .E835 2017 | DDC 174/.4–dc23
LC record available at https://lccn.loc.gov/2016016281

ISBN: 978-1-138-12296-3 (hbk)
ISBN: 978-0-367-02683-7 (pbk)

Typeset in Goudy
by Wearset Ltd, Boldon, Tyne and Wear

Contents

Notes on contributors vii
Preface x
Acknowledgements xi

1 **Introduction** 1
ADRIAN WALSH, SÄDE HORMIO AND DUNCAN PURVES

2 **Do not ask for morality** 9
JOHN BROOME

3 **The ethics of discounting: an introduction** 22
MARC D. DAVIDSON

4 **Climate change, intergenerational equity, and the social discount rate** 41
SIMON CANEY

5 **When utility maximization is not enough: intergenerational sufficientarianism and the economics of climate change** 65
SIMO KYLLÖNEN AND ALESSANDRA BASSO

6 **A new defence of probability discounting** 87
KIAN MINTZ-WOO

7 **Climate change mitigation, sustainability and non-substitutability** 103
SÄDE HORMIO

8 **Dimensions of climate disadvantage** 122
JOHN O'NEILL

9 **Moral asymmetries in economic evaluations of climate change: the challenge of assessing diverse effects** 141
BLAKE B. FRANCIS

10 **The ethical failures of climate economics** 162
CLIVE L. SPASH AND CLEMENS GATTRINGER

11 **A Lockean approach to greenhouse gas emission rights** 183
HANS-PETER WEIKARD

12 **Climate change policy, economic analysis and price-independent conceptions of ultimate value** 198
ADRIAN WALSH

Index 219

Contributors

Alessandra Basso is a PhD student at the Academy of Finland Centre of Excellence in the Philosophy of the Social Sciences. Her research focuses on the philosophy of measurement and the philosophy of the social sciences, in particular of economics.

John Broome is Emeritus White's Professor of the University of Oxford, Visiting Professor of Philosophy at Stanford University and Adjunct Professor of the Australian National University. He holds a PhD in economics. Until 1995 he was employed as an economist first at Birkbeck College, London, and then at Bristol University. Since that time he has worked in philosophy, first at St Andrews and then at Oxford. His present interests are in normativity, rational and reasoning, and also in the ethics of climate change. His most recent books are *Climate Matters: Ethics in a Warming World* and *Rationality Through Reasoning*. He was a lead author for the Fifth Assessment Report of the Intergovernmental Panel on Climate Change.

Simon Caney is Professor in Political Theory at the University of Oxford and Fellow and Tutor at Magdalen College. He works on issues in contemporary political philosophy, and focuses in particular on issues of environmental, global and intergenerational justice. Recent articles have appeared in *Philosophy & Public Affairs*, *Social Philosophy and Policy* and *Journal of Political Philosophy*. He is completing two books – *Global Justice and Climate Change* (with Derek Bell) and *On Cosmopolitanism* – both of which are under contract with Oxford University Press. He is the author of *Justice Beyond Borders* (Oxford University Press, 2005).

Marc D. Davidson holds an endowed professorship in the philosophy of sustainable development from a humanistic perspective at Maastricht University. He is also a researcher and lecturer in environmental ethics and economics at the University of Amsterdam (UvA).

Blake B. Francis is a PhD Candidate in the philosophy department at Stanford University. He received his MA in Philosophy from the University of Montana. His research interests include political philosophy, ethics and environmental ethics. He is currently working on his dissertation, "Climate change and the moral significance of harm".

Clemens Gattringer studied economics and is currently completing the master program "Socio-Ecological Economics and Policy" at Vienna University of Economics and Business. He has worked on governance of social sustainability aspects in global supply chains as a research assistant at the University of St. Gallen. Currently he is writing his master's thesis on an interdisciplinary approach to conceptualize marine plastic pollution.

Säde Hormio is a researcher in the Climate Ethics and Economics project at the University of Helsinki. She is finalising her PhD on climate ethics in the Social and Moral Philosophy discipline in the Department of Political and Economic Studies.

Simo Kyllönen is a PhD candidate in Social and Moral Philosophy, at the University of Helsinki. He has published on environmental political philosophy, intergenerational justice and climate change.

Kian Mintz-Woo is a doctoral student in an interdisciplinary climate project at the University of Graz. He previously read ethics for the BPhil. In climate ethics, his focus is on intergenerational distribution, especially methodological issues of discounting and cost-benefit analyses. His doctoral thesis defends the role of economic experts in determining the parameters relevant to intergenerational distribution. This research touches on issues in philosophy of science (economic and normative expertise), metaethics (decision-making under normative uncertainty) and climate economics (discount rates).

John O'Neill is Hallsworth Professor of Political Economy at Manchester University and Director of the Political Economy Institute. He has written widely on philosophy, political economy and environmental policy. His books include *Markets, Deliberation and Environment* (Routledge, 2007), *The Market: Ethics, Knowledge and Politics* (Routledge, 1998) and *Ecology, Policy and Politics: Human Well-Being and the Natural World* (Routledge, 1993). He is co-author of *Environmental Values* (Routledge, 2008) with Alan Holland and Andrew Light. He has co-authored a number of reports on environmental valuation and on climate change and justice.

Professor Clive L. Spash is an economist, who researches, writes and teaches on public policy with an emphasis on economic and environmental interactions. Over 30 years he has worked on a range of subjects, including the ethics of human induced climate change, plural values related to biodiversity, interdisciplinary research on human behaviour and the transformation of the world political economy to a more socially and environmentally just system. Currently he holds the Chair of Public Policy and Governance at the Institute for Multi-Level Governance and Development at Vienna University of Economics and Business.

Adrian Walsh is an Associate Professor in Philosophy at the University of New England (Australia) and a Research Fellow at TINT at the University of Helsinki. He works mainly in political philosophy and the philosophy of economics. He is currently working on a book on water and distributive justice.

Hans-Peter Weikard has studied agriculture, economics and philosophy in Göttingen, Germany. Currently he is Associate Professor in Natural Resource Economics at Wageningen University, Netherlands. His main areas of study are international environmental agreements and the distribution of scare resources with the tools of game theory and social choice theory.

Preface

This book was born out of two interdisciplinary seminars held in 2014. The first one was the Climate Ethics and Climate Economics workshop in April adjoined as part of the European Consortium for Political Research (ECPR) Joint Sessions 2014 in Salamanca. Spurred on by the invigorating discussions, the participants decided to put together more workshops, with Ethical Underpinnings of Climate Economics following in Helsinki in November that same year. Without the organisers of these workshops the collaborators of this book would not have come together: Matthew Rendall (University of Nottingham), Dominic Roser (University of Oxford), Säde Hormio (University of Helsinki), Simo Kyllönen (University of Helsinki), Aaron Maltais (Stockholm University) and Joanna Burch-Brown (University of Bristol). We would also like to thank all the participants at the workshops for making them so enjoyable and worthwhile.

The Helsinki workshop that this book was named after was organized as part of the Climate Ethics and Economics project, led by Aki Lehtinen and funded by the University of Helsinki. The three-year project (2014–2016) is based at the Social and Moral Philosophy discipline in the Department of Political and Economic Studies. The workshop itself was made possible by funding from the Academy of Finland Centre of Excellence in the Philosophy of the Social Sciences, which also helped to host the event.

We would also like to thank the following people for their help in preparing the manuscript: Margaret Farrelly from Routledge and John Davies.

Last – but by no means least – the editors would like to thank all the contributors to this volume for their time in not only writing their chapters, but also providing each other useful comments and feedback along the way.

Acknowledgements

We would like to thank the journal *Politics, Philosophy and Economics* for granting permission to republish Simon Caney's article "Climate Change, Intergenerational Equity, and the Social Discount Rate".

1 Introduction

Adrian Walsh, Säde Hormio and Duncan Purves

Climate change is one of the most crucial problems facing the global community at the present time. Climate change will affect not only the well-being of future generations but the prospects of those who are currently alive. At the time of writing this introduction (March 2016), news outlets across the world were reporting that global temperatures for February of this year showed an unprecedented upward spike.[1] According to NASA data, it was 1.35°C warmer than the average February during the baseline period of 1950–1981. Even more disturbingly, this is the biggest temperature anomaly since records began in 1880. At the same time, Arctic sea-ice cover recorded its lowest ever February value. Many commentators in those reports spoke understandably of a climate emergency at our very doorstep. These alarming statistics illustrate the rapid changes occurring across the globe and demonstrate the urgency of the climate challenges that confront us.

In responding to climate change and in formulating climate policy, economic analysis and economic solutions will undoubtedly be two of the key tools employed by policymakers. They will be central to the solutions that governments and other relevant institutional agencies develop to the challenge of climate change. Indeed climate economics has been at the heart of much of the recent policy debate. One need only think of the impact in contemporary debates over climate change of Nicholas Stern's 2006 report, *The Stern Review of the Economics of Climate Change* to realise the influence of economic theory and economic analysis on public policy.[2] Equally William Nordhaus's work in books such as *A Question of Balance* and *The Climate Casino* have had a tremendous influence on public debates over climate change.[3] Economic analysis will undoubtedly be at the heart of government assessments of how best to deal with these problems. As John Broome notes in *Climate Matters*:

> the advice of economists is already deeply embedded in the political processes surrounding climate change, and economic system it has created. The governments of the world have put in place a framework for responding to climate change founded on economic principles. The moral problems of climate change arise within the context set by this framework. You need to understand it if you are to bring your moral thinking to bear accurately upon climate change.[4]

But is economics itself up to the challenge? Is economics as it is currently practised "up to the task" of responding to the ethical and practical problems raised by climate change?

In considering the suitability of the economic framework for responding to climate change, we need, amongst other things, to reflect upon the aims or goals of our responses to climate change. What is the goal of climate policy? Presumably one aim is to foster and maintain decent levels of well-being across the globe, which is an aim that is fundamentally ethical and normative in nature. There are a range of specific ethical concerns that arise once we focus on the goal of human flourishing, including, for instance, the nature of the obligations we have to future generations or how the costs of mitigation and adaptation should be spread across societies and across nations.[5] But one might well wonder whether there are methodological or structural features of economic theory as it is currently understood which stand in the way of realising the kinds of outcomes required by ethics. If there are such obstacles how might they best be overcome? To take but one example – and this is an example which is discussed at length at a number of points in this book – orthodox economic theory employs a social discount rate which prioritises present wants or well-being over future ones. One influential justification for such discounting is the assumption (held by many economists) that as the standard of living improves future generations will be better off than present ones. Accordingly, we should give greater weight to the wants and needs of those who are living now. However, the assumption that future generations will be better off than the present generation is hardly uncontroversial. What if the emission of carbon creates a context in which future generations are, all things considered, worse off than present ones? Are we justified in discounting future needs over present ones if we find ourselves in a situation where our choices makes the lives of future generations far worse than they would otherwise have been? If we regard the wants and needs of future generations as significant – and surely we should – then we need a social discount rate that recognises the possible harms being done by present generations to our distant (and not so distant) descendants. This is but one instance where the relevance of ethical considerations to the basic theoretical assumptions of climate economics should be clear; and there are many other such cases. Climate change with its potential for damage to human productive activity – and the need it might well create for us to change how we live, consume and produce – renders questionable many of the assumptions underpinning economic theory.

In this book we explore the ethical underpinnings of climate economics as part of a larger and more long-term project of ensuring that economic theory is capable of meeting the challenges associated with climate change. More modestly, this book begins to outline the conditions under which the discipline of economics is capable of playing a positive and significant role in the response to climate change. There are good reasons for doing so. The first of these is simply a matter of realpolitik. The political reality is that economic theory and economic analysis will continue to be highly influential in government decision-making for the foreseeable future. The marked influence of economics on government policy is unlikely to change. Given that fact we need to ensure that the economic analysis, as employed by policymakers, is able both to recognise and to accommodate the moral demands that an adequate response to climate change must address. Second, as a number of authors in this volume note, economics has much to offer in terms of our understanding of the nature of the problems that face us and in terms of how best to respond. Questions of economic efficiency for instance are vital in determining the correct course of action when faced with a range of possible paths in the use of social resources. Equally, economic solutions to coordination problems have often been highly successful when employed in a range of social situations. As John Broome notes economic theory "provides essential tools" for thinking about how to respond to climate change.[6] Thus, over and above the practical point that economics will continue to be a leading source of policy advice, and hence that it needs to be shaped to fit the contours of the current climate problem, there are positive reasons for endorsing its use in climate policy.

This volume, then, is focused on how we might best develop climate economics so as to deal with the ethical challenges of climate change. It is not an exercise in foundational critique in which philosophers attempt to establish the fundamental mistakes of climate economics (although some of the essays are quite damning). Nor should it be thought of as an attempt by economists to demonstrate that the ethical questions raised by moral philosophers are either irrelevant to the issues under examination or can be accommodated by economic theory without the need for any changes whatsoever to their basic assumptions and methodologies. Clearly, there are important and daunting ethical challenges that the emergence of significant threats to our climate raises for economic theory in general. In order to deal with those, economists need to think more carefully about the ethical underpinnings of their discipline. Thus this volume – which grew out of an interdisciplinary workshops attended by both philosophers and economists – represents amongst other things a call for greater dialogue between philosophers and economists to ensure that the climate economics we do in fact use is "fit for purpose".

With these preliminary remarks in mind, let us now consider briefly the contents of each of the chapters of this book.

John Broome's starting position in Chapter 2, "Do not ask for morality", is that we cannot solve climate change simply by appealing to the morality of individuals, as the economic infrastructure itself needs to change and that requires social cooperation on a large scale. He argues that the slow progress of climate negotiations has shown that neither can we rely on nations' moral motivation to respond adequately with the urgency required. Rather than making moral appeals in vain, he advocates from a realpolitik point of view that we should instead concentrate on a different message: no sacrifice is necessary to solve the problem. According to Broome, no generation needs to sacrifice its own interest, and climate change can be brought under control without a sacrifice in consumption. The key to changing the inefficient current situation is to shift from conventional investments towards reducing emissions. This does not solve the maldistribution of well-being, but that is a separate problem that needs a moral response. The investments necessary for building solar or wind farms, or insulating buildings, will be compensated by the current generation reducing the amount of resources bequeathed to future generations. Broome writes that financing this operation will require an increase in public debt, and the world's financial system needs to be strengthened to make this possible. He thus ends his chapter by calling for the creation of a World Climate Bank.

Marc D. Davidson, in Chapter 3, "The ethics of discounting: an introduction", offers an accessible and comprehensive introduction to the discounting debate. He begins by explaining Ramsey's model of economic growth, as it is vital to understanding the central disagreements in ethics and economics over discounting the future. While many of the disputes (such as whether the discount rate should be based on preferences revealed by markets or on moral principles) predate climate ethics, the literary review shows how climate change has made these debates more urgent. Davidson explains why the choice of discount rate is not simply a matter of efficiency or consumer sovereignty, and illustrates how different moral theories lead to different discount rates. He argues that there are two widely held moral intuitions that are usually in conflict: we ought to reduce the long-term risks of climate change faced by future generations, yet we have no duty to increase our general savings rate across the board. Deontological approaches are capable of reconciling these, but are mostly foreign to the framework of standard welfare economics, unlike consequentialism and welfarism. Davidson concludes that while all these theories concentrate on our duties, more research into our intergenerational preferences and how the prospects of future generations affect our well-being would be timely.

Simon Caney discusses our obligations to future generations. His Chapter 4, "Climate change, intergenerational equity, and social discount rate" considers three kinds of considerations that have been put forward to guide the types of action that one generation should take if it is to treat both current and future people equitably. In particular it examines the implications of pure time discounting, growth discounting and opportunity cost discounting for climate policy. He argues that pure time discounting gives us no reason to delay aggressive mitigation policies, while the other two give little or no reason for the same. Caney also critically engages with Broome's argument that some of the costs of mitigation could be passed on to future generations, looking at it from the viewpoint of intergenerational prioritarianism, egalitarianism and sufficientarianism. While he agrees that Broome's argument is defensible, there are two major caveats: the assumption of continuous economic growth, and the possible limits of being able to pass some of the costs of mitigation to future generations.

Simo Kyllönen and Alessandra Basso, in Chapter 5, "When utility maximization is not enough: sufficientarianism and the economics of climate change", examine a range of problems that the evaluation of climate policies raises for standard economic methods of evaluation. In response a number of writers have suggested that the economics of climate change must go beyond the narrow utilitarian view which underlies standard economic modeling. Kyllönen and Basso explore the possibilities that a "sufficientarian" approach to intergenerational justice – which has become increasingly popular amongst climate ethicists – provides for doing so. They argue that sufficientarianism has many advantages over utilitarianism and prioritarianism in dealing with the specific intergenerational issues related to climate change. Kyllönen and Basso note the increasing willingness of environmental and climate economists to re-examine the central assumptions of economic evaluation in sufficientarian ways. After exploring some of the limitations of standard economic theory in dealing with distributional issues, they argue that devising an economic evaluation of climate policies based on sufficientarian ethical principles provides a plausible way of dealing with distributional issues in general, but also particular questions of intergenerational justice and climate change.

In Chapter 6, "A new defence of probability discounting", Kian Mintz-Woo offers a novel argument for the standard economic practice of discounting value on the basis of probability. Probability discounting (or probability weighting) in decision-making is multiplying the value of an outcome by one's subjective probability that the outcome will occur. The chapter defends probability discounting both negatively, from arguments by Simon Caney, and with a new positive argument. The argument is that, given that we can limit our deliberation and consideration to that which we are morally responsible for and that our moral responsibility for outcomes is limited by our subjective probabilities, our subjective probabilities provide a sound moral basis for probability discounting.

Säde Hormio's Chapter 7, "Climate change mitigation, sustainability and non-substitutability", explores the ethical issues around substitutability and its relevance to discounting practices in climate economics. Substitutability is about some form of capital being a substitute for another, so that consumption of one can be compensated with additional stocks of the other. Discounting implicitly makes the assumption that natural capital is always substitutable with man-made capital, but this is questionable, especially when it comes to life-supporting critical natural capital, some of which climate change puts under jeopardy. Hormio writes that it is a given that future generations need to be taken into account when discussing climate change policy options as cumulative emissions continue to warm our planet over millennia. Future populations will bear the environmental cost of current emissions, while the generations alive today will make decisions on their behalf over whether to invest into mitigation or direct resources to consumption, be it anything from material wealth to education. She argues that even though empirical data about the preferences of future generations is impossible to obtain, a compelling case can be made for substantial investments into mitigation on intergenerational justice grounds alone.

John O'Neill, in Chapter 8, "Dimensions of climate disadvantage", explores issues of climate justice and, in particular, the ways in which some individuals and communities will be more disadvantaged by climate change than others. In doing so he draws on a distinct set of debates in economics and ethics about well-being, inequality and disadvantage, engaging in particular with the "capabilities" approach to well-being. Most academic and policy debates surrounding the harmful impacts of climate change have, for good reasons, focused on international and intergenerational effects of climate change. However, O'Neill argues that discussions of climate injustice must also pay attention to the fact that these negative impacts will be differentially spread within societies. He develops a multi-dimensional approach to climate disadvantage, both about the dimensions of well-being that are threatened by climate change and the personal, environmental and social factors that determine how vulnerable different groups are to those threats. While extreme weather events such as floods and droughts will generally increase in frequency and intensity with climate change, how badly individuals and communities will be disadvantaged by these events will be affected by both their exposure to them and their prior vulnerabilities. Distributions of exposure and vulnerabilities mean that climate change will disproportionally harm those from already disadvantaged groups.

In Chapter 9, "Moral asymmetries in economic evaluations of climate change: the challenge of assessing diverse effects", Blake Francis considers the moral difficulties posed by comparing "diverse effects" of a climate policy. When assessing climate change policy, decision makers face the challenge of comparing diverse effects – comparing potential gains in agricultural productivity, biodiversity and sea level stability from mitigation policy against the risk of higher energy/transportation prices, lost employment opportunities and reduced competition in certain markets. Economic methods present a solution, but are criticised for their "aggregative character". The chapter offers an alternative diagnosis of economic methods based on the differences or "asymmetries" in the moral significance of harms and benefits. It argues that while some economic methods fail to accommodate harm/benefit asymmetry, it is possible to design aggregation methods to be more morally sensitive.

In "The ethical failures of climate economics", Chapter 10, Clive Spash and Clemens Gattringer cast doubt on the prevailing view that economics is a mere positive science, devoid of any moral assumptions. The chapter proceeds by surveying various moral assumptions made by climate economists and then demonstrating that these assumptions are at least controversial, if not implausible. Among the issues discussed are intergenerational ethics, and how future generations are included into economic models, with a debate centred on choosing the appropriate discount rate; interregional justice and equity in mitigation and the urgency attributed to impacts; the current international presumption that development is the same as economic growth; incommensurability in the context of compensation and the distinction between basic maintenance of living standards and liability for harm; and, finally, the way in which conceptualizing uncertainty as risk in economics encourages a narrow consequentialist approach to climate management.

In Chapter 11, "A Lockean approach to greenhouse gas emissions", Hans-Peter Weikard explores the question of what the proper basis of the distribution of emission rights might be. He suggests that the Lockean theory of property rights can assist in the establishment of principles upon which such emission rights can be based. Weikard suggests that in the recent literature on climate justice in general – and more specifically the question of greenhouse gas emissions – the Lockean perspective has been overlooked. Property rights are, of course, central to many solutions proposed by climate economists; however, those arguments typically justify property rights in utilitarian rather than in Lockean terms. The main argument of this chapter is based upon Locke's Second Proviso which claims that private appropriation of goods can be justified if "enough and as good" is left for others. The chapter uses the case of greenhouse gas emissions to develop a Lockean theory of just appropriation that incorporates efficiency considerations and introduces elements of welfarism into a natural rights view. The chapter is thus focused on both the development of ideas in political theory and questions the ethics of climate economics.

Adrian Walsh's Chapter 12, "Climate change policy, economic analysis and price-independent conceptions of ultimate value", which begins with a detailed examination of debates within economics of the "paradox of value", ultimately explores the question of what role economics should play in climate policy. Walsh suggests that the paradox of value raises two important issues. First, its treatment of the history of economics explains, at least partially, why many economists are reluctant to endorse price-independent conceptions of value. Second, it provides a model of a form of reasoning that is required if we are to deal adequately with climate change. Walsh argues that attempts within economics to avoid such normativity fail. The chapter then is part of a more general concern with the role of economics within our all things considered climate policy and, more specifically, with ensuring that economics is not regarded as the *sole* determinant of such policy.

It must be noted that the topics discussed herein do not in any sense exhaust the ethical issues that need addressing. Take for example the fact that the present mal-distribution of resources across the globe is being exacerbated by climate change. How, then, do we factor equity into economic evaluations of the socially optimal course of action? These are difficult questions, all the more so because climate change itself is so intertwined in existing inequalities in consumption and power. It is therefore no surprise that incalculable hours have been spent negotiating over which countries should pay for mitigation and adaptation efforts and how many resources should be directed to these efforts. A related question is, how should the distribution of mitigation and adaptation costs between generations be accomplished?[7] Another important issue concerns how economists value life. Typically economics – and climate economics – is taken to assume a preference satisfaction view of well-being, reflected by willingness to pay, but is this view correct? Relatedly, how can the real value of non-market participants such as non-human entities be captured by economic metrics?

This volume is ultimately about the role of economic evaluation in policy-making – with the central concern being how economic theory might best serve the political process involved in responding adequately to climate change.

In order to do so, policymakers need to be made aware of the ethical assumptions built into economic theory, and so economists (and philosophers) should attempt to make these transparent. None of these dilemmas will be solved adequately without considerable interdisciplinary discussion between moral theorists and climate economists. It is the hope of the editors that this volume, in its own modest way, has a role to play in facilitating such a discussion.

All of the chapters, then, are focused on the relationship between climate economics and ethics. It is the sincere hope of the editors that the book will help foster dialogue between philosophers and economists about the aims and methods of climate policy and in this small way contribute positively to the search for solutions to the challenge of climate change.

March 2016

Notes

1 See, for instance, www.smh.com.au/environment/climate-change/spike-in-global-temperature-fuels-climate-change-fears-20160317-gnl7do.html.

2 Nicholas Stern, 2007, *The Economics of Climate Change: The Stern Review*, Cambridge University Press, Cambridge.

3 Nordhaus, 2008, A *Question of Balance: Economic Modeling of Global Warming*, New Haven: Yale Press and W.D. Nordhaus, 2013, *The Climate Casino: Risk, Uncertainty, and Economics for a Warming World*, New Haven, Yale.

4 John Broome, 2012, *Climate Matters: Ethics in a Warming World*, W. H. Norton, New York, 36.

5 For an excellent overview of the ethical issues raised by climate change see Stephen M. Gardiner *et al.* (eds), 2010, *Climate Ethics: Essential Readings*, Oxford University Press, Oxford.

6 John Broome, 2012, *Climate Matters: Ethics in a Warming World*, W.H. Norton, New York, 36.

7 One suggestion that has recently gathered interest is the idea of "borrowing from the future" that also John Broome writes about in his chapter. Through the creation of new debt financing institutions, the costs of mitigation investments are to be passed on to future, but questions remain, see Aaron Maltais (2015) "Making Our Children Pay for Mitigation", in Maltais, A. and McKinnon, C. (eds), *The Ethics of Climate Governance*, Rowman & Littlefield Publishers, Inc, Maryland, 91–109.

2 Do not ask for morality

John Broome

Private morality and its limitations

Each of us ought to avoid emitting greenhouse gas. We have a moral duty not to harm other people, and particularly not to do so for our own benefit. The greenhouse gas we emit spreads around the world and contributes to global warming, which is harmful. Emitting greenhouse gas harms people by this means, so morality requires us not to do it.

True, there are exceptions to the duty not to harm other people. You may harm someone in self-defence, for example. It is sometimes claimed that there is an exception when the harm is trivial; it is said to be morally permissible to do trivial harms to other people if it brings you significant benefits. That may be so. But the harm done by an individual's greenhouse gas emissions is not trivial. They do only a very little harm to each person, but added up over everyone it amounts to a significant harm. I estimate that the gas each of us emits during our lifetime will shorten people's lives in total by a few months. This is not trivial. So the harm done by greenhouse gas does not fall under the triviality exception, if there is one, and nor does it fall under any of the other exceptions to the duty not to harm. Morality does indeed require us not to emit greenhouse gas. I recommend you to meet this duty by reducing our emissions and offsetting any that cannot be eliminated.

The moral duty not to harm other people is a duty of *justice*. This means we owe it to people, as individuals, not to harm them, and they have a right not to be harmed by us. Besides moral duties of justice, we also have moral duties of *beneficence* (Broome 2012). These are duties to make the world better and not worse, so far as we can. In emitting greenhouse gas, we are probably also failing in a duty of beneficence, because our emissions probably make the world worse on balance, and we could reduce them.

You might think the duty of justice to avoid doing harm is merely a part of the duty of beneficence, because to make the world better you must avoid doing harm. But actually the duty of justice is distinct. Sometimes you should avoid doing harm even if you do it in order to make the world better on balance. This is shown by a well-known example invented by Judith Thomson (1985): a surgeon has in her hospital five patients, each needing an organ transplant.

One needs a liver, one needs a heart, one a lung and so on. Each will die unless he or she gets the organ they need. The surgeon kills an innocent visitor to the hospital, extracts her organs and uses them to save the five patients. In this way she saves five lives at the cost of one. So she makes the world better on balance. Nevertheless, what she does is plainly wrong. How so? Because she violates her duty of justice towards the innocent victim. She has a duty not to harm her, even though by harming her she can do more good on balance. This shows that the moral duty of justice is different from the moral duty of beneficence, because justice can pull against beneficence.

I conclude that our emissions of greenhouse gas are immoral on two counts: they are unjust, and they violate our duty of beneficence. If we as individuals were all to do our moral duty, we would not emit greenhouse gas, and the problem of climate change would be solved. So should we aim to control climate change by promoting morality? This is a question about the generic 'we': the community. Should we aim at reducing climate change by promoting people's morality, making people virtuous?

No. Perhaps we should try to make people virtuous. But we should not try to use this as our means of controlling climate change. The reason is that we would fail. According to the Intergovernmental Panel on Climate Change, to have a reasonable chance of keeping climate change within reasonable bounds, emissions of greenhouse gas by the end of this century must be zero (IPCC 2014). This means that nearly all of us in the world would need to be virtuous by then, if we were to solve climate change that way. But we cannot achieve that. We cannot possibly persuade nearly all of the world's population to be virtuous. We cannot even get the message to very many people, and few of them would be persuaded anyway.

It is similarly immoral to drive very fast on the roads; it exposes other people to danger. But we do not rely on morality to make the roads safe. Why not? Because it would not work. People are in practice not influenced enough by moral considerations. Instead we employ the power of the state to compel people to drive more slowly. We impose speed limits and punish people who exceed them. Dealing with climate change also requires the power of the state to compel people to reduce their emissions.

The need for the state to deal with climate change is much stronger than it is for safety on the roads. It is easy for people to drive more slowly, but it is extremely hard for people to cut their emissions of greenhouse gas to zero by their own efforts. Given the way the world is now, it would require a huge sacrifice of their quality of life. Indeed it cannot be done at all without a restructuring of society and without new technology. For example, how could you survive through the winter without emitting greenhouse gases? You could not use fossil fuels for keeping warm. You could use biomass that you grow during the summer, or wind power, or something else. But these renewable sources of energy need more space than most people have access to. So you probably cannot survive the winter using only your own resources. You need the opportunities of a new economic infrastructure to supply you with carbon-free energy. To build a new infrastructure requires social cooperation on a large scale.[1]

Government morality and its limitations

We therefore cannot deal with climate change by appealing to the morality of individuals. A successful response can come only from social organizations of many people together. In practice it will have to come from nations. How can we get nations to act on climate change? Again, we could ask for a moral response. Morality applies to nations as much as to individuals. Just as there are moral reasons why an individual should not emit greenhouse gas, there are moral reasons why a nation should not. Moreover, nations, like individuals, can be motivated by moral reasons. For example, European governments recognize that their citizens should reduce their emissions, and they use their coercive power to make sure they do. European governments use regulations and taxation to achieve this result.

Is this the right way to deal with the problem of climate change: to appeal to the morality of nations? This has been the main appeal for the past twenty-five years of international negotiations, and it continues. At the UNFCCC meeting in Paris in 2015, nations were asked to present voluntary plans for reducing their emissions. Many made promises. Many are already implementing policies to reduce emissions. Why do they do that? It is not in the direct interest of any of them to do so. Each nation emits greenhouse gas because it benefits from doing so: its emissions provide energy for its citizens to use for their own benefit. A nation's emissions do harm by causing climate change, but most of the harm is borne by people elsewhere rather than by the nation's own citizens. Most of the people who will suffer from the effects of greenhouse gas are not yet even born. So it is not in any nation's interest to reduce its own emissions. Why do they do it, then? I assume they are morally motivated to some extent. They recognize the damage their emissions are doing to the world and to future generations. They recognize that, on moral grounds, they ought not to do this damage, and they volunteer to reduce it. They are willing to impose on their citizens the cost of reducing emissions for moral reasons.

So it seems that some nations, represented by their governments, are not without morality. They are encouraged to act morally by the moral actions of some of their own citizens. This is perhaps the most effective sort of moral action an individual can take in response to climate change. As individuals, we cannot do much directly towards solving the problem by reducing our own emissions, because too few of us will actually do it. But reducing emissions has the further effect of showing that we care about controlling climate change. By this demonstration, individuals can have an indirect effect that is much greater than our direct one. We can influence our governments to act morally. They can do so by imposing emissions reductions on all the individuals who make up the nation.

So the morality of nations, like the morality of individuals, has the potential to solve the problem of climate change. However, this is not a realistic prospect. Nations are responding morally to climate change to some extent, but not enough. In the face of what has to be done, existing efforts have been far too little. The promises made at the Paris UNFCCC meeting were too small. Twenty-five years of negotiations have achieved little. Nations may be willing to ask their people for some sacrifices, but not sacrifices on the scale that are required. We need a different approach from the moral one.

Appealing to self-interest

It is very commonly assumed that, in order to deal with the problem of climate change, a sacrifice is required from the present generation, for the sake of improving the lives of people in the future. A burden must be borne to control climate change. For some time, the aim of international negotiations was described as 'burden-sharing'. But an elementary piece of economics shows that this assumption is mistaken. Greenhouse gas is what economists call an 'externality'. When you are deciding whether to do something that causes greenhouse gas to be emitted (take a flight or buy a computer, say), you balance the cost of doing so against the benefit you expect from it. But you do not bear all the costs of what you do. The gas spreads round the world and does harm everywhere. This harm is part of the cost; it is called an 'external cost'. Those who emit greenhouse gas generally ignore its external cost. Either they do not know about it, or they do not care about it: they care only about the cost to themselves. So in their decision-making they do not correctly balance the benefit of their act against its true cost.

The result is that people cause more greenhouse gas to be emitted than is efficient in the economists' special sense of 'efficiency'. Economists call a situation 'inefficient' when a change could be made that would make things better for some people without making them worse for anyone (they call this a 'Pareto improvement'). When there is an externality, the outcome is inefficient in this sense (though there are a few exceptions, and I shall mention one). Because greenhouse gas is an externality, it leads to a situation that is inefficient in this sense. It would therefore be possible to eliminate the inefficiency without a sacrifice on anyone's part. The present generation does not need to make a sacrifice.[2]

People are so used to thinking that a sacrifice is required that they are often surprised by this, so I shall spend some time explaining it. It is helpful to use an analogy. Imagine two islands. The wind blows from Windward Island to Leeward Island. The Windward Islanders have some industry that brings benefit to themselves but it creates smog. The wind carries the smog down to Leeward Island, where it does harm to the Leeward Islanders. This harm is an external cost of the Windward Islanders' industry. The Windward Islanders are analogous to the present generation, their smog is analogous to greenhouse gas, and the Leeward Islanders are analogous to future generations.

Because of the externality, the situation for the Islanders is inefficient. It would be possible to improve the lives of some people without anyone making a sacrifice. Here is how. The Leeward Islanders could pay the Windward Islanders a fee to reduce their emissions. They could choose a fee that is sufficiently small to make it worth their while to pay it for the sake of reducing the smog. The Windward Islanders have till now been emitting smog at no cost to themselves, so even a small fee would make it worth their while to reduce their emissions. The Windward Islanders would then be better off because they would be more than compensated by the fee for reducing their emission. The Leeward Islanders would be better off because the cleaner air they receive would more than compensate them for the fee they pay. There would be a Pareto improvement.

How does this work between generations? You will immediately see a defect in the analogy. Later generations cannot pay a fee to earlier generations to reduce their greenhouse gas emissions. To create a Pareto improvement a transfer would be required from later generations to earlier ones, and later generations cannot make this transfer. Imagine now that the wind blows so strongly from Windward Island to Leeward Island that the Leeward Islanders cannot send anything against the wind to the Windward Islanders. They cannot pay them a fee, and so cannot compensate them for reducing their emissions. No Pareto improvement is possible in this new situation. The externality is still there, but this is one of those exceptional cases where an externality does not create inefficiency. It seems analogous to the situation between generations.

But let us extend the analogy some more. Suppose that, as well as sending smog to the Leeward Islanders, the Windward Islanders regularly send them nice gifts, which they float down on the wind. Now the inefficiency reappears. The Leeward Islanders cannot send the Windward Islanders a fee to compensate for reducing their emissions, but the Windward Islanders could compensate themselves by withholding some of their gifts. They could decide on their own account to reduce their emissions and compensate themselves that way. Provided they do not withhold too much, they will improve life for the Leeward Islanders. The Leeward Islanders will receive fewer gifts, but they will be more than compensated by their cleaner atmosphere.

Our intergenerational situation is analogous to this one. We regularly send gifts to future generations. We leave them artificial capital in the form of economic infrastructure: roads, factories, farmland, cities and so on. We also leave them natural resources that we could have used for ourselves but choose to leave in the ground for them. So here is something we could do: we could reduce our emissions of greenhouse gas. Other things being equal, that would be a cost to us: it costs something to build wind farms and solar farms, and to transform our way of life to one that does not depend on fossil fuel. But we could compensate ourselves for this cost by leaving fewer gifts to our descendants: we could reduce the amount of other natural and artificial resources that we bequeath them.

Look at it this way. As economists classify things, the goods produced each year by an economy are divided into two parts. One part is consumption: these are the goods that are used by people to give themselves a good life. The other part is investment: these are the goods that are used to build the potential for making more goods in the future. We can change the nature of our investment. Instead of conventional investment in cities, infrastructure and so on, we can start investing more in reducing emissions of greenhouse gas by insulating buildings, constructing windmills and so on. We can switch from conventional investment towards green investment that reduces emissions. Looked at in this way, it is easy to see how the change can be made without a sacrifice on our part. We switch investment but leave our own consumption alone. To be sure, we shall have to change the sorts of things we consume. We shall have to consume fewer goods that are produced with fossil fuel. But, by consuming other sorts of goods instead, we can ensure that the benefit we get from our consumption is not diminished.

Dealing with climate change can bring a great benefit to the world by removing the externality, and this benefit can be distributed to everyone. Nobody in any generation need suffer. It is really true that the present generation does not need to make a sacrifice in responding to climate change. We therefore do not have to appeal to anyone's morality.

There can be a Pareto improvement. But we must recognize that this opportunity is limited by the ability of the present generation to compensate itself for reducing its emissions. I have mentioned one means of compensation, to reduce its conventional investment. Were investment controlled by a world government, that could easily done: the government could simply make the switch in investment. In our capitalist world it is not so easy. I shall come later to practical means of making it possible. But there are moral issues to think about first.

Injustice

A Pareto improvement is possible. It does not follow that we should aim for a Pareto improvement as our strategy for dealing with climate change. Climate change damages the human world in several ways. Two of its bad consequences are that it leads to injustice, and it contributes to the global maldistribution of well-being. A Pareto improvement does not directly address either of these bad consequences. This is as an objection to the strategy of aiming for a Pareto improvement. How important is it?

Injustice first. Suppose you regularly inflict harm on someone unjustly. Perhaps you prevent your neighbour from sleeping by making a lot of noise. Suppose now that your neighbour pays you to stop the noise. If you accept her offer, the result is a Pareto improvement. You are better off, because you evidently think it worth stopping for the sake of the payment. Your neighbour is better off because she would not have paid you to stop if they had not thought it worthwhile. But the outcome is unjust. The harm you did was unjust to begin with, and the Pareto improvement does not correct the injustice. It perpetuates it.

For the same reason, the Pareto improvement I have described for climate change does not correct injustice between people. People who emit greenhouse gas do harm to others, and this is unjust. The Pareto improvement involves a transfer from those who are harmed to those who do the harm. It makes both better off, but it does not correct the injustice; it perpetuates it.

This injustice caused by climate change is mainly between people who live at the same time. For more than one reason, there is less injustice between people of different generations. One of the reasons can be revealed by the islands analogy again. If the Windward Islanders float gifts to the Leeward Islanders, they compensate them to some extent for the harm caused by smog. This helps to cancel the injustice the Windward Islanders cause; compensation is a way of cancelling injustice. If the gifts are enough, they may fully cancel the injustice. Analogously, we are passing resources to future generations through our conventional investment. Indeed, it may be that we fully compensate them for the harm we do them. Common opinion among economists is that the world economy will continue to grow despite climate change, and that future people will be better off than we are. Since growth is caused by investment, this suggests that we are more than fully compensating our successors for the damage we do them through climate change.

Still, even if there is no intergenerational injustice, there is a genuine injustice between contemporaries. This will be perpetuated if those who suffer from greenhouse gas emisssions end up paying those who emit it to reduce their emissions. The big emitting nations already owe compensation to other nations for the harm they are doing them, so justice requires a payment in the opposite direction.

However, it is possible to mitigate and perhaps even eliminate this injustice. A very great benefit is to be gained by removing the externality of greenhouse gas. This benefit is available to be shared among contemporary people. Those who have emitted a lot of greenhouse gas should not expect a big share of it. Most of the benefit should go to those who have suffered the most; I see no reason why it should not be enough to compensate them fully for past injustices. In effect, it means that future generations within the emitting nations are able to compensate those who have suffered from past injustice.

Maldistribution

Next maldistribution of well-being. Maldistribution is often called 'distributive injustice', but it is distinct from the injustice I have just considered. Think about the islands once again. The Windward Islanders send pollution to the Leeward Islanders. This is an injustice done to them because it harms them. But this injustice may not add to maldistribution. Indeed, it may actually improve the distribution of well-being. Perhaps the Leeward Islanders are much better off than the Windward Islanders. If so, the pollution reduces the degree of inequality between the islands. It benefits the worse-off people and harms the better-off, making the distribution more equal. This is an improvement in distribution.

Maldistribution is a bad feature of the world. Reducing maldistribution is a way of making the world better. The moral duty to reduce maldistribution is a duty of beneficence rather than a duty of justice. In the case of the islands, if the Leeward Islanders are much better off, the Windward Islanders' pollution may actually improve the world. If it does, the duty of beneficence is in favour of this pollution because it reduces maldistribution. But the pollution is nevertheless unjust; it is opposed by a duty of justice. The Windward Islanders should not harm the Leeward Islanders, because doing so is unjust. This is similar to the surgeon example, where justice and beneficence pull against each other.

How does climate change affect maldistribution? There is great maldistribution among contemporary people, and climate change contributes to it. By and large, the big emitters of greenhouse gas are better off than those who suffer from the effects. So climate change adds to inequality within the present generation, contributing to maldistribution. However, climate change is not a major source of our present maldistribution. That arises from the long history of colonialism and 200 years of very unequal economic development. The effects of climate change are too recent to have added greatly to maldistribution among contemporaries.

Between generations things are different. Common opinion among economists is that, despite climate change, future people will on average probably be better off than present people. Our economic activity, which benefits us, creates climate change that diminishes the quality of life of future people. Since those future people will be better off than us, climate change diminishes intergenerational inequality. This might seem to be an improvement in distribution, since inequality is a bad thing.

But to draw that conclusion is to ignore another consideration. Equality of well-being is not all that matters. The total of people's well-being is also a value that we should care for as part of beneficence. This means that there is something to be gained by delaying consumption of goods. We possess a productive technology that can, in effect, convert a quantity of goods at one time into a greater quantity of goods at a later time. Delaying consumption of goods consequently adds to the total of goods that are eventually consumed. It is therefore better on balance to allow future generations to consume more than earlier ones. The best distribution, taking account of the two values of total well-being and of equality in well-being, gives more well-being to future people than to present people.

Therefore, by damaging the well-being of future people, climate change may actually increase maldistribution between generations, even though it increases equality. Whether or not it actually increases maldistribution between generations depends on what the intergenerational distribution would be if there were no climate change. This counterfactual judgement seems impossible to make.

But cost–benefit analysis done by economists does give us a related piece of information. It tells us that the best way of responding to climate change, aiming to achieve the best possible distribution of well-being, involves a sacrifice by the present generation. Nicholas Stern (2007) and William Nordhaus (2008: 180) – leading economists who have investigated this question – agree about this, even though their conclusions are quantitatively very different. Stern's conclusion implies a much greater sacrifice by the present generation than Nordhaus's does, but they both favour a sacrifice. The agreement between these authors is perhaps one of the reasons why the pressure in international negotiations is towards sacrifice by the present generation. If your aim is the best outcome, a sacrifice is called for.

These economists' conclusions are illustrated in Figure 2.1. The horizontal axis of the diagram shows the consumption of the present generation; the vertical axis the consumption of a future generation. Given the world's resources and technology, some combinations of present and future consumptions are possible and others are not. The less one generation consumes, the more the other can consume. The downward-sloping line in the diagram is a 'possibility frontier', which marks the boundary of the combinations that are possible. This line slopes more steeply than 45 degrees because reducing present consumption by some amount allows future consumption to be increased by a greater amount.

'Business as usual' in the diagram marks the position where nothing is done about climate change. Because climate change leads to inefficiency, it is below the possibility frontier; it is possible to increase both generations' consumption together. A Pareto improvement is possible.

The curves in the diagram illustrate schematically the values that underlie Stern's and Nordhaus's cost–benefit analyses. They are contours of value: they connect together points in the diagram that these economists respectively consider to be equally valuable. Both contours are bowed downwards to reflect the value each economist gives to equality between generations. Nordhaus's curve is generally steeper than Stern's because Nordhaus gives less value than Stern does

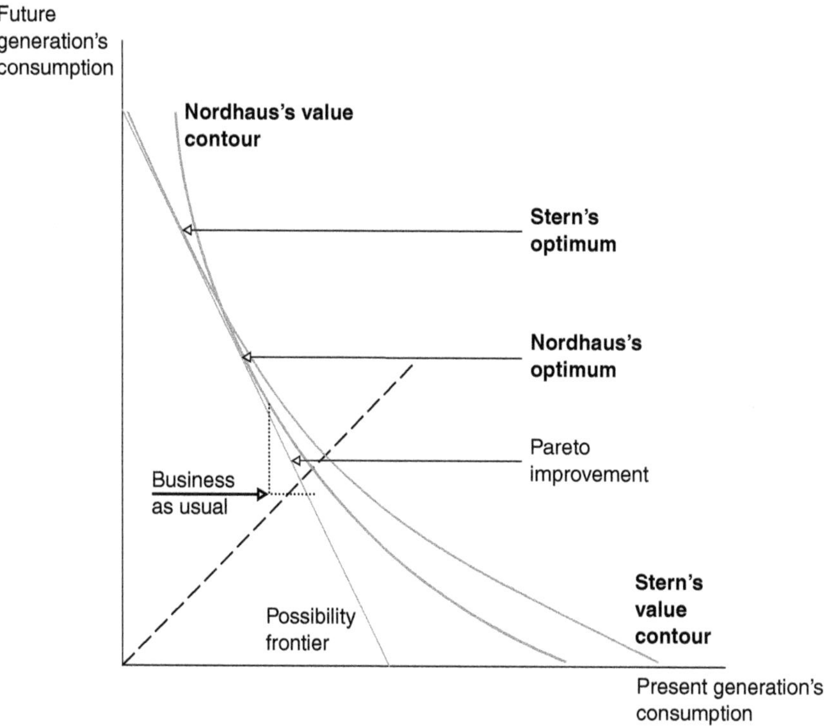

Figure 2.1 Future generation's consumption.

to future consumption compared with present consumption. The points where the two contours touch the possibility frontier represent the best possible outcomes from the two economists' respective points of view. Both points lie to the left of business as usual. This shows that the best response to climate change demands a sacrifice of consumption from the present generation, according to both economists.

So, although a Pareto improvement is possible, according to Stern and Nordhaus it would not be the best response. The best response calls for a sacrifice from the present generation. The Pareto improvement leads to maldistribution of well-being. It leads to a distribution that gives more to the present generation than is ideal.

Just as the injustice of a Pareto improvement can be mitigated, this maldistribution can also be mitigated by an appropriate distribution of the great benefits that will be realized by removing inefficiency. Most of the gains can be directed towards less well-off people and towards future generations. Nevertheless, it remains true that a Pareto improvement will not achieve the best result. It will lead to maldistribution. This undoubtedly counts against it.

But not enough to reject it. The history of failed negotiations about climate change shows that, if we aim for the best result, we shall not achieve it. The best result requires a shift of resources from the present towards the future. This is unattainable. To continue to strive for it is to make the best the enemy of the good. We have a much better chance of attaining an agreement that does not ask for a sacrifice from anyone.

One of the problems facing the world is climate change; another is the maldistribution of well-being. Both are very hard to resolve. If we continue to aim for the best result from our response to climate change, that is in effect to try and resolve both problems together. To aim for the best is to weigh down the effort to deal with climate change with the further aim of correcting the world's maldistribution. If climate change were largely responsible for maldistribution, there would be a case for doing so. But it is not. Maldistribution arises from a long history and has little to do with climate change. The problem of climate change requires a solution very urgently. Maldistribution should be tackled separately.

Dealing with maldistribution requires a moral response by governments. It requires them to sacrifice some of their people's well-being for the sake of others'. But dealing with climate change does not require a moral response. Climate change can be dealt with in a way that promotes everyone's self-interest. At present we are asking unsuccessfully for morality. We should abandon this high-minded approach in favour of self-interest.

The need for borrowing

Abandoning this approach will make the negotiations easier, but it will not make them easy. At least three difficulties remain. First, there is the commons problem. I have explained that a Pareto improvement is possible. This means that reducing emissions of greenhouse gas can be in everyone's interest. But it is not in any nation's individual interest to reduce its own emissions. Each nation can benefit from activities that cause emissions, and it does not itself bear all the costs of the emissions it causes. The costs are borne by all the people who suffer the effects of climate change. So each nation has an incentive to emit more, even though it would be good for every nation if every nation emitted less. The atmosphere is a sort of common resource, into which nations can freely dump their greenhouse gas. Because it costs them nothing to do so, they have an incentive to overuse the common. This is the commons problem. It has to be overcome.

The only solution to the commons problem is international cooperation. Nations must agree together to reduce their emissions, and must trust each other to do so. Each nation must agree through negotiation to some particular reduction. This is not burden-sharing among nations, because they will all end up better off, bearing no burden. It is sharing the benefit of dealing with climate change, rather than sharing the burden. But still it is a problem of distribution between nations. It is a matter of bargaining, and a good result cannot be guaranteed. I hope that bargaining about the distribution of a benefit will go more smoothly than bargaining about the distribution of a burden. But it is not easy. That is the second difficulty.

The third difficulty is one of economic practice. How is it possible to implement the Pareto improvement I have described? We know what has to be achieved in gross terms. Investment has to be shifted away from conventional investment in roads and bridges to green investment in wind farms and insulation. How can that be achieved in practice?

If there were a world government that controlled investment, it could just make the switch. It could command a redirection of investment. This simple fact tells us that the difficulty is not one of the real economy. From a real, technological point of view, the switch is possible. The difficulty is a financial one: how to achieve the switch in a capitalist economy where decisions about investment are made by capitalists who choose the most profitable investments. At present conventional investment is most profitable. How are capitalists to be persuaded to switch to green investments instead?

First, there will have to be a carbon price. On this nearly all economists agree. The externality problem is that people do not pay the full cost of the greenhouse gas they emit. That causes inefficiency. Efficiency will not be achieved except by internalizing the externality, as economists put it. People must be made to pay the full cost of their emissions, including the external cost they impose on other people. Emissions must have an appropriate price attached to them. This can be achieved by means of a carbon tax, by cap and trade or in some other way. Once there is a carbon price, it will give an incentive to people to live their lives in a less carbon-intensive way. They will look for ways of reducing their emissions. This will make green investment more profitable, and give capitalists an incentive to switch to it.

However, a carbon price is in itself against people's interests. When people who previously paid nothing for emitting greenhouse gas find they have to pay a price to do so, that makes them worse off. But we are aiming for a Pareto improvement, where no one is worse off. To achieve this result, people will have to be compensated in some way for paying the carbon price. This can be done. Their other taxes, such as income taxes, can be reduced, or some compensating subsidy can be given them. But this compensation will cost money. The revenue from the carbon tax itself will be available to finance some of the cost, but it will not be enough to pay for all the subsidy that is required. So how can the compensation be financed?

By loans. Governments will need to borrow. They will need to issue bonds, and to pay interest on them that is sufficient to persuade capitalists to buy them. An inevitable effect of governments' borrowing will be to push up interest rates. This in itself discourages conventional investment. In effect, it offers capitalists an alternative asset to invest in. Rather than building conventional capital, they can buy bonds instead. When they do, the capitalists' money will end up in the hands of governments. Governments can then use it to compensate people for paying the carbon price. They could also use it directly to build wind farms and other green investments.

The conclusion is that to manage the switch of investment in a capitalist economy will involve government borrowing. People sometimes describe this as borrowing from the future. Since future people will benefit from green investment, we get them to pay for it. But it is not literally borrowing from future people. We cannot do that. Borrowing is always a transaction between contemporaries, and so is repaying a loan. When the government loans come to be repaid in the future, they will not be repaid by a future generation as a whole. The repayment will be made by some members of a future generation (the inheritors of the debt) to others of their contemporaries (the inheritors of the bonds).

Because of the need for borrowing, this way of managing the transition will require an increase of government debt. It is conventional wisdom these days, particularly in Europe, that governments cannot bear more debt. That is false at present in Europe, where many governments are able to borrow at trivially low interest rates. But it will indeed be difficult for governments to borrow a sufficient amount of money for the very long-term projects that are required to improve the climate. A government can borrow only if investors trust it to repay the debt when it falls due. The bonds issued by governments to finance green investment will have to be extremely solidly founded. Few governments have the stability and credibility to issue these bonds. They will need to be supported by a new, international financial institution that has enough solidity to bear them.

We already have a World Bank and an IMF, which were created to help finance the reconstruction of the world's economy after the Second World War. We now need a World Climate Bank. A well-founded World Climate Bank would make it possible to respond to climate change in a way that requires sacrifice from no one. Creating this bank should be a central aim of international negotiations about climate change.

Conclusion

We should give up trying to solve the problem of climate change by appealing to the morality of governments. Instead we should concentrate on building the institutions that will make it possible to solve the problem without asking for morality.

Notes

1 This chapter was originally a talk given at the conference 'How to Think the Anthropocene' in Paris in November 2015. I owe a great deal to Duncan Foley, who first brought me to see the point. A fuller version of the argument appears in our joint paper "A world climate bank" in *Institutions for Future Generations* (forthcoming), edited by Iñigo González-Ricoy and Axel Gosseries. Research was supported by ARC Discovery Grant DP140102468.

2 This point has been particularly stressed by Duncan Foley (for example, see Foley 2009).

Bibliography

Broome, J. (2012), *Climate Matters: Ethics in a Warming World*, New York: W. W. Norton.

Foley, D. (2009), 'The economic fundamentals of global warming', in J. M. Harris and N. R. Goodwin (eds), *Twenty First Century Macroeconomics: Responding to the Climate Challenge*, Cheltenham: Edward Elgar, pp. 115–26.

IPCC (2014), 'Summary for policymakers', in IPCC, *Climate Change (2014), Mitigation of Climate Change. Contribution of Working Group III to the Fifth Assessment Report of the Intergovernmental Panel on Climate Change*, Cambridge and New York: Cambridge University Press, pp. 11–12.

Nordhaus, W. (2008), *A Question of Balance: Weighing Options on Global Warming Policies*, New Haven, CT: Yale University Press.

Stern, N. (2007), *The Economics of Climate Change: The Stern Review*, Cambridge and New York: Cambridge University Press.

Thomson, J. J. (1985), 'The trolley problem', *Yale Law Journal*, vol. 94: 1395–415.

3 The ethics of discounting[1]

An introduction

Marc D. Davidson

Introduction

Economists differ widely in their recommendations as to how much effort should be put into reducing greenhouse gas emissions. They differ in their recommended reduction *targets* and in the corresponding carbon *prices* to guide policy instruments such as taxes. Among the best-known exponents of opposing views are Nicholas Stern of the London School of Economics and William Nordhaus of Yale University. According to Stern, the social cost of carbon is about $85 per tonne of CO_2 (Stern 2007: xvi), while Nordhaus offers a value of $7.40 per tonne of CO_2 (Nordhaus 2008). In line with these values, Stern advises radical action now, while Nordhaus advises very modest climate policy. Laymen might easily conclude that this disagreement derives from controversy about human influence on the climatic system, particularly given the disproportionate attention given in the media to 'climate sceptics'. Although some economists do indeed consider the IPCC's assessment of the science of climate change 'too alarmist' (Tol 2014) or, on the contrary, stress the importance of low-probability catastrophes for climate cost–benefit analysis (CBA) (Weitzman 2009), Stern and Nordhaus hardly disagree on the actual science of climate change. In fact, as the IPCC already noted in 1995 (Arrow *et al.* 1996), most disagreement among economists originates from their use of different *discount rates*, the parameter used in CBA to compare future and present gains and losses. A discount rate of 5 per cent, for example, implies that a cost of $100 next year is valued equally to a cost of $95 this year, and that a cost of $100 in *two* years' time is valued equally to a cost of about $91 this year.

There are two related reasons why the choice of discount rate is of decisive importance in climate economics. First, in the case of climate policy the time spans separating costs and benefits may be very long indeed. Because of the inertia of the climate system, cause (emission or mitigation) and effect (climate damage) may be separated by *millennia*. Over such a time period a small change in the discount rate applied has huge consequences for the outcome of CBA: at a discount rate of 1 per cent, $1000 in 200 years' time is valued as $137 today; at a discount rate of 5 per cent, $1000 in 200 years' time is valued as only $0.06 today. Second, since cause and effect may be separated by millennia, it is future generations in particular that will be affected by our present choices. This makes the comparison of present and future costs and benefits pre-eminently an issue of ethics, and thus also subject to moral dispute. Although this dispute has a pedigree going back at least to the eighteenth-century writings of Jeremy Bentham and David Hume (Robinson 1990), the debate has intensified over the last decades given its importance for energy and climate policy. The literature shows a wide variety of opinions. See for landmark overviews e.g. Lind *et al.* (1982), Price (1993), Arrow *et al.* (1996) and Portney and Weyant (1999). Some authors dispute that the discount rate is a matter of ethics and argue that the discount rate should be deduced from the market interest rate. Others have argued for different discount rates on the basis of different moral theories such as utilitarianism, prioritarianism and deontological approaches.

The purpose of this chapter is to provide an introduction and a literature review with respect to the issues involved in the longstanding debate in ethics and economics on whether discounting the future is morally justifiable. Section 1 will first offer a short introduction to Ramsey's neo-classical model of economic growth. Understanding the basics of Ramsey's model is pivotal for understanding both the vocabulary of the discounting debate and the complicated relation between ethics and efficiency. Subsequently, Section 2 describes the *prescriptive–descriptive* debate: the debate between those who argue that the discount rate ought to be based on preferences revealed through actual saving behaviour and those who argue that the discount rate ought to be based on moral principles. A variety of these moral principles is successively discussed in Sections 3 to 7. Section 7 offers some concluding remarks.

The Ramsey model of economic growth

In the discounting debate two different 'discount rates' are often confused: the *consumption discount rate* (CDR) and the *marginal rate of return on alternative investments* (MRRI). The CDR expresses how we value future changes in consumption in comparison with changes in the present.[2] The notion of 'consumption' as used in economic parlance should be interpreted very broadly: from market purchase of goods and services such as food and shelter to feeling safe from dying in a flood disaster. In other words, consumption encompasses anything for which there is a willingness to pay, thus including non-market goods. In standard (financial) CBA, however, as employed by businesses to choose between alternative investment options, future costs and benefits are not discounted against the CDR, but against the MRRI, which expresses the fact that there are *opportunity costs* involved in spending money on one project rather than another. If such a CBA yields a negative outcome, this means there is an alternative investment available that offers a higher rate of return. Discounting at a lower rate than the MRRI could therefore result in *inefficient* investment decisions. In fact, in such a CBA there is no issue of comparing consumption at different points in time, only of choosing the investment option with the highest rate of return.

It has been argued that in the case of CBA of climate policy the same procedure should be followed (see e.g. Birdsall and Steer 1993; Nordhaus 1997). Future generations would want us to make the best investments, and depositing money in the bank at an interest rate of 4 per cent would offer better returns than a climate investment with a lower internal rate of return of 2 per cent, for example. These economists therefore believe discounting is not a matter of ethics, but merely of efficiency.[3] Future costs and benefits, including climate damage, should *always* be discounted against the MRRI, they hold. Other economists have argued that future climate damage should be discounted against the CDR, but that the MRRI should be taken as a *proxy* for this rate. In this case, too, there would be no moral choice involved. To discuss the respective merits of these two positions, we need first to sketch Ramsey's neo-classical model of the economy (Ramsey 1928). The Ramsey model elucidates the decisions of households to either consume or save and invest, how MRRI and CDR are related, and the basic components of the CDR.

The Ramsey model starts out from the fact that households obtain returns to capital and labour, and can choose to consume or save these returns:

$$y(K(t)) = c(t) + \acute{K}(t) \tag{1}$$

where $K(t)$ is capital available at time t, $y(K(t))$ are the returns on capital at time t, $c(t)$ is consumption at time t, and $\acute{K}(t)$ are savings at time t.

In this choice between consumption and saving, households face an intertemporal optimization problem as to how to optimize utility over their lifetime. The model assumes, however, that households do not simply *maximize* intertemporal utility but prefer present over future utility, i.e. that they hold a *pure rate of time preference*. Such a pure rate of time preference is generally attributed to erroneous overestimation of the value of benefits occurring earlier in time (temporal myopia) or weakness of the will (akrasia) and impatience. The intertemporal welfare function (W) is thus given by

$$W = \int_{t=0}^{\infty} u(c(t))e^{-\rho t}\,dt \tag{2}$$

where $u(c)$ is the utility accruing from consumption, $c(t)$ is the consumption at time t, and ρ is the pure rate of time preference. This is also called the *discounted utility* model (Samuelson 1937). Utility (u) is usually a concave function of consumption (c), for the higher the level of consumption, the less additional consumption offers people additional utility: better an additional dollar as a poor student than as a well-paid doctor. Since people generally expect to become wealthier in the future, i.e. to have higher consumption levels, this gives people a second reason besides impatience to discount future consumption compared with present consumption. The consumption discount rate CDR thus reads:

$$\text{CDR} = \rho + \mu\, g \tag{3}$$

where ρ is the pure rate of time preference, μ is the absolute value of the elasticity of marginal utility (a measure of the relative effect of a change in consumption on welfare) and g the expected growth rate of consumption.[4]

Because of their positive CDR, consumers require a reward for postponing their consumption. Producers are willing to pay this reward because capital is productive, i.e. there is a positive MRRI. The outcome of this supply and demand for capital is a market interest rate (i) (Fisher, 1907). In a world without market failure, taxes or risk, i equals both CDR and MRRI.

$$i = \text{MRRI} = \text{CDR} = \rho + \mu\, g \tag{4}$$

Finally, the equilibrium between MRRI and CDR also determines the choice between consumption and saving in formula (1). If MRRI were *larger* than CDR, people would increase their savings and vice versa. A typical savings rate is in the order of 20 per cent, and the consumption rate therefore is about 80 per cent (see e.g. Lind 1982; Pearce and Ulph 1999; Moore *et al.* 2004; Stern 2007: 161). In other words, when households spend \$1, at the margin they cut back 80 cents on alternative consumption and 20 cents on savings.

This highly simplified model of the economy shows why it is incorrect to discount climate damage against the MRRI in climate CBA. Discounting against the MRRI would only make sense when two alternative investment options are being compared, as in the case of a company performing a CBA of particular investment options. In the case of climate policy, however, the alternative to investing in climate mitigation is not another investment, let alone an investment with a similar duration of centuries to millennia. As the simplified Ramsey model shows, climate policy will primarily displace present *consumption* and only to a limited extent alternative investments. If a government provides society with incentives to invest in climate mitigation, through carbon taxes or by prescribing new technologies, for example, and society faces higher costs as a result, this does *not* lead to society reducing its savings by an equal amount (see also Lind 1982; Arrow 1995). Instead, society reduces its consumption and savings in a ratio of about four to one: for each additional dollar spent, people reduce their consumption by eighty cents and their savings by twenty cents.

Since climate policy displaces both present consumption *and* alternative investments, we cannot discount future climate damage either simply against the CDR or against the MRRI. To perform a CBA of climate policy we must first calculate the changes in consumption over time that result from alternative policy options, based upon factual and expected saving rates and MRRIs. Subsequently, we must compare the consumption streams by discounting future consumption against the CDR and perform summation over the consecutive years. This is in fact the procedure followed in Integrated Assessment Models (IAMs) such as DICE/RICE (Nordhaus and Boyer 2003; Nordhaus 2008), FUND (Tol 2002, 2006) and the PAGE model (Hope 2006) used in the Stern Review (Stern 2007).

Note that even if present-day society were to put money in an investment fund earmarked to compensate future generations for climate damage – a ‘Fund for Greenhouse Victims' (Cline 1992: 265) – this would be a pledge impossible to fulfil. As Lind argues (1995: 382; see also Price 1973: 394; d'Arge *et al.* 1982: 255; and Cline 1999: 134):

> we would have to find a way, say through a trust fund, to guarantee that the returns on this additional investment were fully reinvested and not returned to the income stream where they would mostly go to consumption with only a relatively small part being reinvested. Without this continual reinvestment, the arithmetic of compounding which is fundamental to the 'give them the cash' alternative does not work. Furthermore, this policy would have to be sustained by successive governments for a hundred years. Even if this generation were to set up such a fund, it could not commit the governments of future intervening generations to do so. There would be every incentive for some future generation to break the chain of intergenerational transfers and consume all or part of the resources in the trust fund.

The prescriptive–descriptive debate

The previous section showed that the correct approach to climate CBA is to calculate the consequences of different policy options for consumption over time and discount future changes in consumption against the CDR. As formula (4) shows, however, there is a relation between the CDR, the MRRI and the market interest rate. Some economists have consequently argued that the observable market interest rate *reveals* society's CDR and should be taken as a *proxy* for CDR. Others disagree and argue that the CDR can be chosen independently on the basis of moral considerations. This disagreement is known in the literature as the *prescriptive–descriptive debate* (Arrow *et al.* 1996). According to the descriptive view, the choice of the consumption discount rate ought to be based on the preferences society reveals through the intertemporal choices made in actual saving behaviour reflected through capital markets, thus respecting principles of democracy and consumer sovereignty (see e.g. Bauer 1957: 113–14; Eckstein 1957: 57–8; Marglin 1963: 97; Pearce *et al.* 1989: 132–3; Manne *et al.* 1995). Marglin, for example, called basing the discount rate on one's own moral view 'an authoritarian rejection of individual preferences' (1962: 197) and considered it 'axiomatic that a democratic government reflects only the preferences of the individuals who are presently members of the body politic' (1963: 97). More recently, the descriptive approach has been advocated by Nordhaus (2007) and Weitzman (2007: 712), among others. In response to the moral choices made by Stern in his Review (Stern 2007), Nordhaus (2007: 691) remarks that:

> The Review takes the lofty vantage point of the world social planner, perhaps stoking the dying embers of the British Empire, in determining the way the world should combat the dangers of global warming. The world,

> according to Government House utilitarianism, should use the combination of time discounting and consumption elasticity that the Review's authors find persuasive from their ethical vantage point.[5]

Against this descriptive view there are various counterarguments, however. The first is that the CDR that people reveal through capital markets (formula 4) only expresses their preferences regarding the trade-off between present consumption and *their own* future consumption (Schelling 1995: 396). Preferences regarding the trade-off between present consumption and the consumption of future generations, as in the case of climate policy, are not and cannot be expressed through capital markets. Although we may be willing to save for future generations, out of moral concerns for example, we may consider the welfare of future generations as a public good to which we are only willing to contribute if we know that others are doing the same, rather than free-riding on our efforts (Sen 1961, 1967; Marglin 1963). Sen called this the 'isolation paradox'. In that case, we face a social or prisoner's dilemma that we can only resolve through coordinated action established through political and democratic processes. Consequently, moral preferences regarding the trade-off between present consumption and the consumption of future generations are likewise expressed by way of political and democratic processes instead of through capital markets. It has been argued, moreover, that, if people's preferences count, it is problematic that future generations are themselves unable to express their preferences in capital markets (see also e.g. Sen 1961: 482; Price: 1973; Krutilla and Fisher 1975: 61).

Finally, it should be remarked that, even if the market interest rate did reveal society's preferences regarding the trade-off between present consumption and the consumption of future generations, a government could still draw its own conclusion on the basis of moral arguments. Democracy interpreted as majority rule may require governments not to translate advice that conflicts with society's preferences into action, but this is unrelated to the question of whether or not the advice itself is sound (Parfit 1983: 32). To make a comparison: if the majority of citizens in society believe climate change to be a hoax, that is no reason for economists to base their integrated assessment models on such beliefs. Instead, economists base their models on their own assessment of the state-of-the-art of climate science. Likewise, governments and economists can show society what they believe to be the best policy, based not only on the best science but also on the best moral arguments (see also Broome 2012: 110–11). In fact, this view is not contradictory with Marglin's plea for consumer sovereignty and democracy (1963: 97–8), which, according to him:

> is not to suggest a simplistic 'recording machine' theory of government, in which the government plays only the passive role of registering and carrying out the articulated desires of the members of society. I certainly would allow an educational role for government, including the education of today's citizens to the 'rightful claims' of future generations.

To conclude, the choice of discount rate in climate CBA is not a matter of mere efficiency, nor can the rate simply be deduced from capital markets. Given the fact that those reaping the benefits of today's greenhouse gas emissions differ from those bearing the costs of climate change (future generations), the choice of discount rate is a *moral* choice. While in the Ramsey model as a description of the actual economy formula (3) *describes* how people discount their own future consumption in comparison with present consumption, the same formula has been used to discuss how we *ought* to discount the consumption of future generations relative to our present consumption. In the intergenerational context, however, the meaning of the parameters changes: ρ does not simply denote impatience regarding changes in our own well-being, but becomes a parameter for our concern for future people's well-being, while μ does not simply express the relative effect of a change in consumption on welfare, but may become a parameter for aversion to intertemporal inequality (Dasgupta 2008). The following sections discuss a number of moral approaches that have been adopted to address this issue.

Classic utilitarianism

Since it is primarily in economic analysis that the discount rate plays a central role, until recently it has first and foremost been economists who have discussed the morality of discounting the future. Unsurprisingly, therefore, it has been the moral theory most compatible with mainstream economic theory that has received most attention: classical utilitarianism. According to utilitarianism, the right act is the one that maximizes utility (or happiness, well-being or other comparable measure) for all concerned. Classical utilitarianism dovetails well with economic theory both in its 'calculation units' (utility) and its aims of maximization and efficiency. The recommendations of classical utilitarianism for discounting are straightforward. The pure rate of time preference, ρ, is set to zero, mindful of the observation by Henry Sidgwick (1874) that 'the interests of posterity must concern a Utilitarian as much as those of his contemporaries'.[6] In other words: changes in future utility count as much as changes in present utility.

However, classical utilitarianism supports the second term in the Ramsey equation (3): μg. If future generations are wealthier than we are today and there is a diminishing marginal utility of consumption, then discounting of future consumption is required so as to maximize utility over time.[7] Marshall (1890) already observed that 'a pound's worth of satisfaction to an ordinary poor man is a much greater thing than a pound's worth of satisfaction to an ordinary rich man'. It should be noted, though, that discounting for higher consumption levels in the intergenerational context is at odds with the idea that interpersonal comparisons of well-being are impossible, one of the basic ideas that initiated the development of positive welfare economics (Pareto 1906). Nevertheless, a CDR equal to the expected growth rate of consumption times the absolute value of the elasticity of marginal utility has been advocated by for example Pigou (1920), Ramsey (1928) and Harrod (1949) in the general discounting debate and by for example Cline (1992), Schelling (1995), Azar and Sterner (1996), Broome (1992, 2004) and Stern (2007) in the climate debate. Note that most economists assume a positive g, i.e. that growth in average per capita income will continue into the distant future. In traditional economics it is generally assumed that environmental problems are *marginal* perturbations of the economic system, i.e. that economic growth is not substantially affected. Particularly in *ecological economics* this assumption has been questioned: climate change and the depletion of natural resources may result in economic decline and thus *negative* discount rates (O'Neill 1993: 51–2; Dietz and Asheim 2012).

Basing the CDR in climate CBA on classical utilitarianism has received a number of criticisms. The first has been that classical utilitarianism is too demanding. Although utilitarianism allows future consumption to be discounted to allow for the fact that future generations may be wealthier than we are today, we could still be obliged to substantially reduce our present consumption and start massive saving programmes. Since capital is productive, investment almost always results in greater utility for future generations than the utility we would ourselves derive from present consumption of that capital (Koopmans 1960, Koopmans *et al.* 1964; Mirrlees 1967; Rawls 1971: 286–7; Olsen and Bailey 1981; Manne 1995; Nordhaus 2007: 694; Hampicke 2011:, 47). According to Dasgupta (2008: 155), the consumption discount rate proposed by Stern (2007) on the basis of utilitarian principles implies a 97 per cent saving rate out of income. Although according to Dietz and Stern (2008: 106) such an outcome depends upon specific model assumptions, including those regarding technical progress, it is nevertheless obvious that applying a zero pure rate of time preference across the board in governmental policy would imply a massive increase in investments compared to the application of a pure rate of time preference of a few per cent based upon market interest rates. Moreover, if utilitarian reasoning were applied to the intergenerational context, there would be no reason not to apply it in the *international* context as well. Based on the same diminishing marginal utility of consumption, utilitarianism would advocate a massive international redistribution of wealth. Although Peter Singer (1972) has indeed advocated such a redistribution, most people consider treating other people's utility entirely on a par with one's own too demanding. Restricting the application of utilitarian reasoning to the discount rate to be used in climate CBA would be inconsistent, however. Finally, utilitarianism has been criticized for failing to respect people's *rights* (see e.g. Rawls 1971). This criticism is further explained in the section 'Rights and duties'.

Discounted utilitarianism

As a solution to the problem of 'overdemandingness' of classical utilitarianism, Arrow (1995) and Beckerman and Hepburn (2007) have advocated *discounted* utilitarianism, not merely as a *description* of actual behaviour (see the Ramsey model), but also as a *prescriptive* position.[8] Discounted utilitarianism is the view that we ought to maximize utility but are allowed to attach a lower weight to utility the further it occurs in the future. Discounted utilitarianism thus morally justifies the use of consumption discount rates close to the market interest rate and thus arrives at policy recommendations similar to those by 'descriptionists' such as Nordhaus. Arrow (1995: 8) finds a justification of discounted utilitarianism in obligations regarding oneself:

> It is a conflict between a basic principle of morality, as seen by many philosophers and others, that of universalizability, and a principle of self-regard, of the individual as an end and not merely as a means to the welfare of others.... One can only say that *both* the universal other and the self impose obligations on an agent.

In this position, Arrow sees support in Scheffler's claim that each person has an 'agent-centred prerogative' allowing each agent to devote energy and attention to his or her own projects and commitments (Scheffler 1982). Scheffler's ideas do not lend themselves for Arrow's purposes, however. As Caney subtly remarks (Caney 2008: 550; see also Dasgupta 2008: 146), '[t]he whole point of [Scheffler's] argument is that persons do not have a duty to maximise well-being. That is why his book is entitled *The Rejection of Consequentialism* (1982).'

Beckerman and Hepburn (2007) look for support for a pure rate of time preference in the works of David Hume (1967 [1738]):

> A man naturally loves his children better than his nephews, his nephews better than his cousins, his cousins better than strangers, where every thing else is equal. Hence arise our common measures of duty, in preferring the one to the other. Our sense of duty always follows the common and natural course of our passions.

However, as Beckerman and Hepburn (2007) themselves observe:

> Of course, the fact that our moral intuitions and our sense of justice reflect human nature as it has evolved though time in a way that prevents anarchy and promotes co-operative solutions to repeated 'games' does not necessarily give it irresistible normative value. Hume is famous for deploring the tendency of people to jump readily from 'is' propositions (such as comments on human nature) to 'ought' propositions (e.g. op. cit., Book III, Part I, sec. I).

In other words, from the observation that we do care more about those near to us, it does not follow that such 'passions' are also justified. Moreover, even while one may have 'special obligations' to one's own group, as Beckerman and Hepburn believe, this does not mean we cannot have other obligations that are universal, such as respect for other people's rights (see the section 'Rights and duties'). Without acknowledging obligations that do not depend on special ties, an agent-relative ethics would justify 'tribalism, racism or nationalism'. As Parfit (1983: 36) argues:

> Perhaps the U.S. government ought in general to give priority to the welfare of its own citizens. But this does not apply to the infliction of great harms. Suppose this government decides to resume atmospheric nuclear tests. If it predicts that the resulting fallout would cause several deaths, should it discount the deaths of aliens? Should it therefore move the tests to the Indian Ocean? It seems plausible to claim that, in such a case, the special relations make no moral difference. We may take the same view about the harms that we impose on our remote successors.

All in all, the amalgam between classical utilitarianism and the notion that we are allowed to treat people unequally seems an ad hoc solution to the problems of classical utilitarianism. As Rawls remarks: 'Unhappily I can only express the opinion that these devices [counting the well-being of later generations for less] simply mitigate the consequences of mistaken principles' (Rawls 1971: 297; see also Roser 2009: 15; Moellendorf 2014: 116).

Prioritarianism, Rawls's difference principle and sufficientarianism

While discounted utilitarianism assumes a positive pure rate of time preference, there are other approaches that adhere to a zero pure rate of time preference, but that unlike classical utilitarianism do not take μ equal to the absolute value of the elasticity of marginal utility. One of these approaches, advocated for example by John Broome, is *prioritarianism* (Broome 1991, 2012: 145–8; Parfit 1997). According to this theory, it is morally more valuable to increase the well-being of someone who has less well-being than to add to the well-being of someone who already has a lot. That means that a prioritarian would set μ higher than the absolute value of the elasticity of marginal utility. For an application of prioritarianism to the discount rate, see Adler (2009), Adler and Treich (2015) and Asheim (2012).

Others have questioned the necessity to save for the future altogether, such as Baumol (1968: 800):

> A redistribution to provide more for the future may be described as a Robin Hood activity stood on his head – it takes from the poor to give to the rich. Average real per capita income a century hence is likely to be a sizeable multiple of its present value. Why should I give up part of my income to help support someone else with an income several times my own?

There are two moral theories to back up Baumol's thoughts: *Rawls's difference principle* and *sufficientarianism*. In *A Theory of Justice* the political philosopher Rawls (1971) rejected utilitarianism and argued for a society in which the position of those who are least well-off is optimized (according to the 'maximin criterion' or 'difference principle'). Although Rawls himself saw reasons not to apply the difference principle in the intergenerational context, other authors did, arriving at a high or even infinite value of μ (see e.g. Solow 1974; d'Arge *et al.* 1982; Pearce 1983; Buchholz and Schumacher 2010; see for further discussion also Arrow 1973; Dasgupta 1974). If future generations are wealthier, *any* expenditure on mitigation will worsen the position of the least well-off generation, the present. The same conclusion would be reached by sufficientarians, according to whom social benefits and burdens should be redistributed only in so far as redistribution is required to let people attain a sufficient level of well-being (Frankfurt 1987; Crisp 2003; Page 2007). For a discussion of a sufficientarian approach to discounting, see e.g. Meyer and Roser 2009; Rendall 2014; Kyllönen and Basso 2016.

Although it is not a criticism of the applied moral theories per se, Price and Nair (1985) and Schelling (1995) have warned of a a fallacy of composition if a single discount rate is used for the anticipated higher wealth of future generations. Even if average per capita income were to rise in every country over the coming centuries, it could still be the case that those investing in mitigation today are wealthier than those reaping the benefits in the future. The present income of the average inhabitant of the United States could be higher, for example, than the income of the average inhabitant of Bangladesh in 100 years' time. In that case, the discount rate based on marginal utility comparisons should be negative. It is therefore necessary to disaggregate.

Rights and duties

What the previous approaches all have in common is that they assume a *single* discount rate for different changes in consumption occurring in the same future year, independent of whether we are in any way causally responsible for the future changes and whether these involve the violation of rights. According to a deontological ethics, however, we have perfect duties not to harm others in bodily integrity and personal property, while we have no duties to redistribute our wealth to people who are already better off than ourselves.[9] Deontology therefore reconciles the two moral intuitions that we have a strong duty to reduce the risk of climate change we impose on our descendants, but have no duty to increase our savings rate across the board as implied by classical utilitarianism.

Previously Parfit (1983) was cited, who in the context of the discounting debate already noted that harms we impose on future generations may require a different treatment than general benefits we bestow on them (see also Sen 1982: 344–8). Some authors, however, have considered the whole procedure of CBA and thus including discounting inappropriate in the case of climate damage, since the harm to future generations caused by climate change violates their *basic human rights*. According to Spash (1993: 128) (and see also Spash 1994; Caney 2008, 2009):

> Accepting an inviolable right of future generations to be free of intergenerational environmental damages has serious policy implications. If it were accepted, compensation would no longer be used to justify environmental degradation in violation of such rights, although there would still be some role for compensation. Irreversible damages, already underway, which could not be prevented by stopping pollutant emissions or other actions would require compensation ... all actions known to cause long-term environmental damages would have to be stopped. Under the theory I am advocating here, the current generation would be obliged to identify all activities causing long-term damages and ban them regardless of the cost.

Problematic with this view is that it is impossible to prevent all damages from occurring. As far as our knowledge permits, damage to future generations is a continuous function of our present emissions and we cannot reduce all our emissions to zero. Davidson (2006) has therefore proposed a middle road between a deontological and utilitarian approach similar to the 'reasonable man standard' in positive law. The reasonable man or reasonable person standard is a legal fiction: a person appropriately informed, capable, aware of the law and fair-minded. The reasonable man is allowed to exercise self-interest and is not required to give his money to the poor. He exercises due care, however, to ensure that his acts do not injure others. He may weigh up the risk itself and the cost of alleviating it (see also Nozick 1974: 79–80). According to the Second Restatement of Torts (§ 291) of US common law, for example:

> Where an act is one which a reasonable man would recognize as involving risk of harm to another, the risk is unreasonable and the act is negligent if the risk is of such magnitude as to outweigh what the law regards as the utility of the act or of the particular manner in which it is done.

The reasonable man standard allows *no* discounting for either empathic distance or wealth differences, however. The reasonable man standard applied to climate CBA is therefore more stringent than classical utilitarianism, but less stringent than the complete ban of harmful activities as advocated by Spash.[10] Davidson (2014) furthermore shows that applying a zero consumption discount rate means that future generations are automatically largely compensated for climate damage that remains unmitigated. It should be noted, though, that positive law only requires compensation of residual damage in the case of strict liability, but not in the case of negligence liability.

Concluding remarks

This chapter has offered an overview of the debate in ethics and economics about whether discounting the future is morally justifiable. It has shown why the choice of discount rate is neither a mere matter of efficiency nor one of consumer sovereignty, and how application of various moral theories leads to different rates. Most theories face the problem of reconciling the moral intuitions that we ought to reduce the long-term risks of climate change faced by future generations, but we have no duty to increase our general savings rate across the board. Deontological approaches are able to reconcile these two intuitions, but are generally foreign to the framework of standard welfare economics that is primarily based on consequentialism and welfarism (Stern 2007: 29).

There is one perspective that has been given little attention in the literature, however. All moral theories that have been discussed in this chapter differ in their definition of our *duties* towards future generations. There is also a broader view on morality, though, an all-inclusive theory of conduct that includes views on the good life (see also Mackie 1977: 106). We may care about our descendants, for example, not only because we *owe* it to them, but also because our ability to give meaning to our lives depends on the existence of a future in which our present-day projects can be continued and flourish (see e.g. Partridge 1980; Heyd 1992). The prospects of future generations may therefore affect our own well-being here and now. According to John O'Neill (1993: 54–5):

> the standard perspectives on time preferences make sense only if one pictures a person's life as consisting of a series of momentary acts of desire satisfaction. Given such a life a pure-time preference for consumption now over consumption in the future makes sense. However, it does so at the cost of coherence in a person's life. Just as such a picture of lives across generations isolates each generation into itself, such a picture of an individual's life isolates each act into itself. A strong sense of identity across time is lacking...
>
> Our concern with the future is, hence, a concern with now: how well our life at present is proceeding depends on its relation to a projected future.

Psychological studies have already shown that, if people can choose between different time series of consumption of which the total consumption is equal, they may prefer increasing over decreasing series, implying a *negative* pure rate of time preference (Loewenstein and Prelec 1991). Such preferences for improvement may be related to one's views on meaning in life, and may describe not only preferences regarding the course of one's own life, but also the course of the intergenerational human project.[11] Future research in this direction would certainly be a welcome addition to the existing literature.

Notes

1 This chapter draws upon earlier work: Davidson 2015.

2 Note that the CDR is also often called the social rate of time preference (SRTP). Sometimes it is also called the 'social discount rate', but this latter term is ambiguous. Various authors use the term 'social discount rate' to denote a *weighted average* of the CDR and the MRRI. This social discount rate is used in CBA if one does not compare the consumption streams through time that result from different policy

decisions (see below in this section for further discussion), but directly compares discounted future costs and benefits against present costs and benefits (see Lind 1982, 1990: S-11; Davidson 2006).

3 Note that underlying the aim of efficiency itself is already the moral assumption that efficiency and maximizing welfare is worth aiming for (see e.g. Baum 2009).

4 Note that this so-called Ramsey equation holds only under conditions of certainty. An uncertain future can give rise to precautionary savings and consequently a lower *CDR* (see e.g. Kimball 1990; Gollier 2010).

5 The term 'Government House utilitarianism' is from Williams (1973: 139), describing the paternalistic morality agreeable to colonial administrators, overruling the morality of the common man.

6 See also Jeremy Bentham (1789), who on the one hand acknowledged the existence of pure time preference when stating that the value of pleasure or pain depends upon 'its propinquity or remoteness' (Chapter IV, §2 and §17), but at the same time argued that the government ought to make efforts to inform people of the negative consequences of their time preferences (Chapter XV, §24).

7 Beckerman and Hepburn (2007: 195) make the interesting observation that the marginal utility of consumption depends largely upon the consumption level of one's peers. Since the people we compare ourselves with are generally contemporaries, inequality in consumption between generations is likely to be less important than inequality within a generation.

8 Dietz and Asheim (2012) have investigated 'sustainable discounted utilitarianism', an approach that gives priority to the future in conflicts where the future is *worse* off than the present. In this approach the utility discount rate is set to zero if present utility exceeds future welfare, for example if the future consequences of climate change entail that present utility exceeds future welfare. If the future is better off, however, then 'sustainable discounted utilitarianism' coincides with discounted utilitarianism.

9 Deontologists would therefore disagree with Schelling (1995: 396–7), who framed climate mitigation as 'sacrifices' we are making to 'redistribute our income' to future generations, comparable to the sacrifices we make for 'foreign aid programmes'. As Cline (1998: 100) responded, '[s]urely there is an ethical difference between refraining from conveying a gift, on the one hand, and imposing a damage, on the other'. For Cline (2012: 7) this is an additional reason to apply his 'preferred approach with zero pure time preference' in the case of climate damage.

10 See Spash (2002: 243) for a less stringent view.

11 Spash (1993: 120, note 7), for example, notes how 'the Russian people made extreme sacrifices after their revolutio'n in order that their descendants might be better off'.

Bibliography

Adler, M. D. (2009), 'Future generations: a prioritarian view', *The George Washington Law Review*, vol. 77: 1478–520.

Adler, M. D. and Treich, N. (2015), 'Prioritarianism and climate change', *Environmental and Resource Economics*, vol. 62(2): 279–308.

d'Arge, R. C., Schulze, W. D. and Brookshire, D. S. (1982), 'Carbon dioxide and intergenerational choice', *American Economic Review*, vol. 72(2): 251–6.

Arrow, K. J. (1973), 'Rawls' principle of just savings', *Swedish Journal of Economics*, vol. 75(4): 323–35.

Arrow, K. J. (1995), 'Intergenerational equity and the rate of discount in long-term social investment', *IEA World Congress*, December 1995. Available at: www-siepr.stanford.edu/workp/swp97005.pdf (accessed 27 May 2016). Reprinted as Arrow K. J. (1999),

'Discounting, morality, and gaming', in P. R. Portney and J. P. Weyant (eds), *Discounting and Intergenerational Equity*, Baltimore, MD: Johns Hopkins University Press, pp. 13–21.

Arrow, K. J., Cline, W. R., Maler, K. G., Munasinghe, M., Squitieri, R. and Stiglitz, J. E. (1996), 'Intertemporal equity, discounting, and economic efficiency', in J. P. Bruce, H. Lee and E. F. Haites (eds), *Climate Change 1995: Economic and Social Dimensions of Climate Change*, Cambridge: Cambridge University Press, pp. 125–44.

Asheim, G. B. (2012), 'Discounting while treating generations equally', in R. W. Hahn and A. Ulph (eds), *Climate Change and Common Sense: Essays in Honour of Tom Schelling*, Oxford: Oxford University Press, pp. 131–46.

Azar, C. and Sterner, T. (1996), 'Discounting and distributional considerations in the context of global warming', *Ecological Economics*, vol. 19(2): 169–84.

Bauer, T. (1957), *Economic Analysis and Policy in Underdeveloped Countries*, Durham, NC: Duke University Press.

Baum, S. D. (2009), 'Description, prescription and the choice of discount rates', *Ecological Economics*, vol. 69(1): 197–205.

Baumol, W. J. (1968) 'On the social rate of discount' *The American Economic Review*, 58(4) 788–802.

Beckerman, W. and Hepburn, C. (2007), 'Ethics of the discount rate in the *Stern Review on the Economics of Climate Change*', *World Economics*, vol. 8(1): 187–210.

Bentham, J. (1948 [1789]), *An Introduction to the Principle of Morals and Legislations*, Oxford: Blackwell.

Birdsall, N. and Steer, A. (1993), 'Act now on global warming – but don't cook the books', *Finance and Development*, vol. 30: 6–8.

Broome, J. (1991), *Weighing Goods*, Oxford: Blackwell.

Broome, J. (1992), *Counting the Cost of Global Warming*, Cambridge: The White Horse Press.

Broome, J. (2004), *Weighing Lives*, Oxford: Oxford University Press.

Broome, J. (2012), *Climate Matters; Ethics in a Warming World*, New York: W. W. Norton.

Buchholz, W. and Schumacher, J. (2010), 'Discounting and welfare analysis over time: Choosing the η', *European Journal of Political Economy*, vol. 26(3): 372–85.

Caney, S. (2008), 'Human rights, climate change, and discounting', *Environmental Politics*, vol. 17(4): 536–55.

Caney, S. (2009), 'Climate change, human rights, and moral thresholds', in S. Humphreys (ed,), *Human Rights and Climate Change*, Cambridge: Cambridge University Press, pp. 69–90.

Cline, W. R. (1992), *The Economics of Global Warming*, Washington, DC: Institute for International Economics.

Cline, W. R. (1998), 'Equity and discounting in climate-change decisions', in W. D. Nordhaus (ed,), *Economics and Policy Issues in Climate Change*, Washington, DC: Resources for the Future, pp. 97–104.

Cline, W. R. (1999), 'Discounting for the very long term', in P. R. Portney and J. P. Weyant (eds), *Discounting and Intergenerational Equity*, Baltimore, MD: Johns Hopkins University Press, pp. 131–40.

Cline, W. R. (2012), 'Intergenerational discounting and global economic policies', Remarks at the conference on 'Ethics and Globalization: Tradeoffs Behind Policy Choices', Washington, 7 January, Peterson Institute for International Economics. Available at: http://piie.com/publications/papers/cline20130107.pdf (accessed 28 May 2016).

Crisp, R. (2003), 'Equality, priority, and compassion', *Ethics*, vol. 113: 745–63.
Dasgupta, P. (1974), 'On some alternative criteria for justice between generations, *Journal of Public Economics*, vol. 3(4): 405–23.
Dasgupta, P. (2008), 'Discounting climate change', *Journal of Risk and Uncertainty*, vol. 37(2–3): 141–69.
Davidson, M. D. (2006), 'A social discount rate for climate damage to future generations based on regulatory law', *Climatic Change*, vol. 76(1–2): 55–72.
Davidson, M. D. (2014), 'Zero discounting can compensate future generations for climate damage', *Ecological Economics*, vol. 105: 40–7.
Davidson, M. D. (2015), 'Climate change and the ethics of discounting', *Wiley Interdisciplinary Reviews: Climate Change*, vol. 6(4): 401–12.
Dietz, S. and Asheim, G. B. (2012), 'Climate policy under sustainable discounted utilitarianism', *Journal of Environmental Economics and Management*, vol. 63(3): 321–35.
Dietz, S. and Stern, N. (2008), 'Why economic analysis supports strong action on climate change: a response to the *Stern Review*'s critics', *Review of Environmental Economics and Policy*, vol. 2(1): 94–113.
Eckstein, O. (1957), 'Investment criteria for economic development and the theory of intertemporal welfare economics', *The Quarterly Journal of Economics*, vol. 71(1): 56–85.
Fisher, I. (1907), *The Rate of Interest: Its Nature, Determination and Relation to Economic Phenomena*, New York: Macmillan.
Frankfurt, H. (1987), 'Equality as a moral ideal', *Ethics*, vol. 98: 21–43.
Gollier, C. (2010), 'Ecological discounting', *Journal of Economic Theory*, vol. 145(2): 812–29.
Hampicke, U. (2011), 'Climate change economics and discounted utilitarianism', *Ecological Economics*, vol. 72: 45–52.
Harrod, R. F. (1949), 'Lecture two: the supply of saving', in *Towards a Dynamic Economics: Some Recent Developments of Economic Theory and their Application to Policy*, London: Macmillan, pp. 35–62.
Heyd, D. (1992), *Genethics: Moral Issues in the Creation of People*, Berkeley, CA: University of California Press, .
Hope, C. (2006), 'The marginal impact of CO2 from PAGE2002: an integrated assessment model incorporating the IPCC's five reasons for concern', *Integrated Assessment*, vol. 6: 19–56.
Hume, D. (1967 [1738]), *A Treatise of Human Nature*. London: Clarendon Press.
Kimball, M. S. (1990), 'Precautionary saving in the small and in the large', *Econometrica*, vol. 58(2): 53–73.
Koopmans, T. C. (1960), 'Stationary ordinal utility and impatience', *Econometrica*, vol. 28(2): 287–309.
Koopmans, T. C., Diamond, A. and Williamson, R. E. (1964), 'Stationary utility and time perspective', *Econometrica: Journal of the Econometric Society*, vol. 32(1/2): 82–100.
Krutilla, J. and Fisher, A. (1975), *The Economics of Natural Environments*, Baltimore, MD: Johns Hopkins University Press.
Kyllönen, S. and Basso, A. (2016), 'When utility maximization is not enough: intergenerational sufficientarianism and the economics of climate change', in A. Walsh, S. Hormio and D. Purves (eds), *The Ethical Underpinnings of Climate Economics*, London: Routledge.

Lind, R. C. (1982), 'A primer on the major issues relating to the discount rate for evaluating national energy options', in R. C. Lind, K. J. Arrow, G. R. Corey, P. Dasgupta, A. K. Sen, T. Stauffer, J. E. Stiglitz, J. A. Stockfisch and R. Wilson *Discounting for Time and Risk in Energy Policy* Washington, DC: Resources for the Future, pp. 21–114.
Lind, R. C. (1990), 'Reassessing the government's discount rate policy in light of new theory and data in a world economy with a high degree of capital mobility', *Journal of Environmental Economics and Management*, vol. 18(2): S8–S28.
Lind, R. C. (1995), 'Intergenerational equity, discounting, and the role of cost–benefit analysis in evaluating global climate policy, *Energy Policy*, vol. 23(4–5): 379–89.
Lind, R. C., Arrow, K. J., Corey, G. R., Dasgupta, P., Sen, A. K., Stauffer, T., Stiglitz, J. E., Stockfisch, J. A. and Wilson, R. (1982), *Discounting for Time and Risk in Energy Policy*, Washington, DC: Resources for the Future.
Loewenstein, G. and Prelec, D. (1991), 'Negative time preference', *The American Economic Review*, vol. 81(2): 347–52.
Mackie, J. L. (1977), *Ethics: Inventing Right and Wrong*, Harmondsworth: Penguin.
Manne, A. S. (1995), 'The rate of time preference: implications for the greenhouse debate', *Energy Policy*, vol. 23(4): 391–4.
Manne, A. S., Mendelsohn, R. and Richels, R. (1995), 'MERGE: a model for evaluating regional and global effects of GHG reduction policies', *Energy Policy*, vol. 23(1): 17–34.
Marglin, S. A. (1962), 'Economic factors affecting system design', in A. Maass, M. Hufschmidt, R. Dorfman, Jr H. A. Thomas, S. A. Marglin and G. M. Fair (eds), *Design of Water Resource Systems*, Cambridge, MA: Harvard University Press, pp. 159–225.
Marglin, S. A. (1963), 'The social rate of discount and the optimal rate of investment', *Quarterly Journal of Economics*, vol. 77(1): 95–111.
Marshall, A. (1890), *Principles of Economics*, London: Macmillan and Co., Ltd.
Meyer, L. H. and Roser, D. (2009), 'Enough for the future', in L. H. Meyer and A. Gosseries (eds), *Theories of Intergenerational Justice*, Oxford: Oxford University Press, Oxford, 219–48.
Mirrlees, J. A. (1967), Optimum growth when technology is changing, *Review of Economic Studies*, vol. 34(1): 95–124.
Moellendorf, D. (2014), *The Moral Challenge of Dangerous Climate Change: Values, Poverty, and Policy*, Cambridge: Cambridge University Press.
Moore, M. A., Boardman, A. E., Vining, A. R., Weimer, D. L. and Greenberg, D. H. (2004), 'Just give me a number! Practical values for the social discount rate', *Journal of Policy Analysis and Management*, vol. 23(4): 789–812.
Nordhaus, W. D. (1997), 'Discounting in economics and climate change: an editorial comment', *Climatic Change*, vol. 37(2): 315–28.
Nordhaus, W. D. (2007), 'A review of the *Stern Review on the Economics of Climate Change*', *Journal of Economic Literature*, vol. 45(3): 686–702.
Nordhaus, W. D. (2008), *A Question of Balance: Weighing the Options on Global Warming Policies*, New Haven, CT: Yale University Press.
Nordhaus, W. D. and Boyer, J. (2003), *Warming the World: Economic Models of Global Warming*, Cambridge, MA: MIT Press.
Nozick, R. (1974), *Anarchy, State and Utopia*, Oxford: Basil Blackwell.
Olsen, M. and Bailey, M. (1981), 'Positive time preference', *Journal of Political Economy*, vol. 89(1): 1–25.
O'Neill, J. (1993), *Ecology, Policy and Politics: Human Well-being and the Natural World*, London: Routledge.

Page, E. A. (2007), 'Justice between generations: investigating a sufficientarian approach', *Journal of Global Ethics*, vol. 3(1): 3–20.

Pareto, V. (1906), *Manual of Political Economy*, trans. Schrier A. (1971), London: Macmillan and Co., Ltd.

Parfit, D. (1983), 'Energy policy and the further future: the social discount rate', in D. MacLean and P. G. Brown (eds), *Energy and the Future*, Totowa, NJ: Rowman & Littlefield, pp. 31–7.

Parfit, D. (1997), 'Equality and priority', *Ratio*, vol. 10(3): 202–21.

Partridge, E. (1980), 'Observations: why care about the future?', *Alternative Futures*, vol. 3(4): 77–91.

Pearce, D. W. (1983), 'Ethics, irreversibility, future generations and the social rate of discount', *International Journal of Environmental Studies*, vol. 21(1): 67–86.

Pearce, D. W. and Ulph, D. (1999), 'A social discount rate for the United Kingdom', CSERGE Working Paper GEC 95-01. University College London and University of East Anglia, CSERGE, London.

Pearce, D. W., Markandya, A. and Barbier, E. B. (1989), *Blueprint for a Green Economy*, Abingdon: Earthscan.

Pigou, A. C. (1920), *The Economics of Welfare*, London: Macmillan.

Portney, R. and Weyant, J. P. (eds) (1999), *Discounting and Intergenerational Equity*, Baltimore, MD: Johns Hopkins University Press.

Price, C. (1973), 'To the future: with indifference or concern? The social discount rate and its implications in land use', *Journal of Agricultural Economics*, vol. 24(2): 393–8.

Price, C. (1993), *Time, Discounting and Value*, Oxford: Blackwell.

Price, C. and Nair, C. T. S. (1985), 'Social discounting and the distribution of project benefits', *The Journal of Development Studies*, vol. 21(4): 525–32.

Ramsey, F. P. (1928), 'A mathematical theory of saving', *Economic Journal*, vol. 38(152): 543–59.

Rawls, J. (1971), *A Theory of Justice*, Cambridge, MA: Harvard University Press.

Rendall, M. (2014), 'The sufficiency view as prima facie principle', Paper presented at ECPR Joint Sessions. Available at: www.ecpr.eu/Filestore/PaperProposal/ebc1164e-949b-4218-ba79-022e7201fca1.pdf (accessed 27 May 2016).

Robinson J. C. (1990) 'Philosophical origins of the social rate of discount in cost-benefit analysis'. *The Milbank Quarterly*, 68(2): 245–65.

Roser, D. (2008), 'The discount rate: a small number with a big impact', in Center for Applied Ethics and Philosophy (eds) *Applied Ethics: Life, Environment and Society*, Sapporo: Hokkaido University, pp. 12–27.

Samuelson, P. A. (1937), 'A note on measurement of utility', *The Review of Economic Studies*, vol. 4(2): 155–61.

Scheffler, S. (1982), *The Rejection of Consequentialism: A Philosophical Investigation of the Considerations Underlying Rival Moral Conceptions*, Oxford: Oxford University Press.

Schelling, T. C. (1995), 'Intergenerational discounting', *Energy Policy*, vol. 23(4/5): 395–401.

Sen, A. K. (1961), 'On optimising the rate of saving', *The Economic Journal*, vol. 71(283): 479–96.

Sen, A. K. (1967), 'Isolation, assurance and the social rate of discount', *The Quarterly Journal of Economics*, vol. 81(1): 112–24.

Sen, A. K. (1982), 'Approaches to the choice of discount rates for social benefit–cost analysis, in R. C. Lind, K. J. Arrow, G. R. Corey, P. Dasgupta, A. K. Sen, T. Stauffer, J. E. Stiglitz, J. A. Stockfisch and R. Wilson (eds), *Discounting for Time and Risk in Energy Policy*, Washington, DC: Resources for the Future, pp. 325–53.

Sidgwick, H. (1874), *The Methods of Ethics*, London: Macmillan.

Singer, P. (1972), 'Famine, affluence, and morality', *Philosophy & Public Affairs*, vol. 1(3): 229–43.

Solow, R. M. (1974), 'Intergenerational equity and exhaustible resources', *Review of Economic Studies* (Symposium on the Economics of Exhaustible Resources), vol. 41: 29–45.

Spash, C. L. (1993), 'Economics, ethics, and long-term environmental damages', *Environmental Ethics*, vol. 15(2): 117–32.

Spash, C. L. (1994), 'Double CO2 and beyond: benefits, costs and compensation', *Ecological Economics*, vol. 10(1): 27–36.

Spash, C. L. (2002), *Greenhouse Economics: Value and Ethics*, vol. 1, London: Routledge.

Stern, N. (2007), *The Economics of Climate Change: The Stern Review*, Cambridge and New York: Cambridge University Press.

Tol, R. S. J. (2002), 'Estimates of the damage costs of climate change. Part 1: benchmark estimates', *Environmental and Resource Economics*, vol. 21(1): 47–73.

Tol, R. S. J. (2006), 'Multi-gas emission reduction for climate change policy: an application of FUND', *The Energy Journal*, vol. 27: 235–50.

Tol, R. S. J. (2014), 'UN author says draft climate report alarmist, pulls out of team', Reuters, 27 March, Available at: www.reuters.com/article/2014/03/27/us-climatechange-idUSBREA2Q1FX20140327 (accessed 27 May 2016).

Weitzman, M. L. (2007), 'The stern review of the economics of climate change', *Journal of Economic Literature*, vol. 45(3): 703–24.

Weitzman, M. L. (2009), 'On modeling and interpreting the economics of catastrophic climate change', *The Review of Economics and Statistics*, vol. 91(1): 1–19.

Williams, B. (1973), 'A critique of utilitarianism', in J. J. C. Smart and B. Williams (eds), *Utilitarianism: For and Against*, Cambridge, MA: Cambridge University Press, pp. 77–150.

4 Climate change, intergenerational equity, and the social discount rate[1]

Simon Caney

Introduction

Climate change raises a number of questions of intergenerational equity. One – and the one that attracts the most attention – is the question of what obligations people have to future generations not to engage in activities that will trigger dangerous climate change and thereby impose harms on people in the near and distant future. The question of what we owe to future people is of critical importance when determining mitigation policy for it bears on when any generation should mitigate and by how much. The economic literature on this issue has tended to approach these questions by drawing on the idea of a 'social discount rate'. The aim in this chapter is to examine the normative force of the considerations that are employed to determine the social discount rate. To do so, I will distinguish between three kinds of consideration invoked in analyses of discounting, assessing in each case their plausibility and their implications for climate change policy. The three kinds are, respectively, Pure Time Discounting, Growth Discounting and Opportunity Cost Discounting. I shall defend the following three claims:

A Pure Time Discounting gives us no reason to delay taking action to mitigate climate change (or for adopting a more gradual approach when implementing mitigation policies).

B Growth Discounting and Opportunity Cost Discounting can only justify very limited justification for delaying action to mitigate climate change.

However,

C Growth Discounting might (subject to two conditions), give us reason to pass on some of the costs of mitigating climate change (and adapting to climate change) to future generations.

This chapter has the following structure: Section I sets out four elements that should be part of any account of intergenerational justice. Sections II to IV discuss whether there is any case for Pure Time Discounting across generations, arguing that there is not. The extent to which people should mitigate should thus not be based on a positive pure time discount rate. Section V introduces what is termed Growth Discounting. Section VI argues – on empirical grounds – that Growth Discounting does not justify postponing mitigation or adopting a gradual approach to mitigation (what I refer to as *Delaying Action*). Section VII examines a third reason given for *Delaying Action* – namely Opportunity Cost Discounting and – drawing on the empirical data available – concludes that it too can justify very little, if any, delaying on action. Finally, Section VIII discusses the proposal made by John Broome (2012), among others, that current generations should adopt an aggressive mitigation policy (and thus *Delaying Action* is wrong), but should be allowed to pass on some of the costs of mitigation to future generations (so what I shall term *Deferring Cost* is justified). Broome maintains that this is pragmatically desirable but unjust: but passing on the costs is *not* necessarily unjust, as adduced by four considerations in defence of it, and we shall seek to rebut Broome's reason for thinking it unjust.

The component parts of an account of intergenerational justice

How should we think about the responsibilities that members of one generation have to future people? In what follows, I take it that any account of intergenerational justice must have at least four component parts:

> *variable [1]*. First, it must specify the agent in question and the role that they are occupying for this affects what principles are appropriate. The principles of intergenerational justice that a person adopts in his or her role as a parent will be different from those that are appropriate in his or her role as a government official. My focus here is on what principles of intergenerational justice are appropriate if we see ourselves as representatives of humanity. This chapter thus explores what humanity at large owes to future generations. (Subsequent analyses can then consider what persons – qua family members – owe any descendants they have, and what members of firms – qua trustees of the firm – owe future shareholders, and so on.)
>
> *variable [2]*. Second, an account of intergenerational justice must specify whether we are according equal moral status to all persons (present, current or future). Is it appropriate to ascribe a lower weight to human interests the further they are in the future just because of the fact that they exist further in the future? To put it in the terms employed by economists, a key question is whether a theory of justice should permit, or require, any *pure time preference*.[2]
>
> *variable [3]*. Third, any account of intergenerational justice must affirm a *principle of intergenerational equity*. For example: Should one generation leave future people equally well-off? Or is it required only to leave future people above a certain sufficiency threshold? Or should it seek to maximize total well-being? What distributive principle, if any, should apply?

variable [4]. Fourth, an account of intergenerational justice needs to outline and defend an account of the metric of justice. Should the distributive principle refer to welfare or primary goods (Rawls 1999a: 78–81) or resources (Dworkin 2000: 65–119) or capabilities (Nussbaum 2011; Sen 2009: III) or something else?

This list is not intended to be exhaustive. I shall not, for example, discuss other aspects that a theory of intergenerational equity might include – such as its position on how to respond to risk and uncertainty (see Caney 2009: 176–81), or the Non-Identity Problem (Parfit 1984: chapter 16) and whether it can justify a kind of discounting. These questions are set aside not because they are unimportant – they are of very great significance – but purely for reasons of space.

Of course in determining what obligations current generations have to future generations to mitigate climate change we need to consider the costs and benefits of mitigation and the likely socio-economic condition of future people. Much important analysis of the intergenerational dimensions of climate change has been conducted by economists. The latter, however, tend not to employ the normative framework outlined above but rather couch their arguments in terms of a social discount rate, where this is conventionally expressed as follows:

$$\text{SDR} = \delta + \eta \times (\text{rate of increase in consumption per capita}).$$[3]

The social discount rate is based on a number of different variables: δ, for example, refers to the extent of pure time preference, what I have termed variable [2]; η is much more complex. As Wilfred Beckerman and Cameron Hepburn point out in their very illuminating discussion of the use of η in the *Stern Review*, η is used to reflect three separate values (aversion to inequality over time, aversion to inequality over space, and risk aversion) (Beckerman and Hepburn 2007: 193). Rather than employ the social discount rate, however, we shall use the fourfold normative framework introduced above to consider the kinds of normative consideration that are employed to determine the social discount rate and examine how these bear on the four variables.

Pure Time Discounting: the concept

One key consideration concerns whether current generations may (or indeed should) treat members of future generations as their moral equals, or whether they may (or should) exercise pure time preference. To relate this to my normative framework, the first question we face is how to think about variable [2].

It is useful to begin our analysis by noting the different possible kinds of pure time discount rates.

First, there are those who adopt a zero pure time discount rate.[4] Most notably, Nicholas Stern adopts this in the *Stern Review* (2007: esp. 35–7, 51–4, 60).[5] Similarly *The Garnaut Review* also holds that economic analyses of climate change should not accord less weight to interests the further that they are into the future (2008: 19).

Many economists though defend positive pure time discount rates. There are many possibilities here. Some defend fixed rates whereas others have defended variable discount rates. For example, in *Warming the World* William Nordhaus and Joseph Boyer adopt the following approach: '[t]he rate of time preference starts at 3 percent per year in 1995 and declines to 2.3 percent per year in 2100 and 1.8 percent per year in 2200' (Nordhaus and Boyer 2000: 16).

In addition to this disagreement about the content of the discount rate there is also a disagreement about method. Some adopt what is termed a 'descriptive' approach (where this utilizes the way that people do actually act) whereas others adopt a 'prescriptive' approach (where this explicitly relies on a value judgement about what discount rate is morally appropriate) (Arrow *et al.* 1996: 131–4). Boyer and Nordhaus, for example, use market data to calculate the discount rate (2000: 15), whereas Stern (2007) adopts a prescriptive approach.

Like many philosophers, I take it that it would be wrong to discount for time. There are two reasons for this – what we can term the *Moral Equality Argument* and the *Best Use Argument*. I begin with the former and then turn to the less familiar, but still powerful, second consideration:

Two arguments for a zero pure time discount rate

- *The Moral Equality Argument*. The most common and straightforward argument for a zero pure time discount rate maintains simply that we have no reason to attribute fundamental moral importance to someone's location in time. A person's place in time is not, in itself, the right kind of feature of a person to affect their entitlements. For example, it does not make someone more or less deserving or meritorious. Similarly, it does not, in itself, make anyone's needs more or less pressing. More generally, if we consider the core values and ideals undergirding theories of justice, then temporal location plays no fundamental role. For utilitarians, for example, what matters is 'utility' and 'maximization': time has no fundamental moral significance. Or consider luck egalitarians. If the thought is that no one should be disadvantaged through no fault of their own then, again, temporal location is utterly irrelevant. To penalize someone *merely* because they were born later (and for no other reason) would be to disadvantage them through no fault of their own. More generally, someone's temporal location seems on a par with their racial identity or gender or ethnicity, and in the same way that it is wrong to penalize or discriminate against someone because of their race or gender so it is also wrong to discriminate against someone because of their date of birth. It is not the right kind of property to confer on people extra or reduced moral status.
- *The Best Use Argument*. I believe that the first argument is compelling but it is worth examining whether it can be supplemented. Consider now what

> we might term the *Best Use Argument*. This, as its name suggests, maintains that pure time discounting results in a suboptimal use of resources. It does this because it allows something other than the optimal use of a resource – namely the proximity in time of the enjoyment of that good – to influence the use of that resource. As such it is *bound* to result in a suboptimal allocation of resources.

This point has often been made by utilitarians, such as Jevons (1970) [1879]: 124) and Pigou (1932, §§3–5: 25–8). Pigou writes eloquently about how a positive pure time discount rate can, ceteris paribus, lead to an overuse of natural resources. It is worth quoting him at length:

> This same slackness of desire towards the future is also responsible for a tendency to wasteful exploitation of Nature's gifts. Sometimes people will win what they require by methods that destroy, as against the future, much more than they themselves obtain. Over-hasty exploitation of the best coal seams by methods that cover up and render unworkable for ever worse, but still valuable, seams; fishing operations so conducted as to disregard breeding seasons, thus threatening certain species of fish with extinction; farming operations so conducted as to exhaust the fertility of the soil, are all instances in point. There is also waste, in the sense of injury to the sum total of economic satisfaction, when one generation, though not destroying more actual stuff than it itself obtains, uses up for trivial purposes a natural product which is abundant now but which is likely to become scarce and not readily available, even for very important purposes, to future generations. This sort of waste is illustrated when enormous quantities of coal are employed in high-speed vessels in order to shorten in a small degree the time of a journey that is already short. We cut an hour off the time of our passage to New York at the cost of preventing, perhaps, one of our descendants from making the passage at all.
>
> (Pigou 1932: 27–8, footnotes omitted)

In an earlier article I rejected the *Best Use Argument* on the grounds that it relied upon a maximizing consequentialism (Caney 2009: 168). However, although utilitarians can and do invoke it, it is a mistake to think it depends on utilitarianism. Its power remains even if one is not a maximizing consequentialist. Suppose, for example, that one accepts a sufficientarian account and wishes to ensure that everyone is above a certain threshold standard of living. One is unlikely to be indifferent to the cost of doing so (especially when resources are scarce). What the argument and Pigou's examples establish is that a positive pure time discount rate results in inefficiency: it will be more costly (and perhaps even impossible) if we employ a positive time discount than it would be otherwise.

One particular illustration of the underlying argument – and an illustration that will appeal to non-utilitarians as well as utilitarians – is made by Derek

Parfit (1984: 485). In the course of discussing what he terms the '[t]he Argument from Excessive Sacrifice', Parfit (1984: 484), makes the following interesting point: consider two policies which cost exactly the same amount of money. One averts a 'major catastrophe' but is further off in the future than another one that averts a 'minor catastrophe'. Now, as Parfit points out, if we adopt a positive pure time discount rate we may be compelled to choose that policy that prevents only a minor catastrophe – simply because of its location in time, 'the greater catastrophe is less worth preventing' (1984: 485). But this is obviously absurd.

Note that the *Moral Equality Argument* and the *Best Use Argument* can stand separately from one another. To see this consider the following: Suppose that someone is not persuaded by the claim that future persons enjoy the same moral status as current persons (so they are unpersuaded by the *Moral Equality Argument*). Suppose, however, that this person does think that future persons are entitled to *some* moral consideration (just not *equal* consideration compared to contemporaries) and, in virtue of this, thinks that future people are entitled to a very basic standard of living (minimal sufficientarianism). Now suppose, in addition to this, that there is a resource that is essential for attaining the sufficientarian threshold and that, if people do not overuse this resource at any point, then it can be sustained throughout time and thus meet the needs of future persons. Now suppose, finally, that each generation uses a (high) positive pure time discount rate. In this situation it is quite possible that – because of the high pure time discount rate – earlier generations overuse the resource required by future people, and, thereby, deny future people the minimal sufficientarian threshold. In such a case, one can condemn a positive pure time discount rate because of its suboptimal use of resources (appealing, thus, to the *Best Use Argument*) without also endorsing the *Moral Equality Argument*. Thus, even if one were not persuaded by the *Moral Equality Argument*, one might think that the inefficiencies created by a non-zero pure time discount rate (and Parfit's example) are sufficient to condemn it.

Objections to a zero pure time discount rate

Zero pure time discount rates are, however, controversial – especially among economists, many of whom endorse positive pure time discount rates (e.g. Nordhaus 2008). One can identify two types of objection to a zero pure time discount rate and the defence of it presented above – one methodological and one substantive. On the methodological front, some economists would criticize the reasoning above (especially the first argument) on the grounds that a 'prescriptive' approach is invalid and it is wrong for philosophers or economists to propose their own value judgement (e.g. Nordhaus 2007: 691). They argue instead that we should adopt a so-called 'descriptive' rate, which has been criticised elsewhere (Caney 2008: 542–4).

Let us consider now what I am terming substantive objections. These argue that a zero pure time discount rate is morally problematic in some way. However, as Parfit (1984: 480–6) points out, many of these (if not all of them) turn out *not* really to be arguments against *pure time* discounting, but instead are arguments for a different kind of discounting. To see one example of this, consider the common objection that a zero pure time discount rate is unduly demanding. Many economists argue that such a pure time discount rate requires current generations to make enormous sacrifices for future generations. Why? The reason is that, whereas a resource consumed now may just benefit current generations, if it were invested it could benefit many future people. As such a zero pure time discount rate can lead to those currently alive making large sacrifices for all those who will follow. The only way to avoid this, it is assumed, is to adopt a positive pure time discount rate, which by giving diminished weight to the interests of future generations ensures that their claims do not impose excessive demands on earlier generations.[6]

However, as many (including Broome, Dasgupta, Parfit and Rawls) have observed, this argument is mistaken. Whether an account of intergenerational justice is unreasonably onerous depends not only on whether there is a zero pure time discount rate but also what the content of the principle is (maximizing utility? ensuring a sufficiency threshold? a prioritarian distributive principle? or something else?). To use the terms set out above, variable [3] matters as well as variable [2]. Thus a zero pure time discount rate *in itself* cannot result in any particular demands. It also depends what principle of intergenerational equity is being affirmed.[7] Given this, there are at least three ways of responding to the charge of excessive demandingness:

Response (a): modify the pure time discount rate;
Response (b): modify the distributive principle; or,
Response (c): maintain that there are no limits on what we can fairly demand.[8]

Our first conclusion, then, is that the demandingness argument on its own *cannot* show that a zero pure time discount rate is implausible.

We can, however, go further. For as the critics mentioned above also observe, the most plausible response to legitimate concerns about demandingness is what I have termed option (b) above.[9] To see this, consider the other options, starting with (c). I assume here that there are limits on how much we can reasonably demand of people and thus option (c) should not be endorsed. Let us turn now to (a). We have two reasons for thinking that this would be the wrong option to take. First, note that the demandingness objection does not explain why *location in time* is morally relevant. It makes no reference to time or why time is morally relevant. This provides further support for Rawls's verdict that it is an 'ad hoc' alteration designed to come out with a more attractive conclusion, rather than a direct argument as to why we may disadvantage some because of their place in time (Rawls 1999a: 262). It does not address the issue of why those further *off in time* should have less of a claim on us. To see this consider a theory which limits the demands of a theory by insisting that we should penalize people according to how close in time they are to us and increasingly care about them the further off in time they are. This too could ensure that the demands made on us fall beneath some specified threshold of demandingness to exactly the same extent as one that employs a positive pure time discount rate. Avoiding demandingness gives us no reason to prefer one to another. Crucially *it does not explain why the passage of time is morally relevant*. As such it gives us no reason to endorse (a). Second, and in addition to this, we have good reason to prefer (b) to (a). Those pressing the objection often assume a commitment to maximizing utility. However, since utilitarianism is also demanding, not simply in the intergenerational context, but also within one generation, this suggests that if there is a problem it lies with a commitment to *maximizing* utility. Adding a positive pure time discount rate would not tackle the underlying problem.

These two considerations suggest that adopting option (a) is an implausible way to respond to the demandingness argument, and that we should pursue option (b) This requires us to examine what principles of distributive justice apply across time, and ask whether maximization is an appropriate principle. This takes us to the subject of the next two sections. Having discussed pure time discounting and defended a zero pure time discount rate, let us then consider a second kind of discounting. This second kind focuses not on variable [2] but variable [3].

Growth Discounting: the concept

Some argue that we may prioritize current generations over future generations on the grounds that the latter will be wealthier than us, and it is wrong for the poor to make sacrifices to enable the rich to become richer. Within the economics literature this has been termed Growth Discounting. Nordhaus defines Growth Discounting in the following passage:

> [One] reason for favoring present over future consumption comes from the fact that different generations enjoy different levels of consumption. Industrial countries have witnessed more or less continual growth in living standard for more than a century; thus, the per capita real consumption in the U.S. has growth by a factor of at least four over the twentieth century. Most global change models project continued rapid growth of living standards in the future, and indeed there would be little cause for climate alarm if world output stagnated at its current level. Society might well feel that it is appropriate for later, richer generations to pay a larger fraction of greenhouse gas (GHG) control costs, just as high-income people pay a larger fraction of their income in income taxes. We might then discount future costs if average living standards were improving – a phenomenon called *growth discounting*.
>
> (Nordhaus 1997: 317)

Stern makes the same claim, writing that 'we should discount the consumption of future generations on the basis that they are likely to be richer than ourselves.

This reason for discounting is, and should be, part of most models, including those of the Stern Review' (Stern 2008: 14). The core idea underlying Growth Discounting is, thus, very simple. It states:

> *Growth Discounting*: People in the future will have more economic wealth and it is wrong to make the poor (current generations) pay rather than the rich (future generations).

To relate this to the framework set out in the first section, proponents of Growth Discounting are affirming a broadly egalitarian distributive principle (variable [3]).[10]

Growth Discounting raises at least five key questions:

> *First*, will future generations in fact be wealthier? And will they be wealthier even with the onset of climate change?

> *Second*, even if future generations in, say, 100 years' time are wealthier it is quite possible given human history that in some cases global average wealth (however defined) will be lower in the near future than it is now. Suppose, for example, that a major war breaks out. Growth is never simply a constantly upwards slope; there are major recessions and setbacks. So average wealth at t2 might be lower than at t1. How does this affect the argument?

> *Third*, there is, in addition, considerable risk and uncertainty involved in any predictions about future wealth. This then raises the question: how should we respond to the risks and uncertainties associated with any predictions about future wealth? Is it reasonable to act on the assumption of increased wealth even though there is a risk that future people will be worse off?

> *Fourth*, we need to know what the relationship is between economic prosperity, on the one hand, and the metric of justice, on the other. For example, is the metric of justice defined in terms of the receipt of economic wealth? And, if not, can increased economic wealth be 'converted' so as to protect the goods that *are* included in our best account of the metric of justice? This question takes us to variable [4], as specified above, and illustrates why it is crucial. Suppose, for example, that there is economic growth but that it cannot be used to secure people's just entitlements as to what matters (suppose it provides little help in advancing people's welfare); then the case for Growth Discounting is undermined.

> *Fifth*, even if we know that future generations will be better off why should we engage in Growth Discounting? What is the normative rationale for this?

Suppose that we provide answers to the five preceding questions. We face one more question: what are the implications of an appeal to Growth Discounting for climate policy? Here it is vital to distinguish between two possible lessons that one might draw:

> *The Delaying Action Version*: Growth Discounting establishes that current generations are under a less onerous duty to mitigate and provide adaptation than they would otherwise be. On this view, Growth Discounting provides a justification for delaying action (such as mitigation) and for introducing mitigation measures more gradually over time.

This is the most commonly advanced response to the question I posed above. There is, however, a second possibility:

> *The Deferring Cost Version*: Growth Discounting does not have implications for the extent to which current generations should mitigate; *but* it does establish that some of the cost of combating climate change should be passed on to future generations.[11]

Many assume that to the extent that Growth Discounting is justified it entails mitigating less now. William Nordhaus (2008), for example, clearly thinks that the truth (as he sees it) of Growth Discounting entails that mitigation should be pursued less aggressively than otherwise. It is, however, worth considering the possibility of divorcing the question of 'whether and how much current generations should mitigate' from the question of 'whether and how much current generations should bear a financial burden'. This is what the *Deferring Cost Version* claims. It allows that we should mitigate aggressively now, but then holds (in line with the broadly egalitarian approach associated with Growth Discounting) that some of the costs should be passed on. It has recently been defended by John Broome (2012: chapter 3) (drawing on Foley 2009) and by Matthew Rendall (2011).

In what follows I argue that: the *Delaying Action Version* is implausible but that the *Deferring Cost Version* is more reasonable (though not problem free). In Section VIII I also critically discuss Broome and Rendall's defence of *Deferring Cost*.

Growth Discounting argument 1: Delaying Action

Let us begin then with the *Delaying Action Version* (but not with the normative rationale for Growth Discounting, which follows in a later section). We can assume that those with greater wealth may reasonably be expected to bear a larger proportion of the burden of addressing climate change. I shall, however, dispute the assumption that Growth Discounting provides a plausible case for delaying the introduction of mitigation policies and for introducing them more gradually than would otherwise be the case.

It might be helpful to state at the outset what assumptions a Growth Discounting argument for delaying action would have to make in order to succeed. To secure its conclusion such an argument would need to:

i specify an account of what current and future people are entitled to, including (a) what kinds of advantages they are entitled to (resources? welfare? capabilities?) and (b) how much of them people are entitled to (the account of intergenerational justice);
ii establish that there will be economic growth even with the onset of some climate change that will be sufficient to ensure that future people are able to adapt successfully to climate change so that they can enjoy the entitlements specified in (i); and
iii provide a normative argument showing why future people, and not current people, should bear the costs of ensuring that they enjoy the entitlements specified in (i) (the normative rationale).

A proponent of *Delaying Action* can of course address (i); and, as I will argue later, there are reasons to accept a version of (iii). The vulnerable part of their argument concerns (ii) – namely, the empirical assumption about the effects of delaying action. Assumption (ii) is problematic for four reasons. One worry common to the first three objections concerns the metric of justice (see variable [4] above): the worry is that we have reason to doubt that an increase in material wealth can be 'converted' to protect the standard kinds of interests that many leading accounts (whether welfarist, resourcist and so on) would hold that justice requires protecting:[12]

- First, the IPCC notes that there physical and biological limits to adaptation (Klein *et al.* 2014: 16.3.2.2–3). These include 'ecological limits' to the extent to which human society can adapt to a changed and changing atmosphere (Peterson 2009). Agricultural systems, to take one example, will be severely threatened by dramatic increases in temperature and this imposes some ecological limits on the extent to which we can cope with a hotter world. To put it another way: there are limits to the extent to which the destruction of natural resources can be addressed by the substitution of capital and human resources.[13]
- Second, many climate scientists also note that there are considerable epistemic limits to adaptation (Klein, *et al.* 2014: 16.3.2.1). Existing integrated assessment models operate at the global level and provide projections for global mean temperature increases and sea-level rises. We have much less knowledge about what specific impacts are going to occur and in which specific places at what times. This epistemic problem considerably hampers attempts to prepare for climatic changes.
- A third problem with the idea of growing and then adapting is that a society's ability to adapt depends, to a large extent, on whether it has responsive political institutions at the appropriate levels. The Growth Discounting

> argument for delaying action assumes that increased wealth is sufficient to enable future people to cope with climatic changes. But the existing research on adaptation reveals this to be unduly sanguine. One widely endorsed finding from such research is that the character of existing political institutions and forms of governance play a key role (Brooks *et al.* 2005). As Brooks *et al.* argue, adaptive capacity is a function of a government's ability to implement effective adaptation policies, the degree of political stability, its commitment to investing in adaptation, whether there is inclusive political decision-making processes, and the existence of civil and political rights that enable political participation (Brooks *et al.* 2005: 155). They list eleven vulnerability indicators, of which four concern the nature of the political system – namely, 'voice and accountability', 'civil liberties', 'political rights' and 'government effectiveness' – and an additional variable which is also somewhat separate from economic growth – namely 'literacy' (Brooks *et al.* 2005: 157). Indeed, their conclusion is that '[a]daptive capacity ... is associated predominantly with governance, civil and political rights, and literacy' (Brooks *et al.* 2005: 151).

One final point is that even if we set aside the ecological, epistemic and institutional limits to adaptation and assume that increased wealth can help address climate change and enable future people to enjoy their (as yet unspecified) entitlements, the argument is incomplete. It is widely recognized that delaying action would be much more costly (Stern 2007). Proponents of this argument therefore need to present us with their principle of intergenerational justice and then to show in light of this principle that the increased wealth that they are assuming minus the (increased) cost of addressing climate change leaves future people with their fair share. So even if the three preceding challenges fail the argument is incomplete.

Opportunity Cost Discounting

At this point it is worth interrupting the discussion of Growth Discounting to consider a third additional, distinct, argument for discounting – namely, what has been termed Opportunity Cost Discounting (Mendelsohn 2008a, 2008b). We will consider this here (and then return to the discussion of Growth Discounting) because, although it is distinct from the Growth Discounting argument for *Delaying Action*, it is also employed to defend *Delaying Action*.

What then is Opportunity Cost Discounting? Opportunity Cost arguments take the form of arguing that we should delay doing X and should instead invest the resources that would be devoted to X-ing on the grounds that the return on the investment exceeds the benefit that would have been realized by doing X.[14] In the context of climate change, the argument would be that it is better to delay mitigation and invest in technological innovation because the resources that would be spent on mitigating now will generate much greater mitigation-benefits if we invest instead.

This argument is distinct from the Growth Discounting argument for delaying action for it does not argue – or depend on the assumption – that there will be overall economic growth.[15] It just contends that there would be a greater return if we invested the resources on, say, clean technology than we would if we used those resources to mitigate now and in the near future. Mitigation would thus be cheaper if we waited. For an example of this kind of reasoning consider the following statement from Robert Mendelsohn (2008a: 49):[16]

> Delaying abatement expenditures into the future also allows society to take advantage of technical change. Although there are many potential ways to reduce greenhouse gas emissions, few of them can be adopted quickly on a large scale. Many of the most promising ideas are not yet clearly understood. Over time, however, society can learn which methods are effective and which are not. For example, let us assume that society can improve the effectiveness of abatement in general by 2 percent per year through technical change. That is, every year, the marginal cost of abatement falls by 2 percent. The emissions one could eliminate by spending $100 billion today would cost only $37 billion if we waited for the technology that would be available by 2050. The cost would be only $13.5 billion using the technology of 2100. Combining the advantages of technical change and delay, the present value of the abatement program would be just $5 billion in 2050 and $250 million in 2100. These are huge rewards to society from delaying abatement.

How should we response to this reasoning? Two points are in order. First, we should record that Opportunity Cost Discounting is often very sensible. Second, we should also note that in itself this kind of argument cannot tell us what principles of intergenerational justice apply: it is a technical argument about the most efficient way of meeting a given end and so should be judged normatively (inter alia, how valuable is the end?) and empirically (are its empirical claims correct?). Related to this (and, as we shall see in the next paragraph), the appraisal of Opportunity Cost arguments itself will involve value judgements.

The question here is whether Opportunity Cost reasoning lends support to the kind of delay in mitigating climate change that Mendelsohn defends. I note three reasons for caution. First, he appears to reject zero (or low pure) time discount rates (Mendelsohn 2008b: 309), contrary to the view defended above (in 'Two arguments for a zero pure time discount rate' and 'Objections to a zero pure time discount rate'). If so, this would lead him to attach insufficient weight to future harmful climatic impacts and thus to conclude that there is little harm if we delay action until the end of this century. Second, he also relies on assumptions about the extent to which wealth can enable adaptation (Mendelsohn 2008a: 57) that the last section queried. This too leads him to attach insufficient weight to future harmful impacts.

Once we accept this, and if we take on board the verdict of the *Fifth Assessment Report* of the Intergovernmental Panel on Climate Change, then the

Opportunity–Cost Argument for the kind of delay that Mendelsohn envisages is implausible. For Chapter 12 of the *Fifth Assessment Report* reports:

> To limit the warming caused by anthropogenic CO_2 emissions alone to be *likely* less than 2°C relative to the period 1861–1880, total CO_2 emissions from all anthropogenic sources would need to be limited to a cumulative budget of about 1000 PgC since that period. About half [445 to 585 PgC] of this budget was already emitted by 2011.
>
> (Collins and Knutti 2013: 1033)

On current trajectories this means that humanity would have emitted the total 'cumulative budget' by 2040, thereby committing us within the following 25 years, to a more than 50 per cent chance of a 2°C increase in global mean temperatures over pre-industrial times, and thus the efficiencies promised by Mendelsohn would be too late.[17] Note this projection focuses solely on carbon dioxide. The prognosis is even bleaker if we include other factors. The passage from the IPCC quoted above continues: 'Accounting for projected warming effect of non-CO_2 forcing, a possible release of GHGs from permafrost or methane hydrates, or requiring a higher likelihood of temperatures remaining below 2°C, all imply a lower budget.' (Collins and Knutti 2013: 1033) This further undermines Mendelsohn's argument.

In light of these three considerations we have reason to be cautious about Mendelsohn's Opportunity Cost argument for delaying action. This does not mean that no delay could ever be justified on opportunity discounting grounds, but it does challenge the extent of the delay proposed by Mendelsohn.

Growth Discounting argument 2: Deferring Cost

Having examined whether the Growth Discounting argument and the Opportunity Cost argument justify delaying action and argued that they can justify little to no delay, I now wish to return to the Growth Discounting argument, and explore whether it can justify the term *Deferring Cost*. The earlier arguments did not dispute the normative principle underlying the claim that growth discounting is defensible. They merely queried – on empirical grounds – the assertion that it justified delaying climate action. Here I turn to the normative question. To use the framework introduced in the first section, I shall examine what content we should attribute to variable [3]. What principle(s) of justice apply between one generation and those that come after it? And, do they justify *Deferring Cost*?

Deferring Cost, recall, holds that:

- i the appropriate action is – contrary to the first Growth Discounting argument – to act now and to mitigate climate change; however, it also maintains that
- ii the costs of this mitigation need not necessarily be borne by contemporary generations, but can be passed on to future generations.

Before evaluating this position it is worth making three preliminary points. First, it is important to record that, in virtue of its commitment to [i], the *Deferring Cost* argument avoids all the challenges to *Delaying Action* that were presented in the last two sections. Since it calls for immediate mitigation it is not vulnerable to the ecological, epistemic and institutional challenges to the claim that increased wealth can ensure the necessary protection from climatic changes. Likewise, it avoids the concern that delaying action might be so costly that it denies future people their just entitlements.

Second, however, we do need to clarify in what ways it is possible to defer the costs. Otherwise a critic might argue that though it escapes one kind of practical objection it acquires another. In reply to this some useful points have been made by John Broome. As he notes, we can, for example, abstain from leaving natural resources that we would otherwise leave. Or we can devote fewer resources to investment, and focus instead on current consumption (Broome 2012: 44). More simply, we can run a budget deficit. These points are also noted by Matthew Rendall (2011: 892–3) who also draws attention to ways in which we can pass on costs to the future.[18]

Third, as mentioned above, Broome and Rendall have both defended the *Deferring Cost Version*. However, they do so on different grounds to those presented here. Broome, for example, endorses *Deferring Cost* on pragmatic grounds. His view is that it would be better if current generations acted now and absorbed the cost (what he terms 'efficiency with sacrifice') than if they acted now and passed on the cost to future generations (what he terms 'efficiency without sacrifice') (Broome 2012: 45–6). He thinks that if they made the sacrifice now it would (a) increase total well-being and (b) be fairer (Broome 2012: 46). However, he thinks that, since it is crucial to avert dangerous climate change and, since current governments seem unlikely to act if their citizens must absorb the costs that Broome thinks they ought to, then there is a case for adopting 'efficiency without sacrifice' (2012: 38, 47–8, 155). That way enables humanity to implement an effective mitigation programme that would otherwise not be implemented.

Like Broome, Rendall (2011: 884) also argues that not deferring the cost would be 'politically unrealistic' and he makes that the central reason for passing on some of the cost. However, unlike Broome, he also thinks that requiring current generations to absorb the whole cost would be unfair (Rendall 2011: 884, cf. also p. 893). He does not, however, elaborate on how it would be unfair and he does not appeal to any particular distributive principle to vindicate that claim. The aim in what follows is to do precisely this, and so the following five considerations are adduced in favour of it.

§1–3 Three arguments for Growth Discounting

Many economists have affirmed growth discounting because they endorse a utilitarian approach and they then invoke the principle of diminishing marginal utility.[19] Stated more fully, they reason thus: we should maximize utility, and, *given that* the marginal utility of each extra unit of wealth decreases the wealthier someone is, and, *given that* future generations will be wealthier than current generations, *then* it is wrong to devote resources to future generations. Therefore current generations can discount the resources to be devoted to future generations. I do not wish to rely on utilitarianism to make my case. It is, however, instructive to note that several other distributive criteria would justify deferring some of the cost (and, moreover, that they too can appeal to the idea of diminishing marginal utility).

In particular it is worth noting that growth discounting can draw on three commonly adduced principles. First, it can, for example, be defended by appealing to a prioritarian principle and maintaining that that may be applied over time (*Intergenerational Prioritarianism*). If wealth increases over time, and if we are committed to promoting the condition of the least advantaged, then we have reason to favour current generations.[20]

A similar conclusion is reached if we adopt egalitarian principles and contend that these apply over time. This would, of course, give us reason to embrace the Growth Discounting argument for deferring the cost (*Intergenerational Egalitarianism*).[21]

Third, it is even possible that the intergenerational application of a sufficientarian position would justify deferring the cost (depending in part on how high we specify the threshold) – especially in cases of current non-compliance (*Intergenerational Sufficientarianism*). This last point is less obvious and requires some explanation. Consider the following scenario:

> There are people who are desperately disadvantaged. If they do not increase their use of energy then they will not be able to attain a decent standard of living (the sufficiency threshold). At the same time, if they do increase their use of energy by using fossil fuels in order to attain a decent standard of living then they will make a major contribution to causing dangerous climate change. These people face a potentially tragic choice.

This scenario is very relevant in the world we face today. Many lack access to energy and as a result are unable to meet core needs. At the same time – because there is only a limited amount of greenhouse gases that can be emitted, and because of the noncompliance of others – the amount of emissions required to realize their needs may take us over the safe level.

Suppose, however, that we can in fact ensure that the people in question could both attain a decent standard of living and do so without using fossil fuels. Suppose, in particular, that this is possible because, and to the extent that the poor in this case can restrain their emissions but pass on the cost of mitigation to future wealthier people (including future generations). Suppose, for example, that they can borrow money to purchase clean technology and then pay pack the relevant sum at a much later date. *If* this is possible then it provides a way of realizing both the sufficiency threshold and also not triggering dangerous climate change. It realizes the sufficientarian threshold because not only can the poor develop now but also the deferred cost does not compromise the capacity of future people, who are projected to be wealthier, to meet the sufficiency level. In this kind of case, then, deferring the cost follows from a commitment to *Intergenerational Sufficientarianism*. It is justified as the only way to avoid the tragic dilemma I described above.

We have seen then that there are three routes to the conclusion that if future people are wealthier, then it is just that they should pay for some of the cost that current generations incur by mitigating climate change.

Sometimes people resist prioritarian or egalitarian claims because they object to levelling down. It is therefore worth noting that we are not faced here with an existing situation of inequality and then considering whether to reduce some people who are currently wealthy to much lower levels. The issue we face is a different one: namely, when designing and setting up the system of the burdens and benefits associated with economic cooperation and development over time, what distributive principle should guide that design? Should we *create* one in which the poor make sacrifices to make whoever is born in the future – who will be wealthier than current generations – even more well-off? Or should we instead *create* one which both avoids foisting certain harms on future generations but also avoids bestowing on them certain benefits as well? Putting it in this way makes it clear, I think, that those who live in the future do not have a prior pre-existing claim to those benefits – or that superior standard of living – which we would be taking away from them. Framed like this it would not be wrong to try to design a framework where opportunities to live good and fulfilling lives are shared more equally across time.

Some might appeal to duties or permissions of partiality to provide further support for the conclusion defended here. That is, they might argue that persons have special obligations (or at the very least permissions) to further the interests of those they care for. On this view, persons may (perhaps even ought to) favour themselves and their children and grandchildren over those in the further future. It might then be argued that this gives us an additional reason to endorse *Deferring Cost*.[22]

I shall not rely on this reasoning here. Recall, I am examining this issue from the point of view of *humanity at large* (variable [1] above) and that we are asking what principles of justice should govern the way that members of one generation of humanity should treat those who come after them. Here, an impartial perspective – one that treats all as equal – seems the appropriate one. This then sets out the overarching framework within which individuals (among other agents) are free to act with their fair share of resources. Now duties of partiality do plausibly apply at the individual-level. We think that an individual may favour his or her own children or family and friends when deciding what to leave others in their will. But this individual-level perspective is (a) not the level we are considering in this chapter, and (b) it applies *within* the moral general framework that we are outlining. That is, individuals may be partial to some using their *fair* share of resources as determined by the overarching account of justice. Partiality thus operates within the limits of a fair and impartial background and so I shall not adduce this extra consideration to defend *Deferring Cost*.

§4 The Benefit Argument

Thus far then I have adduced three reasons to endorse *Deferring Cost*. To this we can now add a fourth. To introduce this fourth argument it is worth noting that (as we shall see in more detail in §5) those with concerns about passing on the costs focus on the *harms* that current generations may be creating. They ask why others (future wealthy people) should have to pay people now not to create those harms. We should, however, take into account the bigger picture, examining not just the creation of harms but also the creation of benefits too. For the current generation is not just abstaining from harm creation (hopefully), but it is also creating many positive benefits for future people, such as increased wealth, buildings, infrastructure, culture and so on.

Given this one might then make the following argument: Why is it right that future people can inherit the *advantages* we create but none of the *sacrifices* involved in the creation of those advantages (where one sacrifice is 'abstaining from high emitting economic activities')? Their wealth is not exogenously given. Rather it is inherited and stems from the labour and investment of earlier generations. This adds a further reason then as to why future people should contribute to the costs of mitigating climate change. If they enjoy the benefits should they not pay for some of the cost and sacrifice involved in the safe creation of those benefits? We lack any reason to treat all the benefits that we create in an asymmetric way to all the burdens that we also create. We might call this the *Benefit Argument*.[23]

To anticipate an objection, there will be cases where it is wrong to impose a harm, A, on future people and one cannot argue that imposing that harm A is acceptable because we have also provided a benefit, B. For example, one cannot break someone's leg and give them money and think that the latter outweighs the former, and thereby conclude that that person has not been harmed. In such a case we do not combine a *pro tanto* disadvantage with a *pro tanto* advantage and then just conclude that, all things considered, no harm was done. Their right was violated and, no matter how much money they were subsequently paid, this fact remains unchanged.

However, the case referred to above is different. Imagine, for example, that we mitigate now but decide to pass on some of the cost by not investing in building hospitals for the future. By mitigating we have lessened the chance that they will be exposed to some health threats; and by investing less in building new hospitals, we are making a smaller contribution than we would otherwise do to the very same interest (their health). My broader point here is that, rather than single out harmful effects that result from climatic changes or the costs of mitigation, it makes more sense to look at future people's enjoyment of a total package of benefits and burdens.[24] If people inherit benefits then may they not also inherit some of the costs involved in creating those benefits?

§5 Rebutting an objection

Thus far, I have argued that the central objection to growth discounting lacks force and that deferring the costs enjoys support from four separate considerations (including *Intergenerational Egalitarianism*, *Intergenerational Prioritarianism*, *Intergenerational Sufficientarianism* and the *Benefit Argument*).

But what of Broome's reason for thinking that deferring the cost is unfair. As noted above, although he endorses *Deferring Cost* he thinks it involves injustice. Why? Broome's starting point is the plausible assumption (P) that justice requires that the polluters should not engage in harmful activities. Broome then appears to infer from this the conclusion (C) that justice requires that the would-be polluters should absorb the cost of not engaging in this harmful behaviour (Broome 2012: 46). But this conclusion does not necessarily follow. One can hold that in a just world A would not do X whilst also thinking that in a just world the sacrifice involved for A in not doing X should not be borne solely (or indeed at all) by A. (P) does not entail (C).

In addition to this, we lack reason to endorse (C). Why should we think that justice requires the would-be polluter to absorb the total cost? Someone might say in reply that the Polluter Pays Principle is a well-established principle and that the reasoning underpinning it supports Broome's view here.[25] The Polluter Pays Principle rests on the underlying idea – widely affirmed by egalitarian liberal thinkers like Dworkin and Rawls – that agents should be responsible for their choices. However, as Dworkin (2000: 5–7, chapter 2) and Rawls (1999b: 241–2, 261–2, 284, 369–70) both emphasize, this principle is not the whole of justice; it applies only within a fair basic structure within which agents have a fair share of resources. One cannot then argue that if A acts in a way that results in pollution then A should not do so, and that A should bear the cost of preventing any harm that might ensue. One cannot argue thus because one needs to know whether A was exceeding his or her fair share or not, and whether A enjoyed a fair set of resources. If A lacks his or her legitimate entitlements, then A should be exempted from paying.

Whether current generations should pay should then depend on what we think their fair share is. Suppose that one gave an egalitarian answer to this. Suppose, that is, that one held that persons should enjoy an equal set of advantages and, moreover, that this principle of equality should apply over time (in addition, perhaps, to other principles). Now, if future generations tend to be wealthier than current ones, then – in virtue of the principle of intergenerational egalitarianism – it would be permissible to 'borrow from the future' and thereby act in ways that make the inequality less than it would otherwise be.

In short, then, the principle of responsibility is just one part of a theory of (intergenerational) justice. If one adds in a broadly egalitarian principle of (intergenerational) justice regulating the basic structure (to outline just one possibility), then we can see that it would not be unjust for current generations to transfer the costs of mitigation (and adaptation) to future generations. One central normative objection to the *Cost Version* is thus incomplete. To make the argument complete, the critic would need to show that whatever principle should regulate the basic structure it would not mandate or permit passing on costs to the future.

We can express the same point another way. The critic is assuming that burdens should be allocated according to a pure unqualified version of the Polluter Pays Principle. However, if, as we have elsewhere, a pure unqualified Polluter Pays Principle that takes no account of someone's absolute or comparative standard of living is implausible (Caney 2005: esp. 763, 765), and, if 'Ability to Pay' considerations should play a major role (Caney 2010), then we have the normative basis for thinking that justice permits the poor passing on costs to the wealthy.

There are, however, two major caveats to the growth discounting argument for deferring the cost. The first is that the argument obviously crucially depends on there being economic growth in the future. Many economists take it as a given that there will be continued economic growth. However, if there are constraints that entail that such growth will not continue, then clearly this argument cannot be applied. Second, the argument assumes that it is possible to pass on some of the cost to future generations and there may be considerable limits to this. So the defence of growth discounting argument for deferring the cost is necessarily heavily qualified by these two factors.

Concluding remarks

In this chapter I have sought to examine how we should think about our obligations to future generations. To do so I have examined three reasons often given for devoting resources to current generations over future generations. This leads to conclusions that:

A the first consideration examined (Pure Time Discounting) gives us no reason to delay mitigation; and, in addition,

B two other considerations often invoked – Growth Discounting and Opportunity Cost Discounting – also give us little to no reason to delay mitigation; however,

C the fact (if it is a fact) that future people will be wealthier than their predecessors can justify members of one generation passing on some of the costs of mitigation to members of future generations.

I have adduced four considerations in support of C, and have sought to rebut the main challenge to it. Much more needs to be said in defence of egalitarian and/or prioritarian values in the intertemporal context, but this chapter will hopefully have motivated some support for sharing the burden intergenerationally.[26]

Notes

1 Originally published in *Politics, Philosophy & Economics*, 13(4) (2014): 320–42.
2 Stern defines the 'the pure time discount rate' as 'the rate of fall of the value of a unit of consumption, *simply because it is in the future*, quite separately from the levels of consumption enjoyed at the time' (Stern 2008: 14).
3 See, for example, Arrow *et al.* (1996: 130, 136ff.), Nordhaus (2008: 33) and Stern (2007: 52). This formula can be traced back to Ramsey's (1928) classic discussion. For good overviews and framing of the issues see Broome (1992: chapter 3); Beckerman and Hepburn (2007: 187–210, esp. 190–206); Dasgupta (2008: 141–69); Parfit (1984 480–6); Stern (2007: esp. 35–7, 51–60; 2008: 12–17).
4 See, e.g. Harrod (1949: 40); Jevons (1970 [1879]: 124); Parfit (1984: 480–6); Pigou (1932: 24–30); and Ramsey (1928: 543–59 esp. 543).
5 See also Stern (2008: 14–15).
6 See Arrow (1999: 14–16); Nordhaus (2008: 182–3). For a seminal analysis see Tjalling Koopmans 'Stationary Ordinal Utility and Impatience' (Koopmans 1960: 287–309) and 'Objectives, Constraints, and Outcomes in Optimal Growth Models' (Koopmans 1967: 1–15). Koopmans (1967: 8) refers to 'the paradox of the indefinitely postponed splurge'.
7 See Broome (1992: 106), Dasgupta (2001: 94), Parfit (1984: 484–5) and Rawls (1999a: 262). See also Brennan (2007: 268).
8 Someone might argue that a fourth response is available, namely (d): maintain that there are limits on what we can fairly demand but argue that a zero pure time discount rate issues in prescriptions which are not unfairly demanding. I set (d) aside for it makes the false assumption that the pure time discount rate *in itself* can be demanding or undemanding. My argument in the text is that pure time discounting cannot, on its own, issue in *any* conclusions, demanding or otherwise.
9 See, for example, Broome (1992: 106), Dasgupta (2001: 94), Parfit (1984: 484–5), Rawls (1999a: 262).
10 I am using the term 'egalitarian' widely so that it includes not just strictly egalitarian approaches but also prioritarian approaches and approaches that are concerned that inequalities do not exceed certain limits rather than calling for strict equality.
11 The idea of acting now but deferring some of the costs was suggested to me by Andrew Williams at a seminar in Oxford in November 2005 when I was presenting a different paper to this one (what became Caney 2010). At the time, I assumed that it was not possible to pass on the costs, but now I think that that assumption is questionable, and that it may be possible to pass on at least some of the costs. I am grateful to Andrew for this point, though he should not be held responsible for the way that I am expressing or seeking to motivate support for it.
12 See also Caney (2009: 175).
13 For an important discussion of these concepts see Dobson (1998).
14 For a canonical discussion of "the argument from opportunity costs" see Parfit (1984: 482–4: also Cowen and Parfit 1992: 151–4).
15 That the two arguments are different is made clear by Parfit (1984: 482–4). For an excellent discussion of Opportunity Cost Discounting see Roser (2010).
16 He makes the same argument elsewhere, calling for "investing in capital, infrastructure, and technology", though he also runs it together with a growth discounting argument (Mendelsohn 2008b: 309–10).
17 See http://trillionthtonne.org/ (accessed 26 May 2016).
18 See also the blog comments by Simon Wren-Lewis, Professor of Macro-Economics at Oxford, at https://mainlymacro.blogspot.co.uk/2012/05/government-debt-and-burden-on-future.html (accessed 30 May 2016) and at https://mainlymacro.blogspot.co.uk/2012/10/more-on-climate-change-and-budget_30.html (accessed 7 June 2016). The latter specifically discusses Broome's and Foley's argument. Elsewhere (Caney

2014: 133–4) I have noted some limits on the extent to which one can pass on sacrifices to future generations.

19 See, for example, Garnaut (2008: 19–20), Harrod (1949: 38, 40), Stern (2009: 81).

20 For salient discussion see Gaspart and Gosseries (2007: esp. 204–13). Note that Broome (2012: chapter 8, esp. 145–8) also discusses a prioritarian approach.

21 See, for example, Partha Dasgupta's (2008: 145) argument that

> considerations of justice and equality demand that consumption should be evenly spread across the generations. So, if future generations are likely to be richer than us, there is a case for valuing an extra unit of their consumption less than an extra unit of our consumption, other things being equal.

22 For a powerful statement of this kind of view see de-Shalit (1995: chapter 1). See also Arrow (1999: 14–16).

23 It is similar in spirit to Rawls's (1999a: 96–8) 'Principle of Fairness'.

24 For further argument for this conclusion and for a discussion of when we should treat certain burdens and benefits on their own and when we should treat burdens and benefits as part of an overall package see Caney (2012: xxx).

25 For a qualified appeal to this principle in this context see Caney (2009: 172).

26 I presented earlier versions of this article at the Politics, Philosophy and Economics conference on Climate Change at New Orleans (March 2013), the University of Gothenburg (April 2013) and the University of Copenhagen (June 2013) and thank the participants at all of these for suggestions and objections. I am particularly grateful to Bengt Brülde, Partha Dasgupta, Göran Duus-Otterstrom, Nils Holtug, Robert Keohane, Kasper Lippert-Rasmussen, Sune Lægaard, Søren Midtgaard, Christian Munthe, Jon Quong, John Roemer, Christian Rostbøll, Theresa Scavenius, and Andrew Williams for their very helpful comments. I owe a special debt to my respondent in New Orleans, Tom Christiano, for his probing written comments and objections. I also gratefully acknowledge the funding provided by the Oxford Martin School which enabled me to engage in this research.

Bibliography

Arrow, K. J. (1999), 'Discounting, morality, and gaming', in Paul R. Portney and John P. Weyant (eds), *Discounting and Intergenerational Equity* (Washington, DC: Resources for the Future), pp. 13–21.

Arrow, K. H., Cline, W. R., Maler, K.-G., Munasinghe, M., Squitieri, R., and Stiglitz, J. E. (1996) 'Intertemporal equity, discounting, and economic efficiency', in IPCC, *Climate Change 1995: Economic and Social Dimensions of Climate Change – Contribution of Working Group III to the Second Assessment Report of the Intergovernmental Panel on Climate Change* (Cambridge: Cambridge University Press), pp. 125–44.

Beckerman, W. and Hepburn, C. (2007), 'Ethics of the discount rate in the *Stern Review on the Economics of Climate Change*', *World Economics* vol. 8 no. 1: 187–210.

Brennan, G. (2007), 'Discounting the future, yet again', *Politics, Philosophy and Economics*, vol. 6 no. 3: 259–84.

Brooks, N., Adger, W. N. and Kelly, N. (2005), 'The determinants of vulnerability and adaptive capacity at the national level and the implications for adaptation', *Global Environmental Change* vol. 15 no. 2: 151–63.

Broome, J. (1992), *Counting the Cost of Global Warming* (Cambridge: The White Horse Press).

Broome, J. (2012), *Climate Matters: Ethics in a Warming World* (New York and London: W. W. Norton).

Caney, S. (2005), 'Cosmopolitan justice, responsibility, and global climate change', *Leiden Journal of International Law* vol. 18 no. 4: 747–75.

Caney, S. (2008), 'Human rights, climate change, and discounting', *Environmental Politics* vol. 17 no. 4: 536–55.

Caney, S. (2009), 'Climate change and the future: discounting for time, wealth, and risk', *Journal of Social Philosophy* vol. 40 no. 2: 163–86.

Caney, S. (2010), 'Climate change and the duties of the advantaged', *Critical Review of International Social and Political Philosophy* vol. 13 no. 1: 203–28.

Caney, S. (2012), 'Just emissions', *Philosophy & Public Affairs* vol. 40 no. 4: 255–300.

Caney, S. (2014), 'Two kinds of climate justice: avoiding harm and sharing burdens', *Journal of Political Philosophy* (Special Issue: Philosophy, Politics and Society), vol. 22 no. 2: 125–49.

Collins, M. and Knutti, R. (2013), 'Long-term climate change: projections, commitments and irreversibility', Chapter 12 in IPCC, *Climate Change 2013: The Physical Science Basis. Working Group I Contribution to the Fifth Assessment Report of the Intergovernmental Panel on Climate Change* (Cambridge: Cambridge University Press), pp. 1029–136.

Cowen, T. and Parfit, D. (1992), 'Against the social discount rate', in Peter Laslett and James S. Fishkin (eds), *Justice between Age Groups and Generations: Philosophy, Politics, and Society Sixth Series* (New Haven, CT, and London: Yale University Press), pp. 144–61.

Dasgupta, P. (2001), *Human Well-Being and the Natural Environment* (Oxford: Oxford University Press).

Dasgupta, P. (2008), 'Discounting climate change', *Journal of Risk and Uncertainty* vol. 37 nos. 2–3: 141–69.

Dobson, A. (1998), *Justice and the Environment: Conceptions of Environmental Sustainability and Theories of Social Justice* (Oxford: Oxford University Press).

Dworkin, R. (2000), *Sovereign Virtue: The Theory and Practice of Equality* (Cambridge, MA: Harvard University Press).

Foley, D. K. (2009), 'The economic fundamentals of global warming' in Jonathan M. Harris and Neva R. Goodwin (eds), *Twenty-First Century Macroeconomics: Responding to the Climate Challenge* (Cheltenham: Edward Elgar), pp. 115–26.

Garnaut, R. (2008), *The Garnaut Climate Change Review: Final Report* (Cambridge: Cambridge University Press).

Gaspart, F. and Gosseries, A. (2007), 'Are generational savings unjust?', *Politics, Philosophy & Economics* vol. 6 no. 2: 193–217.

Harrod, R. F. (1949), 'Lecture two: the supply of saving' in R. Harrod, *Towards a Dynamic Economics: Some Recent Developments of Economic Theory and Their Application to Policy* (London: Macmillan), pp. 35–62.

Jevons, W. S. (1970 [1879]), *The Theory of Political Economy*, 2nd edn (Harmondsworth: Penguin).

Klein, R. J. T., Midgley, Guy F. and Preston, Benjamin L. (2014) 'Adaptation opportunities, constraints, and limits', in Chapter 16, IPCC, *Climate Change 2014: Impacts, Adaptation, and Vulnerability. Working Group II Contribution to the Fifth Assessment Report of the Intergovernmental Panel on Climate Change* (Cambridge: Cambridge University Press).

Koopmans, T. C. (1960), 'Stationary ordinal utility and impatience', *Econometrica* vol. 28 no. 2: 287–309.

Koopmans, T. C. (1967), 'Objectives, constraints, and outcomes in optimal growth models', *Econometrica* vol. 35 no. 1: 1–15.

Mendelsohn, R. (2008a), 'Is the *Stern Review* an economic analysis?' *Review of Environmental Economics and Policy*, vol. 2 no. 1: 45–60.

Mendelsohn, R. (2008b), 'Comments on Simon Dietz and Nicholas Stern's *Why Economic Analysis Supports Strong Action on Climate Change: A Response to the Stern Review's Critics*', *Review of Environmental Economics and Policy*, vol. 2 no. 2: 309–10.

Nordhaus, W. D. (1997), 'Discounting in economics and climate change: an editorial comment', *Climatic Change* vol. 37 no. 2: 315–28.

Nordhaus, W. D. (2007), 'A review of *The Stern Review on the Economics of Climate Change*', *Journal of Economic Literature*, vol. XLV no. 3: 686–702.

Nordhaus, W. D. (2008), *A Question of Balance: Weighing the Options on Global Warming Policies* (New Haven, CT, and London: Yale University Press).

Nordhaus, W. D. and Boyer, J. (2000), *Warming the World: Economic Models of Global Warming* (Cambridge, MA: The MIT Press).

Nussbaum, M. C. (2011), *Creating Capabilities: The Human Development Approach* (Cambridge, MA, and London: Harvard University Press).

Parfit, D. (1984), *Reasons and Persons* (Oxford: Clarendon Press).

Peterson, G. (2009), 'Ecological limits of adaptation to climate change', in W. Neil Adger, Irene Lorenzoni and Karen L. O'Brien (eds) *Adapting to Climate Change: Thresholds, Values, Governance* (Cambridge: Cambridge University Press), pp. 25–41.

Pigou, A. C. (1932), *The Economics of Welfare*, 4th edn (London: Macmillan).

Ramsey, F. P. (1928), 'A mathematical theory of saving', *Economic Journal* vol. 38 no. 152: 543–59.

Rawls, J. (1999a), *A Theory of Justice*, rev. edn (Oxford: Oxford University Press).

Rawls, J. (1999b), *Collected Papers*, ed. Samuel Freeman (Cambridge, MA and London: Harvard University Press).

Rendall, M. (2011), 'Climate change and the threat of disaster: the moral case for taking out insurance at our grandchildren's expense', *Political Studies* vol. 59 no. 4: 884–99.

Roser, D. (2010), 'The opportunity cost argument for discounting climate damages: weak premises, strong conclusion?', paper presented at Conference on 'Cost–Benefit Analysis: Uncertainty, Discounting and the Sustainable Future', Eindhoven University of Technology, 12–13 April 2010.

Sen, A. (2009), *The Idea of Justice* (London: Allen Lane).

de-Shalit, A. (1995), *Why Posterity Matters: Environmental Policies and Future Generations* (London: Routledge).

Stern, N. (2007), *The Economics of Climate Change: The Stern Review* (Cambridge: Cambridge University Press).

Stern, N. (2008), 'Richard T. Ely lecture: the economics of climate change', *American Economic Review* vol. 98 no. 2: 1–37.

Stern, N. (2009) *A Blueprint for a Safer Planet: How to Manage Climate Change and Create a New Era of Progress and Prosperity* (London: The Bodley Head).

5 When utility maximization is not enough

Intergenerational sufficientarianism and the economics of climate change[1]

Simo Kyllönen and Alessandra Basso

Introduction

The predicted effects of climate change are potentially catastrophic. They include dramatic lowering of people's living standards and great loss of life. The commonly employed methods of economics, however, pay no specific attention to the effects that are expected to threaten many people's survival and subsistence. Moreover, the most serious effects are likely to be experienced by future people living centuries after us. But, as a result of the common practice in economics to discount the effects on future people, the economics of climate change may give significantly lower weight to those later serious effects of climate change compared to earlier (often lesser) effects.

A number of authors have therefore accused the standard economic evaluation of climate policies of being unable to deal explicitly with the serious ethical issues related to climate change and suggested that the economics of climate change should go beyond standard economic modeling and reconsider the narrow utilitarian ethics underpinning these models (e.g., Jamieson, 2014; Spash, 2002; Stern, 2014a, 2014b; see also the discussion in IPCC, 2014).[2] In this chapter, we take these suggestions seriously. We consider a specific non-utilitarian approach to justice, *sufficientarianism*, that cares especially about the effects on people's basic subsistence.

We begin by discussing the strengths of sufficientarianism in comparison to other ethical theories particularly in the context of intergenerational distribution related to climate change. Although the sufficientarian understanding of justice has provoked some plausible objections when applied among contemporaries, this approach has specific characteristics that speak in its favor when dealing with relations between generations. Moreover, many climate ethicists have advocated sufficientarian understandings of justice (Beckerman and Pasek, 2001; Cripps, 2013; Caney, 2010b; Shue, 2010; Wolf, 2009).

However, little has been done so far to investigate whether and how sufficientarian principles could be used to inform the economic analysis, and what consequences this would have. These neglected issues are addressed in the latter part of this chapter. We argue that accommodating sufficientarian ideals in the economic analysis is possible, but would require major changes in some of the core assumptions and customary methods of climate economics. We explore some recent attempts of environmental and climate economics to refine the standard assumptions (Heal, 2009; IPCC, 2014; Stern, 2014a, 2014b). In particular, we find the use of resource-specific discount rates (Baumgärtner *et al.*, 2015; Drupp, 2015; Heal, 2009; Traeger, 2011) a promising way to integrate sufficientarian principles with intergenerational economic evaluations.

Despite its narrowness, our investigation reveals some of the main conceptual and practical problems that arise when economics aims to address the ethical issues related to the potentially catastrophic effects of climate change. We argue that intergenerational sufficientarianism offers some promising ways for the economics of climate change to overcome these problems.

The appeal of sufficientarianism

The general starting point of sufficientarianism is the observation that what seems to motivate most people in their fight for equality is not equality per se, but rather the fact that some people are in misery or that they do not have enough for a decent life. As Joseph Raz writes, what "makes us care about various inequalities is not the inequality but concern identified by the underlying principle. It is the hunger of the hungry, the need of the needy, the suffering of the ill, and so on" (Raz, 1986: 240).

Following Raz, leading climate ethicist Simon Caney (2010a, 2010b) argues that some human interests are so fundamental that they should be protected by rights which directly represent "moral 'thresholds' below which people should not fall." While Caney's characterization of the threshold is limited to "most modest formulation of human rights," that is, rights to life, health and subsistence, Elisabeth Cripps (2013) has recently introduced a more expansive characterization. Following the capability approach developed by Amartya Sen (1999) and Martha Nussbaum (2006), Cripps suggests a view about fundamental human interests that is based on recognizing certain functionings as necessary for decent human life. These include at least having an opportunity to enjoy continued life of a normal human length, bodily health, bodily integrity, meaningful relationships with others and an ability to pursue a plan for one's own life with an adequate education. According to this view, if the impacts of anthropogenic climate change cause people to be deprived of their meaningful opportunity to exercise any of these functionings, then a serious harm is done to these people and we should refrain from causing it.

The central idea of sufficientarianism is that there is a morally relevant threshold and our main moral concern should be in improving the position of the people below the threshold. What matters, according to sufficientarianism, is that people have enough of what they ought to have for a decent life, and that they live free from deprivation. This positive thesis includes at the same time a negative one as well: according to sufficientarianism, improving the position of the less well-off people above the threshold is of no particular concern (see Casal, 2007; Meyer and Roser, 2009). Due to the negative thesis sufficientarianism has provoked some plausible objections when applied among contemporaries. According to Richard Arneson (1999), the specification of the morally relevant threshold, above which the importance of improving the less well-off person vanishes altogether, is arbitrary and implausible. Particularly, if the threshold includes only the "most modest formulation of human rights," it can plausibly be argued that this sufficientarian approach to justice is too restricted among contemporaries.

However, notwithstanding its problems in relations between contemporaries, sufficientarianism has specific characteristics that speak in its favor in the intergenerational relations. Moreover, as Meyer and Roser (2009) note, the critiques that are often leveled against it do not necessarily apply in the intergenerational context. For instance, equalizing relative differences between people also above some minimum level of basic rights or needs is often taken to be necessary in order to guarantee political equality between people. Yet, as pointed out by Meyer and Roser (2009: 242), because such arguments are about relationships between citizens who are tied together by shared institutions of authoritative decision-making, they do not hold between non-contemporaries. On the other hand, restricting our concern for distributive justice to the satisfaction of fundamental interests or needs may be the best available strategy in the intergenerational context with full of epistemic uncertainties. The particular way of life and understanding of well-being of future people will depend on technological and societal development that we can only predict with great difficulty (see also Shogren, 1999). Therefore we might not be in a position to determine how well off in terms of absolute well-being future people will be but we may well be able to make reliable estimation about whether their fundamental interests or needs are to be satisfied (see Meyer and Roser, 2009).

The reasons lying behind the increasing attraction of sufficientarianism in intergenerational climate ethics becomes evident if we have a brief look at the debate between different theories of justice. Initially, sufficientarian approach was presented as an intuitively plausible way to avoid the problems of other theories of justice (Frankfurt, 1987; Crisp, 2003). Utilitarianism is often criticized for being blind to the issues of distributive justice, because it is concerned solely with the maximization of total utility. Egalitarianism, on the other hand, is claimed to be vulnerable to the so-called leveling-down-objection: even if equality is not the only intrinsic value an egalitarian would hold, an egalitarian has to claim that there is something valuable in the state of affairs that is worse for some and better for no one. For instance, a world where everyone is blind would be more equal in comparison to a world that includes both blind and sighted, and hence it would be better at least in this respect.[3]

Some authors proposed the so-called priority view, according to which people's well-being has a diminishing marginal value, as a way to alleviate the problems of both theories (Parfit, 1997; Arneson, 1999). The priority view can avoid the leveling-down objection, because it does not hold equality to be intrinsically valuable, but has an egalitarian tendency towards more equal distribution: the more equal state of affairs matters only as much as this benefits the worse off.[4]

However, many take the priority view to be inadequate, because it only alleviates the problems of utilitarianism without removing them completely (see e.g., Crisp, 2003). Particularly in the intergenerational context of climate change, in which the decisions of the present generation can affect a very large number of future people, the priority view would actually have implications similar to utilitarianism (see Casal, 2007; Meyer and Roser, 2009). For instance, according to utilitarianism, even a minuscule improvement in the situation of a large number of future generations is able to outweigh the costs to the present people, even if those future people would probably be better off to begin with and even if the costs to worse-off present people would be unreasonably high and would bring the present people in misery. It is true that the priority view helps us to mitigate these unreasonable demands of utilitarianism, because if future people are better off in terms of well-being than the current generation, the priority view allows us to give less weight to improving their well-being (see e.g., Broome, 2012). But as long as the number of future better-off people is sufficiently large (e.g., it is infinite), the priority view would allow the same unreasonable demands on the present generation as utilitarianism does.[5]

In the intergenerational context, utilitarianism and the priority view are also accused of being unable to handle the problems related to a changing population (see e.g., Adler and Treich, 2015; Meyer and Roser, 2009). According to the well-known Repugnant Conclusion, it would be consistent with both theories to maximize the total well-being by levelling down the welfare of future people to barely worth living, if only the population is sufficiently increased (Parfit, 1984: 381ff.). While both theories have tried to avoid the Repugnant Conclusion by appealing either to average or so-called "critical level" versions of their theories, these attempts have their own problems.[6] Since the prioritarians are also committed to the so-called "person-affecting" view of ethics (in contrast to the impersonal view of utilitarianism), the priority view is also vulnerable to another well-known problem, that is, the Non-Identity Problem (see Adler, 2009; Parfit, 1984). According to the person-affecting view, the goodness of an outcome depends solely on how good the outcome is for individual persons (and not on some impersonal goodness, like total well-being, equality of the outcome, or something else). The Non-Identity Problem arises because, in order to determine whether, in accordance with the priority view, an outcome (e.g., of a climate mitigation policy) is better than the alternative (e.g., of a climate polluting policy), we need to be able to compare each individual's position in relation to her position in the alternative outcome. However, in many future-oriented choices (like in the policy choice between mitigation or pollution) a person-level comparison is impossible, because due to the choices made the person might not exist in all alternatives (Parfit, 1984).

Sufficientarianism can be interpreted as an attempt to respond to these problems by amending the priority view with a morally relevant threshold and giving even stronger priority to our concern for the misery of those people who are below the threshold. First, sufficientarianism can circumvent the Non-Identity Problem, since it requires that we are able to compare each person's position only against the threshold, and not against her relative position in alternative outcomes.[7] Second, sufficientarianism can also avoid the Repugnant Conclusion, because people whose life would be barely worth living would also be below the threshold and sufficientarianism would disvalue this shortfall from the threshold level (see Huseby, 2012). Finally, there is the question about the unreasonable demands posed to present generation due to the fact that they may be able to trivially benefit a very large number of future people. Here the sufficientarian respond depends on the specific formulation of the general idea of giving priority to benefitting people who are below the threshold.

According to one formulation, sufficientarianism includes only a kind of further qualification of the priority view: according to sufficientarianism, improving the position of those who are badly-off matters only below the morally relevant threshold, but decreases to zero at the threshold, whereas in the priority view the relatively worse-off have priority even at high levels of well-being. Meyer and Roser (2009) label this as *weak* sufficientarianism, because this formulation still allows trade-offs between benefitting those below the threshold and those above it. According to the weak view, if the benefits to better-off future people (above the threshold) are to outweigh the misery of the worse-off (below the threshold), the number of better-off people will only need to be very much larger. The so-called *strong* sufficientarianism, in contrast, holds that improving the position of those below the threshold has an absolute (or lexical) priority and no such trade-offs are allowed. The strong view is therefore purported to avoid the unreasonable demands objection, because the number of people above the threshold does not matter at all; all we need to care about is the misery of the people below the threshold.[8]

However, it is not completely clear that the strong view can avoid imposing unreasonable demands to present generation either, particularly in the context of uncertainty. In a world of uncertainty, one possible interpretation of the strong sufficientarianism might be that the present generation has a duty to minimize the probability of future people falling below the threshold as close to zero as possible. However, since this would most likely impose an unreasonable burden on the present generation (e.g., as a duty to minimize the possibility of catastrophic climate change close to zero), such a recommendation is a nonstarter. Therefore, a more plausible way to go on is to interpret the duty of the present generation as requiring to keep the probability of future people from falling below the threshold sufficiently small. This is also in line with the language of many real world policy discussions, where the goal of limiting temperature increase to 2°C is interpreted as a goal to stay below 2°C with some sufficiently high probability (e.g., with 70–85 percent) (see IPCC 2014). The problem with this alternative interpretation is that it focuses exclusively on the probability of people falling below the threshold, but does not take into account how far below the threshold those people are, which is also important to sufficientarians. The strong sufficientarian view should be able to weigh how seriously people fall below the threshold. Roser (2014) suggests a view that requires us to keep the risk (defined as probability multiplied by magnitude) of a shortfall below the threshold level sufficiently small. At the same time, however, he also acknowledges how this strategy, while reflecting the central idea of strong sufficientarianism, underscores the general difficulty of the strong view: we are not permitted to exceed the required level of risk by any (marginal) amount, even if that would be extremely costly for us (the present people) or we would have to forego tremendous benefits for the many future people.

Having recognized these possible pros and cons related to weak and strong sufficientarian views, herein we will remain mostly agnostic between these views and seek possible ways to integrate both sufficientarian positions with the economics of climate change. It is worth noting that, even if either of the sufficientarian positions would be unable to avoid completely the unreasonable demands objection, sufficientarianism is able to mitigate the problem in an intuitively plausible way: the burden imposed to present people should never be so great that it would cause them to fall below the threshold (and e.g., lose some of their fundamental interests) (see Meyer and Roser, 2009). Therefore, since sufficientarianism also fares better than alternative theories in relation to other problems of intergenerational ethics, there are strong reasons to take sufficientarianism as a plausible ethical ground for the climate policy evaluation.

Finally, we should note that in addition to weak and strong positions, there are also many other ways to refine the general sufficientarian idea (see Casal, 2007; Crisp, 2003; Huseby, 2012; Meyer and Roser, 2009), but we will concentrate on the following formulation that allows us to compare the alternative outcomes: According to *sufficientarianism, in assessing the goodness of the outcomes priority is given to benefits accruing to persons below the threshold; to benefit persons matters more the farther below the threshold persons are, the more people are being benefitted and the greater the benefits* (Huseby, 2012; Meyer and Roser, 2009). Moreover, in giving the substantive formulation of the threshold we follow the climate sufficientarians introduced in the beginning of this section: *what matters most in the climate policy choices is the satisfaction of the present and the future people's fundamental interests* (either understood in the Caney's modest way or Cripps's more expansive way).

Sufficientarianism and the economics of climate change

Since sufficientarianism proves to be a good candidate for dealing with the intergenerational ethical issues related to climate change, it is worth exploring whether it could be applied to the economics of climate change. The economics of climate change provides cost–benefit analyses of emissions-abatement policies, which consist in calculating the aggregate costs of climate policies and comparing them with the benefits associated with a reduction of the risks related to climate change. To carry out the analysis, economists construct an intertemporal social welfare function that aggregates the welfare of each generation in the alternative policy options and ranks the policy options on the basis of their total (or average) intergenerational well-being. In order to compare the costs and benefits occurring at different times, economists introduce a parameter called the social discount rate (SDR) on the basis of which the present value of expected future well-being is calculated. The higher the SDR, the lower the present value of future costs and benefits.

The present value of future outcomes is highly sensitive to the value of the SDR, especially when dealing with long periods of time, as is the case in the evaluation of climate policies. At the same time, the SDR has a major impact on how costs and benefits of climate policies are distributed among generations. The choice of the SDR is therefore crucial from the viewpoint of intergenerational justice. Later in this chapter we will examine more closely how taking a sufficientarian stance in intergenerational ethics might affect this choice.

The issues about intergenerational distribution in climate economics are also related to a more general question of how to address concerns of equality and justice in economics, whose standard tools are based on utilitarian maximization and hence do not pay any specific attention to the distribution of welfare. Therefore, in order to address the issues of intergenerational distribution, we start by looking more carefully at the discussion about how non-utilitarian concerns of equality and justice can be addressed in the economic analysis (e.g., Atkinson, 1970; Broome, 1991; Dasgupta 2005; IPCC, 2014; Sen, 1997; Stern, 2014a, 2014b).

The problems of the standard economic argument for equality

The standard utilitarian argument for equality is based on diminishing marginal benefit of consumption. According to this argument, in order to maximize total well-being, we should give an extra unit of a resource to the poorest people because they can get most benefit from it. In the economic analysis, the diminishing marginal benefit of consumption is reflected by the curvature of the welfare function, which depends on the elasticity of the marginal benefit of consumption and is expressed by the parameter η, which can be interpreted as an indication of how averse we are to inequality in individuals' consumption. The higher the value of η, the less we care for an additional unit of consumption to the rich than to the poor. In the intergenerational context, the utilitarian argument applies when future generations are expected to be richer than us, that is, when an additional unit of consumption provides a smaller benefit to the richer future people than to the poorer current people.[9]

The problems related to the standard economic way of dealing with equity concerns have been widely discussed in the literature, both generally and in particular with respect to intergenerational distribution in the context of climate change (Dasgupta, 2005, 2008; Heal, 2009; Sen, 1997; Stern, 2014a, 2014b; Sterner and Persson, 2008). As Sen (1997) vigorously notes, the utilitarian argument for equality would work only if each person's function for the marginal benefit were the same. But individuals' functions are different, and often a person who is poor has a lower function, that is, his or her marginal benefit might be low, for instance because he or she is handicapped. The utilitarian argument, however, would direct the resources to *some* other people else whose marginal benefit is higher even if they/those people would be better-off than the handicapped person and all their fundamental interests would be satisfied. According to Sen, this would be clearly against our moral intuitions, which instead suggest that the handicapped person deserves more resources, even if their marginal benefit is low.

In the context of climate change, the problems are also related to potential contradictory impacts that the standard economic framework may have at the intra- and intergenerational levels (e.g., Heal, 2009; Dasgupta, 2008). Since the higher value of η that aims to reflect our aversion to inequality means higher social discount rates if economy is growing, it means inter alia that the current generation should be less concerned about the benefits and costs to future generations. Therefore our stronger concern for equality leads to a less aggressive position on the need for action on climate change. While this result might correctly reflect the consideration that, due to economic growth, future people are on *average* wealthier than current people, it ignores that at the same time the number of people whose fundamental interests are severely affected by climate change might significantly increase (Dasgupta 2008). Yet reports on the impacts of climate change univocally emphasize that it is the poor people (both in poor and rich countries) that are most vulnerable to the effects of climate change (IPCC 2014).

The standard economic way of addressing equality concerns seems therefore inadequate for the context of climate change, where the satisfaction of people's fundamental interests is seriously threatened. If satisfying the fundamental interests has the primary moral weight as climate sufficientarians suggest, it is clear that the utilitarian argument for equality based on diminishing marginal benefit is insufficient.

Towards a sufficientarian interpretation

In order to provide a more convincing way of addressing equality concerns some economists have suggested functions based on the priority view (e.g., Adler, 2009; Adler and Treich, 2015; Atkinson and Stiglitz, 1980). Contrary to the utilitarian argument, the priority view offers a reason to give the unit of a resource to the handicapped worse-off person even if their marginal benefit is low. This is so, according to the priority view, because the worse off a person is, the more the improving of their position (by giving them an extra unit of a resource) counts in the social value of well-being. In other words, the prioritarian welfare function of each individual is strictly concave, but, instead of the diminishing marginal benefit of their consumption, the curvature of the function represents the diminishing marginal social value of their *well-being*.[10] The prioritarian social welfare function then ranks the policy outcomes on the basis of the aggregate social value of the individual's well-being.

The problems related to the priority view, particularly in the intergenerational context, we have discussed above.[11] What about sufficientarianism then? As argued above, sufficientarianism should fare better than prioritarianism in the intergenerational relations. Sufficientarians share with the priority view the same preference for benefitting the worse-off, no matter how low their marginal benefit is: if an extra unit of a resource can satisfy someone's fundamental interest, it is a reason to give the extra unit to that person, even if someone above the threshold would benefit more from that unit. Moreover, the extra unit should be given to the person whose fundamental interests can be satisfied the most by that unit of a resource. In other words, the further below the threshold a person is, the more an improvement in her position should count for the social value of well-being.

But, in contrast to the priority view, the kind of priority that characterizes sufficientarianism is centered on the notion of threshold: sufficientarians give (absolute or relative) priority to improving people's position below the threshold, while above the threshold benefitting individuals counts the same in the social value of well-being, no matter how well- or badly-off they are. How should this threshold-centered notion of priority be understood in terms of economic valuation of well-being? One way to reach this kind of a drastic change in the marginal value of individuals' well-being would be to make individuals' welfare functions very concave around the threshold, that is, the function would be very steep below the threshold and almost flat above the threshold (see e.g., Broome, 1989). Or in the extreme the function would have a kink at the threshold. But, since in these interpretations the sufficientarian function would have the same properties (apart from the possible discontinuity at the threshold) as the prioritarian welfare functions, it would have problems similar to those functions.

Another way is to interpret the threshold as being made of morally weighty *claims* individuals have to resources that are distributed amongst them (see e.g., Broome, 1989, 1991; Wiggins, 1985). In other words, the sufficientarian priority is restricted to people's claims to resources that are necessary to satisfy their fundamental interests below the threshold. Above the threshold, resources can be distributed in accordance with other principles, such as the utilitarian argument of diminishing marginal benefit. To capture the moral seriousness of the dissatisfaction of a person's fundamental interests would include claiming that it is something that directly decreases his or her personal well-being; for instance, it is a harm that an individual suffers. Since this individualistic approach incorporates the injustice related to people's unsatisfied fundamental interests directly into their personal level of well-being, it is able avoid the problems related to prioritarian functions (Broome, 1991: cf. also the discussion in note 14).

It is noteworthy that, according to this interpretation, individuals have claims not to specific resources, but rather to the satisfaction of their fundamental interests. However, it seems obvious that satisfying people's fundamental interests is resource-specific in many significant ways, and this, as we will discuss below, have implications for the economic modeling of the sufficientarian threshold. Think, for instance, how satisfying many fundamental interests is highly dependent on the availability of energy resources.[12] Consider also the fundamental interest in having an opportunity to enjoy life of a normal length (or of a right to not be arbitrarily deprived of such life) (Caney, 2010b; Cripps, 2013) and how some specific resources are crucial for satisfying this fundamental interest, such as an environment devoid of constant occurrences of severely threatening weather events, as well as healthcare and rescue services. It is hardly surprising then, that a growing number of environmental economists have argued that some ecosystem services are necessary for satisfying the fundamental human interests and that substituting these by any other kind of resource may be impossible or significantly limited in practice (e.g., Baumgärtner *et al.*, 2015; Heal, 2009).

Challenges to the standard economics of climate change

According to our interpretation of sufficientarianism, granting people the necessary threshold resources for satisfying their fundamental interests has priority with respect to the allocation of other resources. The short overview of the discussion also shows that at least in theory integrating this interpretation of sufficientarianism with economic welfare analysis might be possible. However, by comparing the interpretation more closely with the standard economic framework utilized in climate economics, it becomes clear that sufficientarianism challenges some core assumptions and methods of this framework.

The economic evaluation of policy outcomes is based on the comparison of different people's well-being and is meant to maximize aggregate intergenerational well-being. The standard economics of climate change, however, focuses on the maximization of *average* generational well-being. As Dasgupta (2008) notes, it appears to be common practice in the economics of climate change (see e.g., the major works of Cline (1992), Nordhaus (1994) and Stern (2007)) to assume that a generation's well-being depends only on its average endowment of resources, which are typically expressed in terms of consumption equivalents. According to Dasgupta, this is the consequence of the emphasis put on the *inter*generational distribution of resources, which leads to neglect of the ethical issues related to the distribution of resources within the same generation, as well as those related to an individual's distribution of resources within his or her lifetime.[13]

The focus on average generation well-being is problematic for sufficientarians, who are concerned with the satisfaction of individual claims below a certain threshold, not with the average endowment of resources available to a generation. In the standard economic evaluation of climate policies, the current generation should save for the future if future generations will be worse-off in terms of the average amount of resources that will be available to them. According to our formulation of sufficientarianism, the current generation instead has an obligation to save for the future if future people will most likely fall below the threshold or will fall farther below the threshold. In other words, for the sufficientarians, generation A is worse-off than generation B if A has more people whose fundamental interests are unsatisfied than B (or the dissatisfaction of the interests is greater).

A second problem for the integration of sufficientarianism with the standard economic evaluation of climate policies is related to the common practice of expressing costs and benefits in terms of so-called "consumption equivalents." This way of proceeding implies that all resources are substitutable: all sources of well-being, ranging from healthcare to luxury goods, are expressed in terms of their consumption equivalents, and therefore, in this framework, a certain amount of luxury goods could substitute for the lack of healthcare. In other words, any kind of resource, including the resources that are necessary for the satisfaction of individual fundamental interests, can be substituted with other resources that have a comparable consumption-equivalent value. This creates obvious difficulties for the integration of sufficientarian ideas of just distribution into the economic evaluation, because it becomes impossible to single out the resources that are necessary for satisfying people's fundamental interests.

The sufficientarian concern for satisfaction of people's fundamental interests would therefore require some fundamental changes in the current practices of economics of climate change. The economic model should be able to "disaggregate" the average generational well-being both in terms of individuals (which of the impacts of climate change affect individuals above/below the threshold, within each generation?) and in terms of resources (which resources are necessary for satisfaction of fundamental interests?).

It is noteworthy that many climate economists seem to share the demand for these changes (e.g., Heal, 2009; Stern, 2014a, 2014b; Sterner and Persson, 2008). Both the problems related to the use of consumption as a proxy of well-being and to the assumption of perfect substitutability have been widely discussed in the literature (Gerlagh and van der Zwaan, 2002; Neumayer, 2010; Sterner and Persson, 2008; Traeger, 2011). The general suggestion that emerges from this literature supports the case of disaggregating the total consumption to different goods that have limited substitutability between each other (Drupp, 2015; Heal, 2009). In the economic literature, there is also a rich history of studies on subsistence threshold which has been increasingly utilized in the recent contributions on environmental and climate economics (see e.g., Baumgärtner *et al.*, 2015; Heal, 2009; Steger, 2000; Stone, 1954; Traeger, 2011).

In the rest of the paper we follow the main ideas of recent literature in environmental and climate economics and explore more carefully the possibility of integrating intergenerational climate sufficientarianism with the economics of climate change. In order to do this, we focus on the choice of SDR, which importantly affects the distribution of the costs and benefits of climate policies among generations and which therefore has attracted great attention among economists and moral philosophers (Broome, 1994, 2012; Caney, 2008, 2014; Dasgupta, 2008; Jamieson, 2014; Nordhaus 2007; Stern, 2014a, 2014b; Weitzman 2007).

Sufficientarianism and intertemporal discounting

The choice of the SDR: Ramsey's formula and its parameters

In order to choose the value of the social discount rate, economists usually employ a formula derived from Ramsey's (1928) optimal savings model: $SDR = \delta + \eta g$. In this equation, the social discount rate is the sum of two terms: the first is the rate of pure time preference δ, and the second is the product of two parameters: the elasticity of the marginal benefit of consumption η, and the rate of growth of consumption g.

Regardless of the method employed for choosing the SDR (e.g., market-based values, ethical justification, surveys), economists usually base their arguments on the standard interpretation of the parameters contained in this formula (Cline, 1992; Nordhaus, 1994; Stern, 2007, 2014a, 2014b; and also commentaries such as Dasgupta, 2008; Weitzman, 2007). In other words, economists seem to think that these parameters help them to decide the value of SDR, because they encapsulate the different motivations for discounting in this context. According to some moral philosophers, δ and η are also taken to represent the fundamental ethical dimensions that are involved in this choice (e.g., Caney, 2008, 2014; Jamieson, 2014).

According to the standard interpretation, δ is the rate at which future outcomes are discounted merely because they are obtained in the future. The choice of the value of the parameter is commonly justified by two main reasons for discounting future well-being: the society cares less about the well-being of future generations just because they are in the future, and/or the society is averse to uncertainty about the existence of future generations.[14]

The choice of the value of the second term of Ramsey's equation, ηg, reflects the above-discussed utilitarian argument based on diminishing marginal benefit of consumption.[15] Recall that, according to this argument, if consumption is expected to grow (i.e., g is positive) and future generations are therefore expected to be richer than us, then an additional unit of consumption provides a smaller benefit to the "rich" future generations than to the "poor" current generation. The future consumption should therefore be discounted by the rate of change of the present value of the marginal benefit of consumption.

Finally, it is worth noting that the value of the SDR depends also on the estimation of the rate of growth. Although the value of g is not directly related to ethical questions, the growth rates of different resources need to be further discussed if we are to use sufficientarianism as a basis for the choice of SDR, because they importantly affect the satisfaction of future people's fundamental interests.

Choosing the SDR on the basis of sufficientarianism

Climate sufficientarians typically endorse generational impartiality, that is, the idea that the moral weight of a person's basic rights and fundamental interests should be the same regardless of the generation to which a person belongs. Caney (2014: 323–4), for instance, argues that people should not be discriminated against because of their time of birth, in the same way in which they should not be discriminated against because of their race or gender. On the basis of generational impartiality, climate sufficientarians argue against discounting future people's rights or interests purely on the basis of their temporal dimension (see e.g., Caney, 2008; Wolf, 2009). Caney provides an additional argument against pure time discounting, which is available for sufficientarians even if someone is not persuaded by generational impartiality: the employment of (high) pure time discounting might lead to overuse of the resources that future generation would require in order to meet a minimal sufficientarian threshold (Caney, 2014: 325). Hence, in either way, sufficientarians defend zero pure time discounting, that is, $\delta = 0$.

Yet sufficientarians may allow, or even require, the employment of SDR on some other grounds. Caney (2008), for instance, makes it clear that his argument for zero discounting is restricted to discounting the "moral weight" of basic rights and acknowledges the possibility of applying a positive discount rate to "resources" that are distributed to members of different generations. Therefore, as far as intertemporal discounting is based on reasons concerning the allocation of resources, Caney seems to accept it.[16] The question arises of what would be the sufficientarian motivations for discounting and how these could be reflected by the SDR.

According to sufficientarianism, the available resources should be distributed so as to (maximally) satisfy people's fundamental interests in any generation. Therefore, if the current generation's use of resources is expected to decrease the satisfaction of fundamental interests in the future, sufficientarianism requires us to relocate resources from current consumption to investments aimed at ensuring the satisfaction of future people's fundamental interests. This principle provides a reason to discount less the future resources that are required for the satisfaction of fundamental interests. On the other hand, if the resources were expected to grow in a way that more fundamental interests will be satisfied in the future, then the current generation would have a sufficientarian reason to discount more the resources of the future people, thereby giving priority to satisfying the fundamental interests of the people in the current generation.

As discussed above, the considerations concerning the distribution of resources among the people are usually reflected by the second term of Ramsey's equation, ηg. However, as noticed, from the sufficientarian point of view there are two problems with the standard use of this term: one is related to the application of the term to the average generational resources, and the other concerns the assumption of perfect substitutability of resources. The application of sufficientarian motivations for discounting, therefore, requires disentangling the term ηg, so as to distinguish between the resources that are necessary for the satisfaction of people's fundamental interests, and the resources that improve people's well-being above the threshold. In addition, recalling the discussion in the previous sections, the term ηg should be able to deal with the limited substitutability of the necessary resources. Finally, we should be able to distinguish between the rate of growth of the necessary threshold resources and the rate of growth of other resources.

In what follows, we focus on the works of a number of environmental economists who put forward a dual-rate discounting model as a possible way to meet these challenges.

Dual-eta SDR

In environmental economics, the idea of using dual-rate discounting has gained increasing attention recently and the specific issues related to climate change have accelerated the interest (Baumgärtner *et al.*, 2015; Drupp, 2015; Gollier, 2010; Traeger 2011; Weikard and Zhu, 2005). The main idea at the basis of these works is that, if resources are less than perfectly substitutable and if they have diverging growth rates, then there should be a distinct discount rate for each of the different resources. The central element of the economic modeling of resource-specific discount rates is the assumption that the discount rate of a resource E (e.g., an ecological resource) is determined by the formula

$$SDR_E = \delta + \eta_{EE} g_E + \eta_{EC} g_C$$

where $\eta_{EE} g_E$ is the elasticity of marginal benefit of consumption of the resource E times the growth of E, while $\eta_{EC} g_C$ is the cross elasticity of marginal benefit of E with respect to some other resource C (e.g., a manufactured good) times the growth of C. Conversely, the discount rate for the other resources C would be

$$SDR_C = \delta + \eta_{CC} g_C + \eta_{CE} g_E$$

where $\eta_{CC} g_C$ is the own elasticity of marginal benefit of consumption of the other resources times the growth of C, and $\eta_{CE} g_E$ is the cross elasticity of marginal benefit of C with respect to the ecological resource E times the growth of E. The resource-specific elasticities η_{EE} and η_{CC} are positive numbers, while the value of cross elasticities between these resources depends on the elasticity of substitution between the two kinds of resource: if E and C are substitutes, the value of cross elasticities are positive numbers, while if they are complements, the cross elasticities become negative (for more detail, see Baumgärtner *et al.*, 2015; Heal, 2009).

The conclusion of the studies applying the dual-rate model is that the SDR_E for the ecological resources should generally be lower than the SDR_C for the other resources.[17] The difference between SDR_E and SDR_C depends on the rate of elasticity of substitution and on the difference in the growth rates of the resources. Moreover, Drupp (2015) suggests that if the model includes the idea that some resources are necessary threshold resources and if the availability of these resources is reaching the critical level, then the difference between the discount rates of these threshold resources and of other resources can become substantial.

These outcomes seem to be in line with the sufficientarian aims. Discounting the necessary resources at a lower rate means that the present value of the effects on future satisfaction of fundamental interests will be relatively higher than the present value of the effects on future consumption of other resources. The greater the difference between their respective discount rates, the more the model prioritizes the effects on the necessary threshold resources.

Let's test this result further by assuming that the substitutability between the necessary threshold resources *E* and the other resources *C* is close to zero, that is, the cross elasticities between *E* and *C* are negative. Assume also that the availability of a large part of the necessary threshold resources is declining, or that they do not grow. Both assumptions seem plausible. We provided reasons in favor of the first assumption above. Considerations in favor of the second assumption can be found in the Millenium Ecosystem Assessment (2015), which reports that 60 percent of the studied ecosystem services were declining globally. According to the IPCC (2014), climate change may also significantly decrease the amount of many necessary threshold resources (e.g., clean drinking water, fertile soil for food production). According to Broome (1994, 2012), moreover, many of the resources that are essential for people's fundamental interests cannot grow, that is, they cannot be converted to produce more goods and services in the future. Think, for instance, of the environmental services that are necessary for the satisfaction of people's interest in a healthy life, such as those provided by a clean atmosphere, which cannot be converted to produce more of these services in the future. Moreover, the benefit people get from these services in terms of being able to live a healthy human life remains constant over time.

With these two additional assumptions, the dual-eta model would imply that the $SDR_E = \delta + \eta_{EE} g_E + \eta_{EC} g_C$ for the threshold resources becomes negative, because both g_E and η_{EC} are negative (η_{EE} and g_C are positive and for sufficientarians δ is zero). A negative SDR_E implies that we should assign greater weight to the effects of climate policies on future generations' fundamental interests than to our own well-being. Moreover, the further in the future consequences occur, the greater their present value becomes. This conclusion seems to be in line with the sufficientarian principles, because it reflects the high priority the sufficientarian view assigns to the satisfaction of the fundamental interests of the future generations that are threatened by climate change most seriously – e.g., 100 years from now and thereafter. Moreover, the declining availability of the threshold resources raises the SDR_C for other resources, because, due to the negative g_E and cross elasticity η_{CE}, $\eta_{CE} g_E$ becomes positive. This implies that we should give even less weight to the future consequences of climate policies on the other resources that are not necessary for the satisfaction of fundamental interests, which is also in line with sufficientarianism.

Overall, the dual-rate discounting model seems to reflect well the main sufficientarian ideas: the more likely it is that the potentially catastrophic effects of climate change will threaten the necessary threshold resources, the greater priority the dual-rate discounting gives to the effects of climate policies on the satisfaction of future people's fundamental interests. In the extreme case of zero substitutability and of critical decline of the threshold resources, the priority (i.e., difference between the distinct discount rates) becomes substantial. Therefore, this model reflects also, to some extent at least, the central idea of strong versions of climate sufficientarianism, such as Caney (2010b), according to which we should give absolute priority to the effects of climate policies that affect future people's fundamental interests below the threshold.

Conclusions

In this chapter, we have given several reasons for applying the sufficientarian understanding of justice in the intergenerational relations related to climate change. Furthermore we have raised the questions of what would be the implications of integrating sufficientarian principles with the economic framework of analysis for the evaluation of climate policies. On the one hand, we have aimed to show ways in which this integration might happen. According to our analysis, one plausible way to understand the sufficientarian threshold in the economic evaluation is to interpret it as being constituted by individuals' moral claims to those resources that are necessary to satisfy their fundamental interests. In this interpretation the dissatisfaction of fundamental interests then decreases directly each individual's personal well-being. On the other hand, our discussion reveals the limits of the standard economic evaluation of climate policies in addressing the specific distributional issues that are of interest for climate sufficientarians. First, the standard assumption that a generation's well-being depends solely on the average endowment of resources available to the generation hinders the application of our sufficientarian interpretation because this interpretation requires that one is able to make a distinction between the resources that are necessary for satisfying people's fundamental interests and other resources. Second, the common practice of expressing all costs and benefits in terms of their consumption equivalents creates a conceptual problem for the application of sufficientarian ideals because it implies that all resources are substitutable. For the sufficientarians, however, granting people the necessary resources for satisfying their fundamental interests have priority with respect to the allocation of other resources and resources cannot therefore be completely substitutable.

These conceptual problems, however, might be overcome. As the recent discussion in environmental and climate economics shows, there seems to be increasing willingness to modify the assumptions of standard economic evaluation in line with intergenerational sufficientarianism. The dual-rate discounting model provides one promising way of choosing the values of the SDR that reflects the main sufficientarian ideas of just distribution. The dual-rate model appears also to provide policy recommendations that are in line with sufficientarianism.

We should admit, however, that the employment of the dual-rate model in practice is most likely to raise several practical problems related to data gathering and data analysis. In particular, we have suggested that a distinction should be introduced in the economic forecast of growth in order to allow a separate estimation of the part of economic growth that concerns resources that are necessary to satisfy people's fundamental interests. Also, determining the resource-specific elasticities of substitution between various resources will require much more information than we currently have at our disposal. Notwithstanding the recent attempts in environmental economics (cf. e.g., Baumgärtner *et al.* 2015; Drupp 2015), it is not yet fully clear how these separate estimations should be done in practice.

Notes

1 Earlier versions of this chapter were presented at The Ethical Underpinnings of Climate Economics, University of Helsinki November 2014 and at the European Consortium for Political Research's Joint Session, Salamanca April 2014. For many helpful comments we would like to thank Kian Mintz-Woo, Dominic Roser, John Broome, Aki Lehtinen, Matthew Rendall, Hans-Peter Weikard, John O'Neill and the other participants of the workshops in Helsinki and Salamanca. In addition, our special thanks go to the editors of this volume for their valuable suggestions that improved the manuscript in many ways.

2 Nicholas Stern (2014a, 2014b) calls for a broad risk-management approach. Some others have described the requirement that the discipline of economics is facing as a shift in focus from obtaining optimality to that of avoiding the worst (Nelson, 2013). IPCC (2014) discusses the possibility of using the prioritarian welfare functions instead of the utilitarian ones.

3 There are several ways that egalitarians can respond to the levelling-down objection. The most obvious one is to admit that equality makes the outcome good only in some respect but not with *all things considered*. For a defense of such a pluralist egalitarian position, see e.g., Fleurbaey (2015).

4 For a recent discussion about the relevance of the distinction between egalitarianism and the priority view, see Broome (2015) and Fleurbaey (2015).

5 For some economists, these "bizarre" results are an outcome of using too low a discount rate. According to Nordhaus (2007: 696), using the low discount rates of the *Stern Review* (Stern, 2007) would "justify reducing per capita consumption for one year today from $10,000 to $4,400 in order to prevent a reduction of consumption from $130,000 to $129,870 starting two centuries hence and continuing at that rate forever after."

6 The main problem with the average versions of utilitarianism and of the priority view is that, according to these versions, the goodness of an outcome depends on the average level of well-being that includes also the well-being of all earlier lived remote people (e.g., the people who lived in Ancient Egypt). Many hold this implausible (see Adler and Treich, 2015; Broome, 2004; Parfit, 1984). The critical level views of utilitarianism or of the priority view set a critical level above which people's well-being have positive value and below which negative (e.g., Broome, 2004, 2010). The major problem of such a view is that in order to avoid the Repugnant Conclusion the critical level needs to be set at a relatively high level of well-being, which opens the view to another counterintuitive implication that Arrhenius (2000) has called Sadistic Conclusion: it would be better to cause extreme agony to the few than reduce the well-being of a large enough population by minuscule amount below the critical level.

7 Meyer and Roser (2009) propose a threshold notion of harm, according to which an action harms a person only if as a consequence of that action the (then existing)

person falls below a certain threshold standard. The threshold notion of harm is purported to be unaffected by the Non-Identity Problem, because according to this notion the identification of harm does not require that we would be able to compare the state of this sub-threshold person to his or her better-off state in a situation that would have obtained in the absence of the harming action. Though the need for a normative standard required by the threshold notion of harm does not yet specify a sufficientarian understanding of the standard, as Meyer and Roser note, the problems of other theories in the intergenerational context support understanding the threshold in a sufficientarian way.

8 Climate sufficientarian positions differ from each other not only in how expansively they characterize the threshold but also in how strongly they prioritize improving the position of those below the threshold. For Caney (2010b: 165), the threshold set by basic human rights is understood in a strong sufficientarian way, that is, satisfying these basic rights has absolute priority, and no trade-offs are allowed between impacts on the fundamental interests and on other interests which lie above the threshold. Clark Wolf's (2009) approach provides an alternative version of strong but *moderate* climate sufficientarianism. Wolf builds his approach by amending Rawls's classic account of intergenerational sufficientarianism with a "Needs Principle." Therefore, his position is not as *extreme* as Caney's, because the sufficientarian principle of satisfying people's basic needs is not the only principle of justice, but a principle within a broader account of justice. Cripps (2013: 15), on the other hand, is more open than Caney and Wolf in accepting at least some trade-offs between benefitting people below and above the threshold. The most explicit weak climate sufficientarian position is represented by Beckerman and Pasek (2001), who argue that the current generation has an obligation to avoid causing the future people to fall into poverty (e.g., due to anthropogenic climate change), but explicitly deny that there is a way to put the interests of people in any lexical order of priority.

9 It is noteworthy, as Sterner and Persson (2008) point out, that the distributional weightings are most commonly used only in the intergenerational context by setting the value of η for the SDR. In other contexts distributional weighting is seldom used in practice.

10 In other words, the prioritarian welfare function $w_i = g(u_i(c_i))$ is a strictly concave transformation to well-being. Under certain assumptions, in order to capture the kind of transformation, this would also mean higher values for η (see Dasgupta 2005, 2008 for a discussion).

11 In addition to problems mentioned above, Broome (1991, 2015) takes the prioritarian welfare functions to be problematic because they address equality in an individually additively separable way. In other words, what matters from the prioritarian view point is how well off each individual is separately and not how well off he or she is compared with others. For many this is problematic because they hold that equality is essentially a relative matter. Moreover, Broome points out that as a result of this prioritarians need a measure of the person's well-being that is distinct from its social value, and in practice it may be difficult to find such a measure. Finally, when making choices under uncertainty the individually separable way to measure equality have results that may look counterintuitive to many. Think of Broome's example of a two-individual population, which involves a policy G that entails outcomes of either (1,1) or (2,2), with equal probability, and a policy H which entails either (1,2) or (2,1), with equal probability. According to Broome, for prioritarians both policy options have the same expected value and they are thus equally good, because they measure well-being in a separable way. Many people would, however, follow egalitarians and hold G better because it entails more equal outcomes (but see Fleurbaey (2015) for discussion of the example).

12 Henry Shue's (2010) distinction between subsistence and luxury emissions is a leading early example of climate sufficcientarianism. According to Shue, it is a historical fact that the dominant form of industrialization is overwhelmingly dependent on fossil energy and people's subsistence is thus possible only through activities that emit carbon. Therefore every human being ought to be allowed at least an equal minimum amount of emissions sufficient for a decent life. However, setting the minimum threshold in terms of emissions has also been criticized. Nicholas Stern (2014a, 2014b) points out that the notion of an emissions-based threshold is based on the assumption that there is a fixed relation between a decent level of living on the one hand, and emissions on the other. But Stern argues that this is not the case and that indeed one of the main aims of climate policy is to alter the multiple existing relations between human well-being and emissions.

13 Dasgupta (2008: 148) argues that, by assuming that a generation's well-being depends only on the average consumption level that is available to that generation, the economic analysis treats in the same way the differences between an individual's well-being in two periods of time and the differences between the well-being of two individuals in two periods of time.

14 The much debated view of the *Stern Review* was that utility accruing to different people at different times should be given equal weight, because the future generations deserve to be treated equally to the present one (Stern, 2007). The Review does not deny that people care less about the further future, but argues that it is not morally justifiable to discriminate between different individuals living at different times. This ethical argument implies $\delta = 0\%$, but the Review chooses a value of δ that exceeds zero in order to account for the possibility of extinction of the human race. The chosen value is $\delta = 0.1\%$, which reflects a probability of extinction of about 10% in the next century (Beckerman and Hepburn, 2007).

15 Moreover, η is also interpreted as an indicator of risk aversion. Assuming that we are to maximize expected utility, since a consumption loss reduces utility more than an equivalent gain of consumption increases utility, higher η implies higher risk aversion. The value of η for evaluation of intergenerational policies, therefore, depends on the combined effect of three different concepts: *intragenerational* distribution, *intergenerational* distribution, and preferences over *risk* (see Beckerman and Hepburn, 2007; Dasgupta, 2008; Jamieson, 2014). The *Stern Review* (Stern, 2007), for instance chooses $\eta = 1$. Later, Stern (2010) defended this choice as a balanced "value judgment" between the different interpretations of the parameter. From the viewpoint of intragenerational distribution, any value higher than one would easily imply tax-transfer requirements that many would find unacceptably demanding. With respect to intergenerational distribution, Stern maintains that the criticism that $\eta = 1$ is too low since it would imply too high savings rates (see e.g., Dasgupta, 2008) is highly depended on the model assumptions and cannot be generalized. Finally, Stern doubts strongly that interpreting η as a parameter of relative risk aversion in the context of expected utility model of individual behavior provides a sound basis for the specification of this ethical parameter in the climate policy context.

16 Wolf (2009) also accepts that, if resources are growing over time, discounting for the rate of interest would be justifiable.

17 Baumgärtner *et al.* (2015), for instance, provide a conservative estimate that on the global average the ecosystem services, such as crop production and renewable water production, should be discounted at the rate that is about 1 percentage-point lower than the one used for manufactured consumption goods. However, if the necessary resources are declining and the substitution possibilities are limited, then the difference may be much larger, according to Drupp (2015) even up to 4 percentage-points.

Bibliography

Adler, M. D. (2009), "Future generations: a prioritarian view," *The George Washington Law Review*, vol. 77: 1478–520.

Adler, M. D. and Treich, N. (2015), "Prioritarianism and climate change," *Environmental and Resource Economics*, vol. 62: 279–308.

Arneson, R. J. (1999), "Egalitarianism and responsibility," *The Journal of Ethics*, vol. 3: 225–47.

Arrhenius, G. (2000), "An impossibility theorem for welfarist axiologies," *Economics and Philosophy*, vol. 16: 247–66.

Atkinson, A. B. (1970), "On the measurement of inequality," *Journal of Economic Theory*, vol. 2: 244–63.

Atkinson, A. B. and Stiglitz, J. E. (1980), *Lectures on Public Economics*, Columbus, OH: McGraw-Hill.

Baumgärtner, S., Klein, A. M., Thiel, D. and Winkler, K. (2015), "Ramsey discounting of ecosystem services," *Environmental Resource Economics*, vol. 61: 273–96.

Beckerman, W. and Hepburn, C. (2007), "Ethics of the discount rate in the *Stern Review on the Economics of Climate Change*," *World Economics*, vol. 8(1): 187–210.

Beckerman, W. and Pasek, J. (2001), *Justice, Posterity and the Environment*, Oxford: Oxford University Press.

Broome, J. (1989), "What's the good of equality?," in J. Hey (ed.), *Current Issues in Microeconomics*, Basingstoke: Macmillan, pp. 236–62.

Broome, J. (1991), *Weighing Goods: Equality, Uncertainty and Time*, Oxford: Blackwell.

Broome, J. (1992), *Counting the Cost of Global Warming*, Cambridge: The White Horse Press.

Broome, J. (1994), "Discounting the future," *Philosophy and Public Affairs*, vol. 23(2): 128–56.

Broome, J. (2004), *Weighing Lives*, Oxford: Oxford University Press.

Broome, J. (2010), "The most important thing about climate change," in J. Boston, A. Bradstock, and D. Eng (eds), *Public Policy: Why Ethics Matters*, ANU E Press, pp. 101–16.

Broome, J. (2012), *Climate Matters: Ethics in a Warming World*, New York: W. W. Norton.

Broome, J. (2015), "Equality versus priority: a useful distinction," *Economics and Philosophy*, vol. 31(2): 219–28.

Caney, S. (2008), "Human rights, climate change, and discounting," *Environmental Politics*, vol. 17(4): 536–55.

Caney, S. (2010a), "Cosmopolitan justice, responsibility and global climate change," in S. Gardiner, S. Caney, D. Jamieson and H. Shue (eds), *Climate Ethics: Essential Readings*, Oxford: Oxford University Press, pp. 122–45.

Caney, S. (2010b), "Climate change, human rights, and moral thresholds," in S. Gardiner, S. Caney, D. Jamieson and H. Shue (eds), *Climate Ethics: Essential Readings*, Oxford: Oxford University Press, pp. 163–77.

Caney, S. (2014), "Climate change, intergenerational equity and the social discount rate," *Politics, Philosophy & Economics*, vol. 13(4): 320–42.

Casal, P. (2007), "Why sufficiency is not enough," *Ethics*, vol. 117(2): 296–326.

Cline, W. R. (1992), *The Economics of Global Warming*, Washington, DC: Peterson Institute for International Economics.

Cripps, E. (2013), *Climate Change and the Moral Agent: Individual Duties in an Interdependent World*, Oxford: Oxford University Press.

Crisp, R. (2003), "Equality, priority, and compassion," *Ethics*, vol. 113(4): 745–63.

Dasgupta, P. (2005), "Three conceptions of intergenerational justice," in H. Lillehammer, and D. H. Mellor (eds), *Ramsey's Legacy*, Oxford: Clarendon Press, pp. 149–69.

Dasgupta, P. (2008), "Discounting climate change," *Journal of Risk and Uncertainty*, vol. 37: 141–69.

Drupp, M. A. (2015), "Limits to substitution between ecosystem services and manufactured goods and implications for social discounting," SSRN Working Paper, available at: http://ssrn.com/abstract=2568368 (accessed 30 May 2016).

Fleurbaey, M. (2015), "Equality versus priority: how relevant is the distinction?," *Economics and Philosophy*, vol. 31(2): 203–17.

Frankfurt, H. G. (1987), "Equality as a moral idea," *Ethics*, vol. 98(1): 21–43.

Gerlagh, R. and van der Zwaan, B. (2002), "Long-term substitutability between environmental and man-made goods," *Journal of Environmental Economics and Management*, vol. 44: 329–45.

Gollier C. (2010), "Ecological discounting," *Journal of Economic Theory*, vol. 145: 812–29.

Heal, G. (2009), "The economics of climate change: a post-Stern perspective," *Climatic Change*, vol. 96: 275–97.

Huseby, R. (2012), "Sufficiency and population ethics," *Ethical Perspectives*, vol. 19(2): 187–206.

IPCC (2014), *Climate Change 2014: Mitigation of Climate Change. Contribution of Working Group III to the Fifth Assessment Report of the Intergovernmental Panel on Climate Change*, Cambridge and New York: Cambridge University Press.

Jamieson, D. (2014), *Reason in a Dark Time: Why the Struggle Against Climate Change Failed – and What It Means For Our Future*, Oxford: Oxford University Press.

Meyer, L. and Roser, D. (2009), "Enough for the future," in A. Gosseries and L. Meyer (eds), *Intergenerational Justice*, Oxford: Oxford University Press, pp. 219–48.

Millenium Ecosystem Assessment (2005), *Ecosystems and Human Well-being: Synthesis*, Washington, DC: Island Press.

Miller, D. (2005), "Against global egalitarianism," *The Journal of Ethics*, vol. 9: 55–79.

Nelson, J. A. (2013), "Ethics and the economist: what climate change demands of us," *Ecological Economics*, vol. 85: 145–54.

Neumayer, E. (2010), *Weak Versus Strong Sustainability: Exploring the Limits of Two Opposing Paradigms*, 3rd edn, Cheltenham: Edward Elgar.

Nordhaus, W. D. (1994), *Managing the Global Commons: The Economics of Climate Change*, Cambridge, MA: MIT Press.

Nordhaus, W. D. (2007), "A review of the *Stern Review on the Economics of Climate Change*," *Journal of Economic Literature*, vol. 45(3): 686–702.

Nussbaum, M. (2006), *Frontiers of Justice: Disability, Nationality, Species Membership*, Cambridge, MA: Harvard University Press.

Parfit, D (1984), *Reasons and Persons*, Oxford: Clarendon Press.

Parfit, D. (1997), "Equality and priority," *Ratio*, vol. 10: 202–21.

Ramsey, F. P. (1928), "A mathematical theory of saving," *The Economic Journal*, vol. 38(152): 543–59.

Raz, J. (1986), *The Morality of Freedom*, Oxford: Oxford University Press.

Roser, D. (2014), "Rights-sensitivity and risk aversion," unpublished manuscript, University of Zurich.

Sen, A. (1997), *On Economic Inequality*, exp. edn, Oxford: Clarendon Press.

Sen, A. (1999), *Development as Freedom*, Oxford: Oxford University Press.

Shogren, J. (1999), "Speaking for citizens from the far distant future," *Climate Change*, vol. 5: 489–91.

Shue, H. (2010), "Subsistence emissions and luxury emissions," in S. Gardiner, S. Caney, D. Jamieson and H. Shue (eds), *Climate Ethics. Essential Readings*, Oxford: Oxford University Press, pp. 200–14.

Solow, R. M. (1974), "Intergenerational equity and exhaustible resources," *The Review of Economic Studies*, vol. 41: 29–45.

Spash, C. (2002), *Greenhouse Economics: Value and Ethics*, London: Routledge.

Steger, T. (2000), "Economic growth with subsistence consumption," *Journal of Development Economics*, vol. 62: 343–61.

Stern, N. (2007), *The Economics of Climate Change: The Stern Review*, Cambridge: Cambridge University Press.

Stern, N. (2010), "The economics of climate change," in S. Gardiner, S. Caney, D. Jamieson and H. Shue (eds), *Climate Ethics: Essential Readings*, Oxford: Oxford University Press, pp. 39–76.

Stern, N. (2014a), "Ethics, equity and the economics of climate change, paper 1: science and philosophy," *Economics and Philosophy*, vol. 30: 397–444.

Stern, N. (2014b), "Ethics, equity and the economics of climate change, paper 2: economics and politics," *Economics and Philosophy*, vol. 30: 445–501.

Sterner, T. and Persson, U. M. (2008), "An even sterner review: introducing relative prices into the discounting debate," *Review of Environmental Economics and Policy*, vol. 2 (1): 61–76.

Stone, J. R. N. (1954), "A note on economics growth with subsistence consumption," *Economic Journal*, vol. 64: 511–27.

Traeger, C. P. (2011), "Sustainability, limited substitutability, and non-constant social discount rates," *Journal of Environmental Economics and Management*, vol. 62(2): 215–28.

Weikard, H. P. and Zhu, X. (2005), "Discounting and environmental quality: when should dual rates be used?," *Economic Modelling*, vol. 22: 868–78.

Weitzman, M. L. (2007), "The *Stern Review of the Economics of Climate Change*," *Journal of Economic Literature*, vol. 45(3): 703–24.

Weitzman, M. L. (2009), "On modeling and interpreting the economics of catastrophic climate change," *Review of Economics and Statistic*, vol. 91: 1–19.

Wiggins, D. (1985), "Claims of need," in T. Honderich (ed.), *Morality and Objectivity: A Tribute to J. L. Mackie*, London: Routledge & Kegan Paul.

Wolf, C. (2009), "Intergenerational justice, human needs, and climate policy," in A. Gosseries and L. Meyer (eds), *Intergenerational Justice*, Oxford: Oxford University Press, pp. 347–76.

6 A new defence of probability discounting[1]

Kian Mintz-Woo

Introduction

Probability discounting (or probability weighting) in decision-making is multiplying the value of an outcome by one's subjective probability that the outcome will occur.[2] The broader import of defending probability discounting is to help justify cost–benefit analyses in contexts such as climate change. This chapter, however, addresses only decisions under risk. Decisions can be made under conditions of certainty, risk, and uncertainty.[3] Under certainty, the decision-maker knows the outcome of any of his or her decisions.[4] Under risk, they know the potential outcomes of any of their decisions, and can assign probabilities to any of those outcomes dependent on particular decisions. Finally, under uncertainty, at least some outcome for at least some decision cannot be assigned a probability. This defence of probability discounting applies only under risk. However, this is not unduly limiting. At a theoretical level, the possibility of probability discounting does not arise under the other conditions. At a practical level, evaluations of climate policy are almost never done under conditions of full certainty, and many are performed under risk. (For an overview of evaluations of climate policy under risk, please see Chapter 3 of this volume.) So addressing probability discounting under risk is widely applicable. The purpose of this chapter is thus to justify the use of probability discounting in contexts of risk – but also cost–benefit analyses more broadly – using a new argument.

While such probability discounting is sometimes taken to be objectionable, it is also sometimes taken to be uncontroversial. This chapter addresses both camps.

As a representative of the first sceptical camp, I consider an objection by Caney (2008, 2009) in the following section.[5] Caney has been particularly influential in the climate debate and argues that, if certain conditions obtain, it is morally impermissible to discount for probability. But his conditions – which are meant to indicate when probability discounting (and cost–benefit analysis) is impermissible – fail, since they overgeneralize. Since climate change is plausibly construed as putting many people's rights at risk, one question which arises is how to assess the risk of a violation compared to a violation which is certain to occur. Caney's answer is that, at least under the assumption that certain conditions ("R1–R4") obtain, there is no difference in how we ought to assess them: even putting human rights *at risk* is impermissible.

These conditions do not manage to do the work that Caney needs, and, more generally, this type of approach is unworkable; each individual action may increase risks of violation only in very small increments and it is only once these risks are aggregated that initially plausible conditions like Caney's R1–R4 are satisfied. At least in theory, cost–benefit analyses with probability discounting are sensitive enough on the individual level to compare the small incremental risks and the marginal benefits of individual actions.

Among those in the second camp who take probability discounting to be uncontroversial, many refer to the decision-theory literature. However, probability discounting has not received a more catholic defense. Here I offer a defense of probability discounting which does not rely upon decision-theoretic axioms that those outside of decision-theory may not accept. My intention in my positive argument for probability discounting is to address those skeptical of probability discounting with a new normative defence. This defense can be taken as complementary to decision-theoretic defences. The complementarity, for those who are already sympathetic to the decision-theoretic defences of probability discounting, lies in this argument's reinforcement of this conclusion.

This argument involves distinguishing between causal responsibility and moral responsibility, where moral responsibility for an effect can be cashed out in terms of blameworthiness and praiseworthiness and causal responsibility for an effect requires only that that effect is part of a causal chain issuing from one's act. With this distinction in hand, moral responsibility can be seen as coming in degrees. Given that we can limit our deliberation and consideration to that which we are morally responsible for, and that our moral responsibility for outcomes is limited by our subjective probabilities, it follows that our subjective probabilities can ground probability discounting.

The concluding section includes some suggestions about what this means for long-term decision-making. The argument allows us to ground probability discounting in normative terms such as moral responsibility. Evaluations of climate change can be grounded, on this argument, in our moral responsibility which – on the assumption that our subjective probabilities decrease with respect to time – itself decreases with respect to time. This argument also shows that it is permissible for individuals to engage in (mini) cost–benefit analyses with probability discounting.

Caney's objections to probability discounting

In an argument against discounting for probability in the context of climate change, Caney (2009: 176) writes "A sound response to the current climate change, I suggest, would prescribe exactly the same course of action … to mitigating climate change as would be appropriate if it were known that the malign effects would definitely occur."[6] Essentially, the point is that, from the perspective of rights-based theories, "high" probabilities of rights violations are just as impermissible to bring about as certainty of rights violations.[7] In effect, this means that cost–benefit analyses should not or need not be performed in these circumstances, and the actions which lead to high probabilities of violations should be avoided.

I begin by addressing Caney's particular conditions for cases where these actions simply should not be performed, before explaining what is wrong with this approach. The problem is that, if we look at practices at the social level using his approach, we lose subtle gradations in levels of risk for individual actions and the corresponding individual benefits of introducing small increments of risk. And, for Caney's approach to work, we *do* have to look at practices at the social level, because his argument is about climate change and any given individual's emissions in isolation do not materially increase the probability of rights-violations (let alone introduce *high* probabilities of rights violations).

Caney suggests four conditions meant to distinguish between cases in which probability discounting is warranted or unwarranted. He writes that the four conditions may not all be necessary, but if all are satisfied in some instance, then this justifies treating risky outcomes the same way as certain outcomes. But Caney's conditions, which are meant to apply to the social practice of excessive carbon emitting, apply in an analogous manner to another case: the social practice of driving cars. The first clarification to make is that the relevant comparison *is* about the permissibility of pervasive social practices. The second clarification to make is that, obviously, driving cars is not in *all* respects analogous to excess emitting, but that the practice satisfies the four conditions Caney endorses, which is enough to show that the argument generalizes beyond what he intends. In other words, this is meant as a *reductio* – someone who endorses the conclusion that the practice of driving cars is impermissible need not be troubled by these remarks. However, there are few who would be willing to endorse this claim and Caney himself denies it (Caney 2009: 179–80).

First, here are Caney's four rights conditions applied to emissions and climate change (2009: 177–9):

R1 The changes to the climate involve both (a) a high probability of severe threats to large numbers of persons' fundamental human rights and (b) a possibility of even more catastrophic threats to fundamental human rights.

R2 Affluent members of the world can abstain from emitting high levels of greenhouse gases, and thereby exposing others to risk, without loss of their own human rights.

R3 The risks of dangerous climate change will fall disproportionately on those whose human rights are already violated.

R4 The benefits that arise when the affluent of the world emit high levels of greenhouse gases falls almost entirely to them, and not to those most at risk from climate change.

Now consider an everyday example of risky behavior: driving cars. This example of a social practice satisfies analogous conditions. This case certainly satisfies (R1): drivers kill many people daily, through either irresponsibility or bad luck. In the United States, the costs amount to tens of thousands of lives, orders of magnitude more of non-fatal injuries, and a total of hundreds of billions of dollars annually in economic losses and social harms. It is not the case that *any given* driver has a very high probability of killing other road users; however, it *is* the case that the *social practice* of driving leads to a high probability of severe threats to the fundamental human rights of many. Caney is right that driving satisfies (R2): "the emissions stemming from driving cars, taking plane flights, poorly insulated housing, and inefficient energy use [must be cut to] avoid dangerous climate change, but the loss involved cannot be said to compromise any human rights" (2009: 179). In defending (R3), Caney appeals to the income disparity between nations more at risk from climate change (mainly in the global south) and those less at risk (mainly in the global north). Since those most at risk from climate change are – independently of climate change – disproportionately poorer, they are more likely to suffer from human rights violations. Similarly, we can consider the risks from driving. On average, those most at risk from the practice of driving cars are those who do not themselves drive cars (the so called "vulnerable road users" such as pedestrians and cyclists) (e.g., Shinar 2012; Tiwari 2015).[8] Those who do not drive cars are *disproportionately* likely to be unable to afford cars so will be – independently of car driving – disproportionately poorer. Thus, by analogous reasoning, they too will be more likely to suffer from human rights violations. However, Caney is aware that driving cars might be a case that satisfies his conditions, and this is not a conclusion he endorses. So he addresses car driving in the discussion for (R4):

> one might think that it is permissible for some to drive motor vehicles even though they pose a fatal threat to some because the risky activity is part of an equitable scheme which is generally beneficial, including to the risk-bearers. Even non-drivers might value the practice of driving – it means that their friends and family can visit, goods can get transported promptly from one end of the country to another, food gets delivered to shops still fresh, business and personal correspondence can arrive swiftly, and so on.
>
> (Caney 2009: 179–80)

The purpose of (R4), Caney continues, is that it distinguishes between cases like climate change and driving. But it is doubtful that such a consideration is enough to distinguish between the two cases.

How can we measure the benefits from excess emissions or driving? We can consider possible worlds in which we do not benefit from the risky behaviors. We are not considering *ideal* possible worlds, but closer *non-ideal* worlds where people also often fail their duties, but scale down dramatically (or even completely) the risky behaviors under consideration. So, in a world where there is (almost) no driving, perishable foodstuffs, for example, would have to be consumed sooner and would have to be sourced locally. In this world, there would be less capability to visit those far away. It would mean that serious injuries might not be treated in time (this is a friendly addition to Caney's argument). If we stopped (almost) entirely the practice of driving cars, Caney is right that some of these costs would be borne by risk-bearers (non-drivers).

However, a world where there were dramatically reduced emissions would similarly have costs which would be borne by risk-bearers (non-affluent countries). Roughly one-third of global emissions stem from transportation. To cut this down significantly would greatly change the world. Assuming that all of the global emissions are scaled down proportionately, this would restrict many aspects of global transportation. For instance, Bangladesh, which is at severe risk from climate impacts, would have limited access to world markets for clothing; the workers in Hong Kong would have limited access to global markets for electronic goods; countries with disparities in resources would be less able to trade. There would also be less transportation that allows for foreign aid and medical support: mosquito nets would be less distributable to sub-Saharan Africa; fewer tetanus and measles vaccinations would be sent to Iraq; in the case of sudden disasters, it would be less feasible to react internationally with aid; and it may not have been possible to eradicate polio. These are just some of the consequences of reducing transportation emissions; reductions in other sectors might well have other impacts for the risk-bearers. In short, like driving, emissions from affluent countries are part of a scheme which generates benefits, including to the risk-bearers.

Obviously, it is only a fraction of the gains associated with excessive emissions that are distributed in these laudable ways, but we are considering a world where all of the activities associated with significant affluent emissions are ratcheted down.[9] My claim is that, just as in (R4), there are substantial gains to non-drivers and society at large from transport as well. Or enough gains that it is plausible that the analogue of (R4) fails in the case of excess emissions.

Caney might respond that these are not the "excessive" emissions he was considering, so they are not part of the relevant social practice. However, this response will not work for three reasons. First, such a response would raise a worry about ad hoc emendations to the theory. If we define "excess" emissions as only the emissions that we have moral or social objections to, then not only would this be less possible to apply, it would invite worries about being merely dialectically motivated.

Second, his R1–R4 are not sensitive enough to pick out the excess emissions generated which are not necessary to maintain the human rights of those emitting, and it is R1–R4 that are under consideration. For instance, they do not distinguish between emissions by the affluent who are travelling with NGOs to distribute bed nets, medicine, trade or aid and those who are merely travelling for holidays.

Finally, and most importantly, he *cannot* add a condition that says we are including only those cases where the emissions are for a sufficiently good cause or have positive outcomes which outweigh their increase to the threats to human rights (via climate change), since that is precisely the kind of cost–benefit analysis condition that he is trying to avoid or supplant with the conditions R1–R4. The purpose of a cost–benefit analysis is precisely to be sensitive to the cumulative effect of smaller (or larger) benefits and costs. On this reading of Caney's argument, his intention is to suggest conditions which supplant cost–benefit analyses by being grounded in human rights. If he appeals to the aggregation of more mundane considerations, then he is engaged in cost–benefit analysis by another name.

So either (R4) is not a plausible condition to determine whether a cost–benefit analysis applies, or, following Caney, it implies that on rights-based theories, drivers are rights-violators to precisely the same extent as if we were all *certain* that we would kill when driving, i.e., it is not permissible to drive cars. Most people would view this as a reduction of Caney's conditions.[10]

This third point leads to a general worry: that, while such a rights-based view does not greatly differ from a probability discounter at the level of social practice – since the non-discounter does take into account that the practice must in aggregate have a "high" probability of threats to fundamental human rights – it does not give any weight to small individual benefits. Thus, this view does not allow one to compare (i) practices where each instance of the practice has an infinitesimal marginal addition to the probability of fundamental violations to (ii) practices where each instance of the practice has a more substantial marginal addition to the probability of fundamental violations. If the practices are widespread enough, the non-discounter will not be able to distinguish between these practices because, in aggregate, both will involve high probabilities of threats to large numbers of persons' fundamental human rights. Furthermore, if we are focussed on rights-violations, we will not be able to compare practices where the *benefits* are minor or major in each instance of the practice, so long as the benefits are never required for upholding fundamental human rights. The type of view that Caney endorses does not allow for fine-grained evaluation, unlike cost–benefit analyses with probability discounting. This coarseness matters, since small costs and benefits can in aggregate be very important, even if they do not directly relate to human rights – for instance, the social benefits of driving and extra emissions.

So far, we have considered why Caney's argument against probability discounting is unsuccessful. But there is more: a positive moral argument that discounting for probability is permissible, which we turn to in the next section.

A positive argument for probability discounting

A moral commonplace in everyday life is that one is not fully morally responsible for *all* the consequences of one's actions. If cashed out in terms of reactive attitudes, we might say that one is not fully blameworthy (or praiseworthy) for indefinitely many effects of one's actions. It is true that one is morally responsible for the immediate and predictable consequences, but, as one's knowledge of the effects lessen, it is less and less reasonable to hold one fully morally responsible.[11]

This commonplace about moral responsibility can ground a defence of probability discounting in rational decision-making. The conclusion to this section will consider how this argument might apply both at the individual level and the social level, with an eye towards social applications to evaluations of climate change policy. Responsibility at the social level, though not argued here, is not unlike responsibility at the individual level. There are some interesting differences, mainly related to greater limitations on individual decision-making, which we discuss in the concluding section.

When I call in sick to work, I am morally responsible for the foreseeable consequences: my colleagues having a larger workload, my boss having to reschedule her meeting, etc. The unexpected effects of these effects I am *less* morally responsible for: my harder working colleague has to miss dinner with her wife; my boss ends up with no space in her agenda. The effects of these effects I am even less responsible for. And, so, when I am deciding whether to call in sick, I do not have to fully include these further effects in my calculation, because I have diminished (or no) morally responsibility for these effects.

Moral responsibility is a complex concept. These arguments are not meant to characterize it, let alone define it. They are based on a particular claim about moral responsibility, which is consistent with many different substantive accounts: that one can have less than full moral responsibility – understood as levels of, inter alia, blame-worthiness and praiseworthiness – for some outcomes. Whatever conditions one takes to be necessary and/or sufficient for moral responsibility, this argument is intended to demonstrate an additional layer: the level of moral responsibility is *lessened* by certain kinds of ignorance. So, although the focus on subjective probability may be surprising in a discussion of moral responsibility, it is best thought of as an emendation. The argument is also meant to apply widely, not just to actions with significant moral import, such as those involving pain and death, but also everyday actions, such as listening to loud music in public.[12] The argument, schematically, is very simple:

1 Sometimes, we do not have full moral responsibility for the effects of our actions.
2 The most plausible explanation for (1) is that moral responsibility is limited by the subjective probabilities of particular effects.
3∴ Moral responsibility is limited by the subjective probabilities of particular effects. (1,2, abduction)
4 It is rational to exclude that which you are not morally responsible for from deliberation.
5∴ It is rational to exclude from deliberation outcomes to the extent that they are limited by subjective probabilities of particular effects. (3,4, deduction)

Premise (1) captures the idea that moral responsibility for effects or consequences of an action are not always full or complete. There is a separate sense of responsibility which *is* always full, which is sometimes called *causal responsib-*

ility, for which *any* effect of one's act is fully one's responsibility. It is in this latter causal sense that responsibility is fully transitive or iterative. For instance, if I scribble down my grocery list and some biologist happens to read the grocery list and has a flash of inspiration and develops a new strain of guava, I (or my writing of the list) might be *causally responsible*, although it would be odd to say that I am *morally responsible*. Common sense has it that there is a sense of responsibility which is not always full, unlike this causal sense. According to this common sense, one can diminish one's responsibility for the effects of an action by showing that one did not know that those effects would follow. In other words, if the effects are surprising or unforeseen, then this can have some exculpatory force. It is this moral sense of responsibility that this argument relies upon, and I use this sense from here on except where explicitly noted.

To motivate Premise (2), i.e., that it is subjective probability that is changing the level of moral responsibility, we will consider several cases. Here is the first:

> **Chemistry – Certainty:** Tamara, a high school student, has a lab experiment to conduct. She is following the instructions she has written down on the chemicals to mix: X and Y. However, she knows that X and Y explode when combined, and when she mixes them, they do indeed explode, leading to significant property damage.[13]

Tamara intuitively is morally responsible (and blameworthy) for this property damage, and also causally responsible. We can change the case so that she does not know about this consequence (i.e., she assigns the probability of an explosion less than 1, maybe even close to 0):

> **Chemistry – Low/High Risk:** Tamara does not know that X and Y explode when combined, but when she mixes them, they do explode, leading to significant property damage. There are two subcases. In the first, Tamara has a low subjective probability that X and Y explode (e.g., she copied her instructions for mixing them out of her textbook or another generally reliable source). In the second, Tamara has a high subjective probability that X and Y explode, although she also does not know (e.g., she knows that sometimes she accidentally writes down chemical Y instead of chemical Z, or that she knows she was not paying full attention when she was taking notes).

In the Low Risk subjective probability case, where Tamara thinks it very unlikely that she has made a mistake, Tamara has less responsibility. In contrast, in the High Risk subjective probability case, where Tamara has reasons to believe that her instructions might be in error, she has greater responsibility.

Since the only differences between Low and High Risk cases is the subjective probability Tamara would assign to the explosion, that is a good explanation for the assigned level of responsibility.

An objector might suggest a different explanation: in particular, that the relevant probability is not subjective probability, but *objective* probability. Such an objector may remind us that individuals sometimes have very inaccurate probability assignments. As Smart (1973: 40) writes,

> The ordinary man is frequently irrational in his moral thinking. And if he can be irrational about morals why cannot he be irrational about probabilities? The fact that the ordinary man thinks that he can weigh up probabilities in making prudential decisions does not mean that there is really any sense in what he is doing.

It is manifest that individual subjective probabilities may diverge significantly from the actual ones. This is true in these Chemistry cases; in fact, the objective probabilities that *X* and *Y* will explode in *each* of these cases is 1 and that objective probability diverges from Tamara's subjective probabilities in each Risk case. However, if you believe that having more or less credence in this outcome (as in High Risk/Low Risk) affects her level of moral responsibility, then it is subjective probability and *not* objective probability that is relevant for responsibility.

An objector could press a separate case. One could say that in Low/High Risk it is relevant whether Tamara has tried to *improve* her subjective probabilities. She is fully morally responsible, one might claim, in all the cases because she should do all that she can to improve her probabilities, say by rechecking about the explosive potential of *X* and *Y* with another authoritative source.[14] In this manner, the "excess" moral responsibility attaches to her epistemic practices.

There are at least three responses to this objection:

- First, one is *epistemically* responsible for assigning the right subjective probabilities, but this is distinct at the point of decision from any *moral* responsibility for acting upon these probabilities. So we can epistemically criticize the individual for having generated the wrong probabilities up to the point of decisions, but the moral responsibility is still a function of the subjective probabilities the individual had assigned at the point of decision. This might also act as a response to someone who endorses *evidential probability*, a theory according to which the correct probability is the probability that draws on the evidence that is available to the individual (e.g., Zimmerman 2008, 2014).[15] On this theory, it is sensible to say that the individual is being epistemically irresponsible (or irrational) if their evidential probabilities diverge from their subjective probabilities. But their moral responsibility is still a function of their subjective probabilities at the point of action.
- Second, it is easy to conflate moral responsibility for some action ϕ-ing and moral responsibility for a different action ψ-ing that would have changed one's information *about* ϕ-ing. These may be conflated, for instance, because, in both cases, the responsibility attaches to the same individual, and ψ-ing affects whether or not the individual ϕs. Because of this potential

conflation, it is important to distinguish between *which party* is morally responsible and *their level* of moral responsibility. For the purposes of this argument, we are primarily concerned with the latter. This account can also handle actions such as updating one's information – one is responsible to the extent that one would have a subjective probability that an action which updates one's information (e.g., ψ-ing) would have the effect in question.[16] To illustrate, suppose that a doctor prescribes some medication believing there are no relevant contraindications. The doctor turns out to be wrong. An objector might say that, even though the doctor had (for instance) a low subjective probability that the medication had contraindications (say, because they had checked the contraindications recently), we are likely to hold him responsible, i.e., blame him. However, it is not important here to determine *whom* we are blaming (that is not in doubt), but *why* and *to what extent* we are blaming. Presumably, the reason we blame the doctor is not for prescribing a medicine they thought was safe. Indeed, *that* act is praiseworthy. We blame the doctor for failing to check the indications. But the subjective probabilities matter again: if there were good (subjective) reasons to think that there were no contraindications, then we should blame the doctor less for failing to check, even if those reasons were ultimately misleading. If we assigned full blameworthiness for failing to check, then we would also have to assign full blameworthiness for failing to *recheck* each time the medicine is prescribed, or perhaps even more often. But this seems implausible; at some point, it no longer makes sense to spend time ascertaining contraindications and to spend time on patients who need it. So the blameworthiness must be diminishing as well. Again, this is what one should accept if one judges Tamara less responsible in Low Risk than in High Risk.

- But these first two responses may be too concessive. A third response would be to try to undermine the intuition that one is morally responsible for poor epistemic practices. For instance, one could argue that such an intuition is problematic, since it is asymmetrical. Epistemic practices which lead to mistaken beliefs in cases with good outcomes do not seem blameworthy in the same manner that practices in cases with bad outcomes seem blameworthy.

The intuition we need to undermine, however, is that, even if Tamara was in Low Risk, she is still morally responsible (blameworthy) for her epistemic state of being in Low Risk. Let us consider a contrasting case:

> **Donation (Low/High Risk):** Meili has several different codes for all the accounts or payments she makes. She intends to load a substantial amount of money onto her prepaid coffee card (e.g., her expected annual coffee budget), but she enters the wrong code and instead sends it to a charity which does good works.[17] She is aware that it is possible that she used the wrong code. There are two subcases. In the first, Meili has a low subjective probability that she used the wrong code (e.g., she recently used her codes

and knows that her recent attempts were successful). In the second, Meili has a high subjective probability that she used the wrong code, although she also does not know she did (e.g., she knows that regularly she forgets which of these codes is which).

For the objector whose intuition is that Tamara has moral responsibility for her epistemic practices which led to her being in Low Risk, an analogous claim about Meili in Low Risk is unconvincing. It sounds absurd to claim that Meili is *morally* blameworthy for failing to check the codes in order to switch her payment *away from charity*. This undermines the intuition in Tamara's Low Risk case, since the intuition does not generalize.

Since it is beyond the scope of this chapter, these are only brief and tentative remarks about how to explain the intuition. One is a (reverse) halo effect. The halo effect is the bias to associate extra positive properties to individuals with positive properties. Reverse halo means that, since we already blame Tamara for causing the property damage, we may be prone to judge her negatively in other ways as well. In particular, we might judge her epistemic practices as morally problematic, even though epistemic responsibility and moral responsibility should be kept separate. A more interesting and speculative possibility is that this asymmetry is connected to the Knobe (2006) effect, whereby attributions of praiseworthiness/blameworthiness (and intentionality) are asymmetrically a function of the moral desirability of side-effects. It is taken as given that this asymmetry is, at least prima facie, problematic. Here, the asymmetry may come from a similar set-up; instead of them being side-effects of a stated goal, the outcomes are accidental outcomes which occur instead of their goals. In short, we blame an individual for not avoiding a negative outcome, whether that outcome was a side-effect of a separate goal or unexpectedly occurred instead of the goal. In the former case, this blame means imputing intentionality to the individual, whereas in the latter case, since blame for the action may be limited by their expectations, the "excess" blame is shifted to subjective probabilities. That this shift is asymmetrical can be seen by considering Donation, and that the shift is asymmetrical suggests that the shift is illegitimate.

Now, we can move on to Premise (4), which tells us that, in deliberation, it is rational to exclude that which you are not responsible for. This premise is probably straightforwardly or conceptually true, but some justification is necessary. Just as it is irrational to spend unlimited time and energy trying to attain certainty about what consequences will follow from an action (recall that the consequences might be extremely spatially or temporally distant), it is irrational to include potential consequences for which one is not responsible. This is most obvious when considering consequences which one cannot affect. Such consequences are not one's moral responsibility and so, given we are finite beings, it is irrational for us to consider them. If we also accept that this is the case with consequences which one could affect, but which are not one's moral responsibility, then this is sufficient for (4). In other words, the reason to adopt Premise (4) is that it unifies or systematizes the considerations that may be permissibly excluded from decision-making. I think it is a sensible limitation on decision-making, as it helps to prevent it from becoming implausibly onerous on finite beings like ourselves.

With (3) and (4), it is easy to see how rational deliberation will limit outcomes to the extent of the subjective probabilities, giving us (5). Finally, since probability discounting is a way of representing this exclusion mathematically, it can be used to exclude outcomes from deliberation. Mathematically, the way to exclude the *outcomes* to the extent given by subjective probability is just to weight (i.e., multiply) the outcomes by their subjective probability. This argument demonstrates that, when decision-making under risk, probability discounting is defensible when taking responsibility into consideration.

Additions and extensions

There are interesting decision-theoretic arguments and axiomatic derivations of the claim that it is rational to weight outcomes by the subjective probabilities that those outcomes will occur. Many of these hold that rationality implies that decision-makers will try to maximize the satisfaction of their preferences, assuming that their preferences are sufficiently coherently structured. These are targeted towards idealized decision-makers with rational preferences. The arguments presented here are targeted in a slightly different manner; they are aimed at interlocutors who find these decision-theoretic conclusions and axioms less plausible. They are more plausible since they are based on the claim that it is rational for decision-makers to *focus* their decision-making by *limiting* things in their decision-making.

Now, in practice, it is important to hypothesize that such cost–benefit analyses are a good model for actual decision-making for individuals, with two considerations or qualifications:

- Individuals have very coarse-grained probability increments, so it is probably descriptively more accurate that individuals work with categories such as "unlikely" or "almost definitely not" or "almost certainly" and that these can only roughly be mapped onto a range of probabilities in percentage terms (e.g., 10–25 percent or 0–10 percent or 90–100 percent, respectively). Responsibility on this argument would then be just as coarse-grained as the probability categories a given individual is working with.
- Individuals tend to round probabilities up and down, such that small probabilities get rounded down to 0 percent (impossibility) and high probabilities get rounded up to 100 percent (certainty) (cf. Kahneman 2011). This matters greatly for simplifying decision-making, since most of the distant consequences or effects of an action are very difficult to predict (or have very small effective subjective probabilities). For individual decision-making, this means that many potential consequences are given negligible probabilities and, due to this psychological quirk, tend to round those to 0 percent, weighting those outcomes by 0 and discounting them from the decision-making entirely.[18]

It seems that both of these considerations make the decision-making account given here descriptively more accurate. But adopting these considerations is more normatively defensible or rational for individuals than for social groups, since a proper cost–benefit analysis involving all of the imaginable or foreseeable potential outcomes – even those with very small probabilities – would be so cognitively taxing for individuals as to be unworkable.

However, when the stakes are high, it is best for individuals to try to mitigate both of these caveats and take the cognitive effort required to do so. Furthermore, at the social and political level, decision-makers should always try to avoid these effects. Social and political decision-making do not, at least in theory, have as many limitations as individuals do in day-to-day decision-making and so should include, with as fine probability assignments as possible, all the outcomes that can be predicted. There may well be practical limitations, but simplifications should be tolerated in fewer cases than for individual decision-making. This is the case with evaluations of projects in the context of climate change.

This argument implies that, if our subjective probabilities of the effects of our climate-altering actions decrease with respect to time, we have decreasing moral responsibility for effects which do occur. As for what the subjective probabilities are, and who the relevant "we" are, reports issued by the Intergovernmental Panel on Climate Change (IPCC) should be seen as a legitimate first approximation of the state of published science so anyone who has reasonable access to the results of these reports should be included in this "we" and the subjective probabilities should reflect the IPCC reports. In fact, due to the level of agreement required for information to be included in the reports, they are likely to be conservative in their assessments.

A final point to make is that the probability discounting endorsed here does not conflict with or double-count probability discounting for axiomatic reasons (for instance). It offers an alternative route to the claim that one ought to discount by subjective probabilities, a route which is meant to be normatively and intuitively acceptable. By buttressing the conclusion in a context divorced from the decision-theoretic axioms, it is intended to make this conclusion more palatable to a wider audience. In this way, we can justifiably use cost–benefit analyses even in contexts which concern costs and benefits over the very long-term, as with climate change.

Notes

1 I would like to thank Joanna Burch-Brown, Marc Davidson, Eike Düvel, Rachel Fraser, Clare Heyward, Alison Hills, Lukas Meyer, Daniel Petz, Thomas Pölzer, Matthew Rendall, Dominic Roser, Harald Stezler, and Teru Thomas for helpful comments and suggestions; audiences at the University of Graz, the University of Oxford, and the European Consortium for Political Research's Joint Session organized by Matthew Rendall and Dominic Roser; and the very helpful editors of this volume. My subjective probabilities are such that responsibility for remaining errors lie with me. Funding from the Austrian Science Fund (FWF) under research grant W 1256-G15 (Doctoral Programme Climate Change – Uncertainties, Thresholds and Coping Strategies) is gratefully acknowledged.

2 It is not meant to be confused with either *utility discounting* or *consumption discounting*, such as discussed in (Broome 1992, 1994; Dasgupta 2008; Parfit 1984; Stern 2007), among many others. In particular, it is not the same as the special category of consumption discounting that Parfit (1984) calls *probabilistic discounting*. The latter picks out consumption discount rates which are justified by reference to probabilities. The type of discounting under consideration could potentially be *used* to justify probabilistic discounting, but it is not directly about discount *rates* at all. The kind of probability in question is also sometimes called *ex ante* probability.
3 See Ellsberg (1961) for a seminal paper on these distinctions.
4 I use the terms "consequence" and "effect" synonymously, but "outcome" indicates the entire set of consequences (or effects) that result from an action. For expositional simplicity, I assume that the probability an individual assigns to an outcome is the same as their credence in that outcome.
5 Caney (2009: 196) agrees that probability discounting only applies under risk, and mentions that this is a limitation, since we do not always have solid grounds for subjective probability assignments, especially in the context of climate change. However, Caney's (2009) argument which I engage with here presumes that we have probabilities of rights violations, so the argument in question does presume decision-making under risk.
6 Caney writes this in terms of money spent, but this means either he is suggesting no *consumption* discounting, which he explicitly denies, or, more plausibly, it is simply a *means* to the morally relevant consequences.
7 Caney is not explicit about what probabilities constitute "high," but for the purposes of the critique here, I do not focus on the arbitrariness of setting any particular special threshold, although I believe that any such specification would invite new objections.
8 Of course, when drivers are not driving cars, they may be at risk just as much as non-drivers. However, *over a lifetime*, or any other given span of time, non-drivers will spend more time than drivers as vulnerable road users and at disproportionate risk.
9 There would be good consequences in these worlds, too. For instance, world wars might become technically infeasible. However, in line with (R4), we are only considering the actual benefits of risky behaviors, i.e., the costs in these possible worlds which are avoided in the actual world.
10 I should point out that I am not making this argument simply because I intend to justify probability discounting; I actually think, to be consistent, that rights-based theorists *should* be this concerned about driving cars, along with many other technologies which are potentially rights-violating. Although it may well not be feasible to go back to a society without *any* rights-endangering transportation technologies, I think rights-based theories lead us to the conclusion that such a society would be in that respect morally superior.
11 Of course, I am not intending to imply that knowing is always extensionally equivalent with assigning a probability of 1, nor that not knowing is in general extensionally equivalent with assigning a probability of less than 1, but using the term in this manner is, I believe, perspicuous in the current context.
12 If one takes the concept of moral responsibility to apply only in a narrow range of morally weighty circumstances, please treat my wider usage as stipulative.
13 Many of the examples in the literature involve death (e.g., Harman 2015; Parfit 2011). I think this is problematic, since we have laws against killing, even when it is accidental or unintended ("manslaughter"), or when it is intended but unsuccessful ("attempted murder"). So one could think that another is morally responsible for some unsuccessful or unintentional killing, when one is instead conflating responsibility for the other's killing for these other legally punishable offences. Another issue is that moral responsibility for murder might be so great that it is difficult to tell the difference between an intuition of complete moral responsibility for murder and (say)

quarter responsibility for murder: both might be so much greater than any day-to-day level of moral responsibility as to be intuitively indistinguishable in the assignment of blame. For these reasons, none of my examples involve death.

14 Sepielli (2009), for instance, distinguishes between *narrow-scope* and *wide-scope* norms, depending on whether the norm applies to an individual given the set of subjective probabilities they have or whether the norm is satisfied by the individual also doing some action which leads them to revise their subjective probabilities. Harman (2015) makes a similar distinction (between "blameworthiness for behavior" and "blameworthiness for causing that behavior"). My first response is addressed to narrow-scopers or those who want to retain Harman's distinction; my second is aimed at undermining these distinctions. One advantage of losing this distinction – making actions aimed at epistemic updating just extra choice possibilities – is that we have a more unified concept of moral responsibility (or blameworthiness) without it. However, both Sepielli's and Harman's discussions are about blameworthiness in the presence of moral uncertainty; mine is about non-moral uncertainty, which I believe to be more relevant in the context of climate change since most plausible moral systems converge decisively on urgent action (e.g., Stern 2014, 2015).

15 Of course, there is the further worry for evidential probability advocates about how to specify which evidence is "available to the individual," but that is well known (e.g., Timpe 2009).

16 On my account, one always has *some* moral responsibility for not gathering more information, but that responsibility diminishes the less helpful one thinks information gathering would be.

17 Let me stipulate that such charities exist, and, in climate contexts, an existence proof for such a good charity is one that helps indigenous people to protect rainforest, CoolEarth, www.coolearth.org.

18 On the assumption that the subjective probabilities will decrease with respect to time, perhaps consistently, these two considerations allow us to answer the worries of Lenman (2000), about one's inability to determine all of the consequences of an action (see also Burch-Brown 2014). If one cannot know all of the consequences of one's actions, Lenman argues, then one cannot ever know that one acts rightly. My argument shows that, even for a consequentialist, it is rational to act even if one does not know rightly since it is rational to probability discount according to one's subjective probabilities. For very difficult to foresee future events, rounding down to 0 percent – even if they may occur – is rationally defensible for finite beings like ourselves.

References

Broome, J. (1992), *Counting the Cost of Global Warming*, Cambridge: White Horse Press.

Broome, J. (1994), "Discounting the future," *Philosophy & Public Affairs*, 23(2): 128–56.

Burch-Brown, J. (2014), "Clues for Consequentialists," *Utilitas*, 26(01): 105–19.

Caney, S. (2008), "Human rights, climate change, and discounting," *Environmental Politics*, 17(4): 536–55.

Caney, S. (2009), "Climate change and the future: discounting for time, wealth, and risk," *Journal of Social Philosophy*, 40(2): 163–86.

Dasgupta. P. (2008), "Discounting climate change," *Journal of Risk Uncertainty*, 37: 141–69.

Ellsberg, D. (1961), "Risk, ambiguity, and the savage axioms," *The Quarterly Journal of Economics*, 75(4): 643–69.

Harman, E. (2015), "The irrelevance of moral uncertainty," in R. Shafer-Landau, (ed.), *Oxford Studies in Metaethics*, Vol. 10, Oxford: Oxford University Press, pp. 53–79.

Kahneman, D. (2011), *Thinking, Fast and Slow*, London: Penguin.

Knobe, J. (2006), "The concept of intentional action: a case study in the uses of folk psychology," *Philosophical Studies*, 130(2): 203–31.

Lenman, J. (2000), "Consequentialism and cluelessness," *Philosophy & Public Affairs*, 29(4): 342–70.

Parfit, D. (1984), *Reasons and Persons*, Oxford: Oxford University Press.

Parfit, D. (2011), *On What Matters*, Vol. 1, Oxford: Oxford University Press.

Sepielli, A. (2009), "What to do when you don't know what to do," in R. Shafer-Landau, (ed.), *Oxford Studies in Metaethics*, Vol. 4, Oxford: Oxford University Press, pp. 5–28.

Shinar, D. (2012), "Safety and mobility of vulnerable road users: pedestrians, bicyclists, and motorcyclists," *Accident: Analysis and Prevention*, 44(1): 1–2.

Smart, J. J. C. (1973), "An outline of a system of utilitarian ethics," in J. J. C. Smart and B. Williams (eds.), *Utilitarianism: For and Against*, Cambridge: Cambridge University Press, pp. 1–74.

Stern, N. (2007), *The Economics of Climate Change: The Stern Review*, Cambridge and New York: Cambridge University Press.

Stern, N. (2014), "Ethics, equity and the economics of climate change, Paper 1: Science and Philosophy," *Economics and Philosophy*, 30(03): 397–444.

Stern, N. (2015), *Why Are We Waiting?*, Cambridge, MA: MIT Press.

Timpe, K. (2009), "Review: *Living with Uncertainty: The Moral Significance of Ignorance*," *Notre Dame Philosophical Reviews*.

Tiwari, G. (2015), "The safety of vulnerable road users: the challenge for twenty-first century," *International Journal of Injury Control and Safety Promotion*, 22(2): 93–4.

Zimmerman, M. (2008), *Living with Uncertainty: The Moral Significance of Ignorance*, Cambridge: Cambridge University Press.

Zimmerman, M. (2014), *Ignorance and Moral Obligation*, Oxford: Oxford University Press.

7 Climate change mitigation, sustainability and non-substitutability[1]

Säde Hormio

Introduction

Climate change policy decisions are inescapably intertwined with future generations. Even if all carbon dioxide emissions were to be stopped today, most aspects of climate change would persist for hundreds of years. Because of cumulative emissions, seas will continue to warm for centuries, and 15 to 40 per cent of emitted CO_2 continue to contribute to warming for more than a millennium (IPCC 2013, 25–6). Anthropogenic climate change thus inevitably raises questions of intergenerational justice and sustainability. The most famous definition of sustainability comes from the Brundtland Report, which defines it as "development that meets the needs of the present without compromising the ability of future generations to meet their own needs".[2] It is clear that climate change poses a serious risk to sustainability. Climate change puts ecosystems under severe stress through increased climate-extremes such as floods, droughts, heat waves and cyclones, and affects crop yields, usually negatively. Melting snow and ice and changing precipitation alter hydrological systems, affecting the quantity and quality of water resources. All of this affects the poor disproportionately, both now and in the future, as they are more vulnerable to climate shocks (IPCC 2014a). Sustainability thus has a strong intra-generational justice aspect to it also, but this chapter will concentrate on the intergenerational side.[3]

While debates around sustainability have been going on for decades, and are perhaps already considered old news in some fields, the concept is very relevant to climate ethics and economics. This chapter argues that since not all natural capital is substitutable, we should invest in mitigation efforts. Climate policies focused mainly on adaptation are not acceptable, although adaptation measures have their role to play, especially as compensatory measures. The role of economics is very prominent in political discussions around climate change mitigation and adaptation. Therefore, to tackle justice issues effectively, one must also look into the ethical assumptions included in economic analyses. The latest Intergovernmental Panel on Climate Change (IPCC) report includes for the first time discussion on how justice questions could be brought into economic calculations that feed into policy recommendations (IPCC 2014b). It is not an easy task, but an essential one.

The chapter proceeds as follows. The second section begins with a short overview of discount rate debate in climate economics, followed by the observation that discounting implicitly makes the assumption that natural capital is always substitutable with man-made capital (Holland 1995; Neumayer 1999, 2007, 2013; Spash 1993). The following section explores the role of substitutability in discussions around sustainability, and explains why non-substitutability matters if we are to take intergenerational justice seriously and invest aptly in mitigation. Non-substitutability simply implies that there are some forms of capital that cannot be substituted by another, and so consumption of one cannot be compensated with additional stocks of the other. The non-substitutability of critical natural capital can be defended without empirical data about preferences or the need to view the environment as a superior good, and the argument is presented through the language of keeping options open. The fourth section anticipates likely objections and tries to clarify the essence of the debate on sustainability. Those alive today make decisions about what natural capital to use and what to save for future. These choices are often represented as different points in a continuum of sustainability: weak sustainability is associated with a high degree of substitutability and therefore a lot of flexibility over what capital to consume, whereas strong sustainability is more stringent on substitutability. While it may be that in economical understanding weak and strong sustainability collapse into one another, philosophically the emphasis is slightly different. Section five discusses how *normative sustainability* can be supported without ignoring opportunity costs and trade-offs. Section six concludes.

Discounting and its implicit acceptance of substitutability

Discounting is a tool in economics that allows effects occurring at different future times to be compared. Due to the cumulative and long-term nature of the problem of climate change, future generations inevitably have to be incorporated into climate economists' models. There is an inherent intergenerational tension, as future populations will bear the environmental cost of today's emissions, while a large part of the current population benefits from the industrial activities contributing to greenhouse gas emissions. Conversely, people in the future will reap the benefits of mitigation efforts, while the current generation bear the costs, as mitigation efforts mean allocating resources away from other things. When economists make cost–benefit analyses to weight these options, they utilise discount rates to compare the costs and benefits of climate change mitigation policies that arise at different times. In discounting, all aggregate costs and benefits are expressed in terms of their present value first. Then discounted values are compared to each other, so that a policy is considered desirable if its net present value is positive.

Discounting is traditionally justified with the assertion that present utility counts more than future utility. In economics, future generations are also assumed to be better off than we are. For example, Geoffrey Brennan (2007: 277–80) argues that, on average, each generation over the past 300 years or so has systematically done better than its predecessors, mainly through gaining socially robust institutions and an ever-increasing stock of knowledge.[4] I remain sceptical of the growth optimism, especially with the possibility of runaway climate change scenarios. In any case, just because the material conditions and medical care of the average person has improved vastly in the past few hundred years, taking a bird's-eye view of history gives us no real assurance that this is a trend that will definitely continue.[5] Importantly, even if economic growth were to continue, it does not mean that it would translate to the benefit of those at the bottom of the ladder, even in the future. However, for the sake of the argument, reservations about this assumption will be left aside for the remainder of the chapter as it is not the only problematic one in discounting, as we will soon see.

The exact value of the discount rate has ethical implications, as it determines how the consequences of mitigation are distributed between generations. When payoffs are in the distant future, seemingly insignificant differences in discount rates can make an enormous difference. This has led Martin Weitzman (2012: 309–10) to argue that it may not be too much of an exaggeration to say that, in climate economics, almost any answer to a cost–benefit analysis question can be defended by the choice of a discount rate. To give a prominent example, the 2006 Stern Review on the Economics of Climate Change (Stern 2007) utilised a low discount rate (1.4 per cent per year) and concluded that we should take immediate action to reduce emission, whereas Nordhaus's (2008) analysis assumed a higher discount rate (around 5.5 per cent per year) and reached the conclusion that only a mild reduction in the short term followed by more significant reduction in the mid-term were economically desirable. The choice of discount rate thus leads to differences in policy recommendations regarding mitigation and adaptation. The majority of debates on climate ethics and economics have thus unsurprisingly centred on the discount rate chosen (in addition to Stern and Nordhaus, see also Azar and Sterner 1996[6]; Brennan 2007; Broome 1992[7], 1994; Dasgupta 2007; Weitzman 2012).

Eric Neumayer (1999: 39) argues that attacking the discount rate ignores the real problem: the premise of perfect substitutability – that natural capital is always substitutable by human capital – which "is the implicit underlying theoretical foundation for discounting". Alan Holland (1995) had observed similarly a few years earlier that one of the framework assumptions implicit in cost–benefit analysis is the homogenising of value and preferences: you cannot compare environmental goods with other goods without a common measure of value. Holland notices that if we are to bring environmental goods into the (hypothetical) market, it amounts to pronouncing them substitutable (others to have discussed substitutability include Spash 1993 and Gardiner 2004). To give an example of how the empirical assumption of natural capital being substitutable by human capital is implicit in discounting, Nordhaus's dynamic optimisation economic growth model meshes together benefits and costs as shares of total output, regardless of whether they are about consumption or connected to environmental amenities. Neumayer argues that this is the first of two closely related ways in which the model implicitly assumes substitutability. The other is that material costs and benefits can substitute for environmental costs and benefits, which is implicitly assumed in the way Nordhaus discounts the future. The model utilises Ramsey's (1928) formula for discounting where the discount rate relates to the growth rate of consumption: future counts less as future generations are presumed to be better off due to increased consumption, so increased consumption is implicitly assumed to perfectly compensate for losses in environmental amenities. (Neumayer 1999, 35–7, 2013: 31–4; Nordhaus 2008).

According to Neumayer (2007, 300–1), the Stern Review missed the opportunity to build a more persuasive case for current generations to take immediate, decisive action on climate change mitigation, as it was too easy for critics to point out that the Review's central message is decisively dependent on the discount rate used. Rather than focusing on the low discount rate and possible substantial losses of output, Neumayer argues that the non-substitutability argument could have provided a much stronger case for the measures recommended by the Review. This is because even in the Review's worst-case scenario, people living in 2200 are assumed to be eight times better off than present generations. In contrast, the non-substitutability argument draws attention to how future generations are harmed by climate change in a way that consumption growth just cannot compensate for.

While Neumayer is seemingly correct in criticising the Stern Review for failing to explicitly problematise the assumption of substitutability, he lacks the apparatus to make his argument persuasive. This is because Neumayer (1999: 41–2) concludes that favouring non-substitutability over "perfect substitutability" is "a matter of belief"[8] at the end of the day, even though "a persuasive case" can be made for the preservation of some (especially life-supporting) forms of natural capital, as the likelihood of these being substitutable is slim (Neumayer 2013: 99). He continues that as there are no "hard numbers" when it comes to climate change, policies cannot be based on them (Neumayer 2013: 44). Economics thus cannot provide a clear answer on what to do about climate change, i.e. to invest heavily in mitigation or not, but it can make the choices more rational and transparent. It is up to us to decide politically if growth in consumption can compensate losses to natural capital. While the question of substitutability of natural capital with human capital cannot be settled by economists or philosophers alone, it does not follow that it is a matter of mere belief and all is up for grabs within political decision-making process. Instead, the next sections demonstrate that a strong case for mitigation can be built based on intergenerational justice.

A matter of intergenerational justice

Considerations of intergenerational justice should compel us to invest substantially in mitigation to protect critical forms of natural capital at minimum, and to keep as many options open for future generations as possible. The idea about freedom of choice in intergenerational justice is of course nothing new. Already in 1987 the Brundtland Report argued that as few future options as possible should be foreclosed.[9] Various arguments have been given to the same effect (in addition to those discussed below, see e.g. Beekman 2004; Dobson 2003; Holland 1999; Norton 1999; Norton and Toman 1997; Weikard 1999). This is not a problem, as the goal of this chapter is not to present some novel argument about intergenerational justice. It is rather to argue that (on a minimal account) the non-substitutability of critical natural capital, and the climate change mitigation investments which that entails, can be defended without empirical data about preferences or the need to view the environment somehow as a superior good.[10]

Capital is a stock that provides flows of service, both current and future. It comes in various forms: natural capital, financial capital, real capital (consumer and investment goods, infrastructure), cultural capital (institutions), social capital (social contacts), human capital (abilities and knowledge, health) and knowledge capital (non-person-bound knowledge). These categories are not absolutely fixed: sometimes it is not possible to give a clear-cut answer whether something is human-made or a form of natural capital. For example, with cultivated natural capital such as farmlands, the difference between natural and artificial is a matter of degree (Tremmel 2009: 66–7). Despite this, natural capital has many distinguishing features that make it different from all other forms of capital. It is essential to human survival and thus has a basic life-support function. Natural capital is a necessary input for production, transformable and deployable by everyone. Some forms of natural capital are limited in supply and there is irreversibility to their destruction, as natural capital such as minerals are not created or produced by humans. Using up natural capital potentially causes dangerous waste and pollution, and there is an inbuilt rivalry in consumption: if we consume more now, there will be less for future generations. Natural capital comes in many forms: plants, species, resources, ecosystems. Some forms of natural capital have more of the distinctive features listed above, while others are more substitutable. Because resources are limited – and uncertainty, ignorance and ubiquitous risk plague our world – we cannot simply preserve all natural capital. Knowing what to preserve is not easy, though: because we do not have perfect information, we also cannot say for certain which forms of natural capital should be preserved (Casal 2011: 313, 2012: 421; Neumayer 1998: 28–9). Natural capital is not equally distributed across people and nations. Paula Casal (2011, 2012) also points out that, while the distribution is arbitrary, natural resources are easy to redistribute compared to, say, natural talents. Therefore there is no *prima facie* reason for them to be a source of inequalities.

Environmental economics began tackling sustainability in the mid-1970s (gaining mainstream popularity in the 1990s) to deal with the issue of how much and in which ways the economy can grow without impoverishing the future. Robert Solow (1974: 41) influentially argued that a finite pool of resources should be used optimally, but if there is elasticity of substitution between natural capital and other capital, the pool can be drawn down as long as the stock of capital is added to. The central tenet of weak sustainability is that we can cause pollution and use non-renewable resources as long as we compensate for this with enough man-made capital, be it infrastructure, material goods, education or advances in medicine. Strong sustainability denies this and maintains that some forms of natural capital are non-substitutable, for example that critical forms of natural capital should be preserved. In a continuum of sustainability, weak sustainability is associated with a high degree of substitutability and therefore a lot of flexibility over what capital to consume, whereas strong sustainability is more stringent on substitutability. However, it should be noted that weak sustainability is also compatible with some limitations to substitutability.[11] Economist Wilfred Beckerman (1994: 200) argues that implicit in any definition of sustainability is the idea that any substitution of natural capital by man-made capital is only justified if it contributes equally to human welfare. Strong sustainability always maintains that some forms of natural capital cannot be substituted (perhaps some man-made capital could be branded as non-substitutable also, like unique artworks or historical buildings). John O'Neill (2014) distinguishes between technical and economic substitutability. A thing that realises the same purpose or a goal is a technical substitute for something (saccharine for sugar). Much of the empirical debate around climate change is about technological substitutability. Technical substitutes are not, however, needed if economic substitutes are available: substituting A with B does not change the overall welfare of the agent. Weak sustainability allows for wide economic substitutability and tends to be linked to high technological optimism, unlike strong.

In economics, the essential problem of sustainability is often presented as lack of decisive information about what future generations would want us to do: their desires and preferences are uncertain to us. Neumayer (2013: 79–80) argues that to defend strong sustainability on empirical grounds, "the proponents of strong sustainability would have to show that individuals have lexicographic preferences with respect to environmental amenities", i.e. they display preference of environmental capital over other capital, and there just isn't empirical evidence to back up the claim. Contingent valuation surveys do indicate that, regardless of costs, substantial minorities of respondents (14–24 per cent of sample) exhibit preferences towards environmental protection. However, these still remain minorities and the preferences indicated remain hypothetical. Neumayer therefore concludes that without "the acid test of real sacrifices" one cannot infer that strong sustainability would in fact be preferred. Daniel W. Bromley (1998) is critical of sustainability and laments that it "is at once a fine idea and a hopeless concept". The present people thus "stand as dictators over the future" as our actions violate all three constituents of freedom: autonomy, opportunity and immunity with regards to the people who come after us. Our dictatorship concerns not so much the amounts of capital to be preserved, but what capital to preserve, what judgements will be of value to the future generations. Maintaining choices for future generations restricts choices for the present people. What sustainability can be, according to Bromley (1998:

234–9), is to provide "suggestion and direction", but what we should do is a question of ethics. I agree we cannot settle the debates of sustainability without basing our arguments on justice.

Usually when natural capital is transformed into man-made capital, it limits the range of options to what use it can be put into. It has been observed that natural capital's paradox "is that the realization of its potential is at one and the same time the limitation of its potential" (Holland 1999: 64). Therefore a balance between natural and man-made capital should exist: if not, we could be locking future generations into a lifestyle of our choice. If we try to act with the best interests of the future generations in mind, surely the best course of action is to keep as many options open for them as is feasible. Since we do not know what future generations want or prefer, it is good that they have options among which to choose. The question here is not about making the wrong decision for future generations; it is about the possibility of exhausting the future generations' opportunities for making any real decisions for themselves. According to Brian Barry (1997: 104–6), we should sustain the conditions that make it possible to realise a range of conceptions of what a good life is: we should not preempt future people's choices, but instead "respect the creativity of people in the future" and maintain equal opportunities across generations. What intergenerational justice demands is that we leave the future generations with a range of choices open to them, instead of some predefined amount of utility. The current generation is not the sole creator of the majority of our capital stock and technology: new generations do not start from scratch. Intergenerational justice, then, requires the maintenance of capital as far as possible, and, when this is not feasible, the creation of additional capital (including technology) and alternative productive opportunities to compensate for the depleted resources and to replace the productive opportunities we have destroyed (Barry 1991: 260–9). Clive Spash (1993: 130) argues similarly when he labels the intergenerational transfers that occur in daily lives – advances in technology, investments in capital and direct bequests – as equity payments that should be made to provide some minimal standard of living. According to Spash, long-term environmental damages are not covered by equity payments, but present a case for liability responsibilities and corresponding compensation. More recently, Joseph Mazor (2010: 408) has argued that present people owe to each other an obligation to conserve natural resources for future people, based on a principled commitment to equal shares to natural resources among contemporaries and the fact that generations always overlap. The older people alive at the moment are thus confronted with demands by their younger contemporaries, who in turn "can anticipate being confronted with the demands of the members of the following generation and so on". O'Neill (2014) makes an important observation that we do not only want to pass on options, but also particulars: this building, this work of art. The relationship between (overlapping) generations is one of deliberation, not of coercion, and the dialogue about the nature of good life is ongoing.

Sometimes options should be closed, of course, for example when doing so eliminates a major threat. If we were given the option of eradicating AIDS or malaria forever, we should do so. However, most of the time when future options are closed, it is for a mundane and simple reason: it is simply inevitable. Whenever we make choices, we incur opportunity costs, i.e. we won't be able to enjoy the benefits that the alternatives would have brought us. We cannot help but close a number of options for future generations in the course of our lifetimes, while opening others:

> Certain alternatives that otherwise would be open for choice in the future are eliminated by acts performed in the present. This is an inescapable fact of life. But another fact of life is that the acts we perform in the present may either increase or diminish the freedom of future generations, depending upon which acts we perform. As civilization develops, later generations are free from certain natural limitations from which earlier generations were not free.
>
> (Lemos 1986: 175)

Climate change, however, is not an inescapable fact of life. Climate change – and environmental damage more generally – runs a great risk of foreclosing a wide range of opportunities to act out, or perhaps even conceive, some versions of a good life for future generations (in a runaway climate change scenario, perhaps it may threaten even life itself). Therefore we have to immediately invest in mitigation. We could complicate the argument by talking about capabilities as the metric of intergenerational justice (Sen 1985; Alkire and Deneulin 2009; Gutwald *et al.* 2011), but the main idea remains the same: intergenerational justice calls for mitigation. In economics, the argument could take the form of the value of capital being a function of the opportunities associated with it. Since future generations cannot have a common social preference ordering with us, the range of choice must be what counts. The range of alternatives in each opportunity set is what allows for freedom of choice to be upheld (Perrings 1994: 96–103). Another possible way of formulating this argument would be to present climate change as a threat to the liberal idea of neutrality.[12] We should try to secure conditions to realise pluralistic ways of conceiving the good life, as destroying certain physical environments irreversibly narrows options (Dobson 2003: 163–9). We might also block future innovations, such as when a plant is found to have new medicinal properties.

Because critical forms of natural capital provide life-support functions, they have lexical priority among natural capital. Such critical forms of natural capital include at least ecosystem services – the benefits we get from ecosystems – for instance, controlling the climate or providing clean drinking water. On the minimal account, intergenerational justice demands that we preserve these for future generations. Without mitigating climate change we are running the risk of serious damage for example to the Earth's atmosphere and climate regulation, critical capital that cannot be substituted. If we had a time machine that could take into account and calculate all future preferences, this would not change the fact that critical forms of natural capital remain non-substitutable, they are not optional: they are the backbone of life on Earth. The important point is that sustainability is a normative issue, not just a technical optimisation puzzle waiting to be solved.

Would you like your sustainability weak, strong or normative, sir?

This section attempts to separate the normative debate around sustainability from the convoluted usage of the terms associated with it. In climate ethics, the debate is essentially about how immediate and drastic the action to reduce emissions should be, i.e. how much to invest in mitigation efforts. Some of the general debate around weak and strong sustainability (largely predating climate ethics and economics) is generated by the genuine difficulty of working in an interdisciplinary field, and I have begun to doubt if it is useful to employ the terms in climate ethics and economics. Not only do they have a different flavour across disciplines, the problem with using such long-debated concepts is that they have come to mean different things to different commentators. For example, some use "strong sustainability" to denote the idea that none or very few forms of natural capital are substitutable, whereas others link it to the non-substitutability of critical forms of natural capital, as we will soon see below. This is why the term *normative sustainability* is introduced, to try to tease out what the weak/strong debate has been about and to defend the importance of normativity in climate policy discussions.

Beckerman (1994: 194–5) has criticised strong sustainability as unacceptable and totally impractical. He questions the sense of conserving all plant and animal species just for the sake of it, and reminds us that about 98 per cent of all species that have existed during Earth's history are already extinct. Still, does anyone lose sleep over dinosaurs? Beckerman brands strong sustainability as "an absolutist concept" and "morally repugnant":

> Given the acute poverty and environmental degradation in which a large part of the world's population live, one could not justify using up vast resources in an attempt to preserve from extinction, say, every one of the several million species of beetles that exist.
>
> (Beckerman 1994: 194)

He clearly defines strong sustainability along the lines of keeping natural capital intact. However, strong sustainability must not be blind to the differences between types of natural capital. Not all natural capital was created equal: some forms are more critical to support life on Earth than others and are therefore always non-substitutable. If we save several million species of beetles, it is of no use if climate change deteriorates the Earth's atmosphere. The key is not to exceed the regenerative capacity of life-supporting, critical forms of natural capital, so that their function is maintained. Harvesting can be done at the optimally sustainable yield, as long as stocks are not deteriorated. In case of sinks, pollution should not exceed the natural absorptive capacity (Neumayer 2013: 26). By emphasising the importance of some forms of natural capital over others, this understanding of strong sustainability avoids the theoretical pitfalls and practical implausibility of preserving everything in nature. As Bromley (1998: 237) puts it, what we should conserve is not species per se (that would be species fetishism), but rather "the conditions for the recreation of ecosystems". This is not to ignore the very real difficulty of identifying the forms of natural capital that must be preserved, or finding suitable measures and indicators to keep tabs on how well we are doing with sustainability.

Beckerman would probably not be satisfied with this response as he has also criticised proponents of strong sustainability for failing "to indicate the criteria that are relevant in deciding when one is faced with 'absurdly strong sustainability' and when one is not – i.e. by what rule does one decide when there may be some trade-off, after all" (Beckerman 1995: 175). What he abhors are those who claim to know what is good for others without detailed logical arguments, and argues that economists show humility to the plurality of values within democratic societies by concentrating on individual preferences, while at the same time being aware of the limitations of this approach.

However, with climate change it is clear to see that ecosystem services are already under serious threat and the uncertainty that plagues our future calls not just for risk management, but the ethical choice of investing substantially in mitigation. In any case, presenting normative arguments does not translate into thinking that one occupies some moral high ground and knows what is good for others. It is – no more and no less – putting forward an argument about what should or should not be done, the strength of which is to be decided in public discourse. What separates normative arguments from merely voicing one's opinion is that the former should come with an explanation of their logic attached. There needs to be nothing suspicious about normativity. Quite the contrary, it is about facing up to the ethical questions that living together in societies present to us. Normative arguments aim to change the way we think and, most importantly, the way we act. They attempt to bring the ethical issues that demand an open debate to the front. This is why philosophers can be wary of the mask of objectivity that ethical issues can take within economic framework. When new circumstances arise, new ethical issues need to be discussed and weighted. This is of course very much the case with climate change at the moment.

The way sustainability is understood in economics can make it seem somewhat redundant to separate weak and strong versions. This is due to both being compatible with limitations to substitutability. The difference is that in strong sustainability a normative line is drawn at some resource *x*, depending on the theory, whereas with weak sustainability the non-substitutability of *x* is always an empirical issue. When economists are wary of strong sustainability, they aren't taking a moral stand against conserving critical natural capital. Beckerman (1995: 178) writes that when a natural resource becomes scarce "its relative price will rise and this will set up a chain of market responses which will tend to discourage its use and encourage the development of substitutes". He continues that, unlike in science fiction, natural resources do not suddenly disappear overnight, and therefore societies have time to adapt to changes in demand and supply.

While Beckerman might be right in most cases, does this really apply to sudden changes in the ecosystem services, such as the ones caused by anthropogenic climate change? Do the markets really have enough time to react, especially as the resource becoming scarce is still (mostly) outside the markets? Even if they did, the argument would remain problematical. After all, it is not purely an empirical issue whether coal is substitutable by solar power, as clean technology needs initial investments to make it a viable alternative. Investments are largely a political decision, as government incentives and available infrastructure affect the kind of energy sources it makes economic sense to concentrate on. Delaying investments in clean technology is an ethical issue also, as mitigation becomes more costly with each passing year. In this way, the substitutability of many forms of natural capital becomes an empirical issue only after the fact, after ethical decisions have already been taken.

While it may be that in economics weak and strong sustainability collapses into one another, philosophically the emphasis between the terms is slightly different. It is not about future shortage of some natural capital that is either met or unmet by technological innovations, thus affecting its market price and demand and supply. Rather, acknowledging the need to maintain critical natural capital like ecosystem services is a normative position about how we are not allowed to knowingly jeopardise the lives and well-being of future people. A line is drawn based on normative arguments over what is an acceptable harm that can be compensated (what is substitutable, if you like) and what is not. Taking an openly normative position, versus belief in the ability of the markets to self-regulate scarcity with market responses, lies at the heart of much of the interdisciplinary literature on strong versus weak sustainability. Due to the various uses of the terms, both of the sides are right in their own way, but the terms also mask this underlying difference across disciplines. There is thus a risk that the commentators speak past each other.

This is why I propose the term *normative sustainability* to refer to the line that can – and should – be drawn over what natural capital must be preserved for future generations based on normative considerations alone, prior to waiting for market signals over substitutability. Where the line is drawn naturally varies between writers, but here it is on risks to critical life-supporting functions. Inflicting harm can only be done when it is unavoidable and even then it should be compensated for. Harm here means depriving someone of a fundamental interest (Cripps 2013: 10–12).[13] On this minimal account, fundamental interests can be linked to life-supporting ecosystem services. Jeopardising them is a risk too big for us to take. That is why normative sustainability calls for urgent and strong mitigation measures on the policy front. Laissez-faire policies based on watch-and-wait and unrealistically high technological optimism are not acceptable.

Why normative arguments about sustainability not need to be unfeasible

This section defends a plausible reading of normative sustainability to anticipate possible objections, in order to show that normative arguments based on intergenerational justice need not disregard the reality of the world we live in, at least when the concept is applied in climate ethics and economics. I begin with some examples of how easily normative arguments can be misunderstood.

Economists tend to see themselves as technicians and therefore some of them view normative arguments with suspicion. I will use Neumayer as an example of an economist who misconstructs normative arguments on sustainability, as he has written a textbook on sustainability that is already on its fourth edition. While he bases his analysis on the economic methodology, he is not blind to normative issues in economics, and considers – but rejects as implausible – arguments based on intergenerational justice by Barry (1991) and Amartya Sen (1984). Neumayer (1999, 2013) claims that they brand any action that could inflict harm on future generations as unjustified and non-compensable. Great opportunity cost is incurred if we decide not to impose any harm on future generations. Instead, everything depends on what is the compensatory benefit (Neumayer 1999: 40). Neumayer writes: "The verdict that any action that inflicts some harm on coming generations is unjustified and cannot be compensated for calls for a virtual standstill in economic actions of the present generation."

It is worth spending a moment to dispel the misunderstandings in Neumayer's reading, as they represent quite a common line of argument in the sustainability literature in economics. The suggestion that philosophers, especially the more environmentally minded ones, are simply widely implausible in their recommendations is nothing new. Indeed, if normative sustainability really demanded avoiding all possible harm to future generations, they would be worse off as technological development would be halted and brakes put on, for example, research on renewable energy sources and medicines. Luckily while intergenerational justice arguments might be thin on practical recommendations, they need not be implausible. Industrialisation and technological advances have raised the living standards, conditions and life-expectancy of people around the world (albeit very unequally), reducing human suffering and making human flourishing possible on a wider scale than ever possible, with the possibility for much more. Normative sustainability simply requires that we take the (however unintended, or conveniently ignored) negative effects of these developments seriously, and do not ignore environmental pollution and degradation. The gravest one of the long-term harm caused is climate change, and it might even have the power to wipe out the gains development has brought. Of course it matters if natural capital is converted into things that benefit humankind now and in the long run, such as education for girls or medical advances, instead of some activity with short-lasting benefits conferred upon only a few individuals. Still not everything is up for grabs: future generations will not be compensated by bigger homes, smarter phones or even advances in medicine if climatic stability is jeopardised.

Neumayer's criticism of Barry and Sen seems to be based on misreading the normative arguments he considers. Sen argues that long-term environmental pollution resulting of deliberate action could be seen as a form of oppression of present generations towards future generations (Sen 1984: 194–6; Sen's 1982 paper quoted by Neumayer is republished in Sen 1984). According to Neumayer, Sen ignores the reality of trade-offs. When quoting Sen to support his point, Neumayer importantly omits the original quote's last sentence: "The avoidance of oppression of the future generations has to be given a value of its own" (Sen 1984: 195). This points to considerations of foreseeable, lasting harm being taken properly into account, but not necessarily overruling everything. In fact, Sen (1984: 199) writes that he does not doubt that compromises can be reached. While Sen was quoted out of context, Barry's argument is completely misrepresented by Neumayer. Neumayer (1999: 40) claims that, according to Barry, any environmental damage imposed on future generations represents a harm that is both unjustified and not amenable to compensation.[14] To support this conclusion, he quotes the example Barry (1991: 264) gives about how doing harm is in general not cancelled out by doing good, and how doing some good does not license one to do harm:

> For example, if you paid for the realignments of a dangerous highway intersection and saved an average of two lives a year, that would not mean that you could shoot one motorist per year and simply reckon on coming out ahead.

However, Barry clarifies that the above example involves "gratuitous infliction of harm" and that the argument *does not apply to resources*. His claim is only that not *all* violations of rights can be acceptably compensated. Barry (1991: 264) continues:

> In the case of resources and future generations, the crucial feature is that we cannot possibly avoid harming them by using up some non-renewable resources … the choice is not between reducing the resource base for future generations and keeping it intact, but between depletion with compensation and depletion without compensation.

Part of the confusion might stem from Neumayer and Barry not spelling out what they mean by harm: I suspect Neumayer's conception of harm might be wider than Barry's. In any case, Barry is clearly not advocating some kind of a standstill in economic actions of the present generations. Quite the contrary, Barry (1991: 265) writes that it is possible that "in the absence of resource depletion, we would in fact be inclined to leave future generations with far less productive potential than, as a matter of justice, we ought to leave them with". Barry thus fully acknowledges the importance of human capital creation: that the generations before us have added to the capital stock that was passed on to us, and that this "thousands of years of technological development" has left us better off (Barry 1991: 266).

One more clarification is required to make clear what is *not* being proposed. Neumayer (2013: 8–10) defines sustainability as development that is able to maintain the capacity necessary to provide non-declining future utility (per capita utility for infinity). But the idea of non-declining future utility is neither convincing nor necessary. Bromley (1998: 238) asserts that the idea "that those of us now alive can never be better off than any representative future generation" places the current people "in a situation of guilt and insecurity". Here we are agreed. It is not irrelevant to intergenerational justice what the starting point of welfare is. But it is not possible to agree with Barry (1997: 106) writing that "unless people in the future can be held responsible for the situation that they find themselves in, they should not be worse off than we are".

To illustrate why we cannot agree, this scenario shows why it would be strange to demand that the baseline can never go down. Imagine some 25-year-period in the future where crop yields across the globe exceed all expectations. This could be due to exceptionally advantageous weather conditions caused by some planetary movements, but in any case something that is outside of human control. Previous records are broken everywhere and food supplies are plentiful, allowing for labour normally spent on agriculture to be utilised elsewhere. Once the weather conditions return to normal, why should there be any intergenerational injustice attached to the next generation not having it quite so easy anymore? This is not to argue that any kind of drop between generations is acceptable: at minimum, we should always aim to secure fundamental interests. Capabilities is (again) one route to try to flesh this out, and could be helped to identify what kind of options we should try to keep open, or try to obtain, for future generations. Inequality among people, or generations, who all do very well, is much less of a problem than inequality among people of whom some are seriously struggling while others have plenty. This is why it is unnecessary to demand that future generations must always be at least as well off as the present generation and therefore non-declining future utility would be misleading as a principle of intergenerational justice. Alas, this is (sadly) not a concern for the present moment, as we are very far away from a world where all are doing well, or even close to such a world.

Concluding remarks

Intergenerational justice demands that we invest in climate change mitigation considerably to preserve non-substitutable ecosystem services, and also aim to leave as many options open for future generations as is feasible. Normative sustainability requires that, at minimum, critical forms of natural capital should be preserved, and that inflicting harm can only be done when it is unavoidable, and even then it should be compensated for. How substantial should investment into mitigation be then? While this is a question for politics, the costliness of mitigation is relative: according to the latest IPCC report the financial sacrifices of the current generation would, for example, be below the recent spending on saving banks in the financial crisis.

Where, then, does this leave cost–benefit analyses in climate economics? We should not get rid of them completely; carefully done they can throw light on areas that require more work and help to identify problematic assumptions. As Robert C. Lind (1982: 24) put it, cost–benefit analysis "need not and cannot provide precise answers to policy questions. Rather it is a procedure that can provide a crude but highly useful picture of the relative merits of alternative policies." While welfare economists are aware that market prices are not perfect price signals (the difficult task of determining shadow prices for goods is a way of trying to represent the full social cost), non-substitutability does not get its proper attention. As discounting presupposes substitutability, non-substitutability of critical natural capital reveals the limits to its usefulness. Because of this, and other problematic assumptions (such as endless growth), the ethical assumptions and normative choices made in the calculations that compare different mitigation options should be made transparent. Policymakers and those who use cost–benefit analyses to guide their decision-making should be made fully aware of what they are comparing.

In any case, discretion is required in using cost–benefit analyses. They should never be viewed as neutral tools for policymakers, as normative considerations always come into choosing the discount rate and in deciding whether this can be uniform across different types of capital. This chapter does not claim that economists are unaware of the value judgements that go into making cost–benefit analyses. But the way they are utilised in the political arena with regards to climate change belies the not-so-objective nature of economics. The ethical choices that go into making the formulas should be spelled out and there should be honesty about the moral implications of different options. In other words, these calculations should come with a warning about their limited applicability. Political decision-making will most definitely be needed and not all decisions around mitigation and adaptation will be easy. Awkward trade-off decisions cannot be avoided and it is unlikely that a neat, clear formula can be discovered that would cover all cases. However, the requirements of normative sustainability underline the importance of taking immediate and decisive action on mitigation.

Notes

1 I would like to thank Hans-Peter Weikard, John O'Neill, Matthew Rendall, Aaron Maltais, Dominic Roser, John Broome, Kian Mintz-Woo, Simo Kyllönen, Duncan Purves, Adrian Walsh and the other participants of the 2014 climate ethics and economics workshops in Salamanca and Helsinki for their helpful suggestions and critique. In addition, I would like to thank Alessandra Basso, Aki Lehtinen, Caterina Marchionni and Michiru Nagatsu for commenting on earlier drafts.

2 WCED 1987: 43. This definition has been hugely influential, but also heavily criticised for being ambiguous enough to encompass a wide variety of non-compatible interpretations (Robinson 2004).

3 IPCC reports show that climate change is already making lives harder for the worst-off. In general, intra- and intergenerational justice issues should both be taken into account when drafting climate change policies. See also note 6 below and Casal (2011, 2012).

4 Brennan argues that the focus on discount rates in intergenerational justice literature is misleading, as prices are relevant to normative reasoning only derivatively, not intrinsically. Moreover, the whole problem might not even exist due to rising welfare. He does, however, allow that climate change might be a legitimate concern for intergenerational justice.

5 To give examples, some countries have experienced a drop in their standard of living in the past decades, such as Tajikistan after the collapse of the Soviet Union. Another example is how the introduction of agriculture originally worsened the average person's physical condition for a long stretch of time (Diamond 1987; Larsen 2006).

6 Azar and Sterner (1996) argue that because developing countries are more vulnerable to climate risks and have less adaptation capacity than OECD countries, the cost to a poor person in a developing country should be valued as a higher welfare cost compared to an equivalent cost to an average citizen of developed countries. Neumayer (2013: 35–9) argues that this reasoning leads to inefficiency problem. With education, for example, real rates of return to investment are very high in poor countries, some 13–26 per cent. Investments in climate change mitigation would be very inefficient in comparison, so the global poor would arguably prefer immediate development assistance.

7 The Nordhaus and Stern debate is about the social discount rate. Another prominent discounting debate is about the pure rate of time preference. Broome (1992), for example, has argued that inter-generational fairness demands that future generations should not be excluded from political and economic decisions made today. The pure rate of time preference should therefore be set equal to zero, since being later in time should not mean that you count for less. Other prominent philosophers who have criticised pure time discounting in economics include Rawls and Parfit. For a summary of their accounts and an overview of the issues involved, see Van Liedekerke (2004). Beckerman (1994: 198–9) argues that using a discount rate does not mean that we value future generations less: on the contrary, it is a tool for maximising future welfare.

8 "Whether one believes in one paradigm or the other is ultimately just that: a matter of belief. Hence there is no clear-cut answer on what to do with global warming." (Neumayer 1999: 41). Neumayer's claim in 2013 is more toned down. He writes that "it is hubris to believe that natural or social scientists can make the decision on what should be regarded as 'unacceptably high' costs in society's stead" (Neumayer 2013: 129). However, the book still misrepresents intergenerational justice arguments.

9

> Economic growth and development obviously involve changes in the physical ecosystem. Every ecosystem everywhere cannot be preserved intact.... Sustainable development requires that the rate of depletion of non-renewable resources should foreclose as few future options as possible.
>
> (WCED 1987: 45–6)

10 I am not taking a stand against theorists who argue that intrinsic value can be found in nature; this chapter leaves the question open. I am merely arguing that normative sustainability can be defended on anthropocentric grounds alone.

11 An anonymous referee rightly pointed out that if a (non-substitutable) resource that contributes to human welfare approaches a critical threshold, the shadow price of that resource rises to infinity in a neoclassical growth model. This limitlessly large marginal rate of substitution would then be a signal of non-substitutability.

12 For a discussion on the common core of forms of liberalism, see Waldron (1987).

13 Cripps's definition is meant to be as uncontroversial as possible. For a broader discussion on harm, see Shiffrin (2012). Harming future generations inevitably raises the non-identity problem identified by Derek Parfit (1984). There is no scope to discuss that here, but for possible solutions see Cripps (2013: 15–18), Harman (2004) or Meyer (2003).

14 In his later work, Neumayer (2013: 79) repeats his criticism of Barry, but with a significant addition: "The problem with Barry's argument is that *taken to its logical conclusion* it would imply that the current generation must not impose any harm on the future [my emphasis]." However, he seems to again ignore Barry's distinction between gratuitous infliction of harm and depletion of resources without adequate compensation.

Bibliography

Alkire, S. and Deneulin, S. (2009), "The human development and capability approach", in S. Deneulin and L. Shahani (eds), *An Introduction to the Human Development and Capability Approach: Freedom and Agency*, Abingdon: Earthscan, pp. 22–48.

Azar, C. and Sterner, T. (1996), "Discounting and distributional considerations in the context of global warming", *Ecological Economics*, vol. 19: 169–84.

Barry, B. (1991), *Liberty and Justice: Essays in Political Theory 2*, Oxford: Clarendon Press.

Barry, B. (1997), "Sustainability and intergenerational justice", in A. Dobson (ed.) (1999), *Fairness and Futurity: Essays on Environmental Sustainability and Social Justice*, Oxford: Oxford University Press, pp. 93–117.

Beckerman, W. (1994), "'Sustainable development': is it a useful concept?", *Environmental Values*, vol. 3: 191–209.

Beckerman, W. (1995), "How would you like your 'sustainability', sir? Weak or strong? A reply to my critics", *Environmental Values*, vol. 4: 169–79.

Beekman, V. (2004), "Sustainable development and future generations", *Journal of Agricultural and Environmental Ethics*, vol. 17: 3–22.

Brennan, G. (2007), "Discounting the future, yet again", *Politics, Philosophy & Economics*, vol. 6: 259–84.

Bromley, D. W. (1998), "Searching for sustainability: the poverty of spontaneous order", *Ecological Economics*, vol. 24: 231–40.

Broome, J. (1992), *Counting the Costs of Global Warming*, Cambridge: The White Horse Press.

Broome, J. (1994), "Discounting the Future", *Philosophy & Public Affairs*, vol. 23: 128–56.

Casal, P. (2011), "Global taxes on natural resources", *Journal of Moral Philosophy*, vol. 8: 307–27.

Casal, P. (2012), "Progressive environmental taxation: a defence", *Political Studies*, vol. 60: 419–33.

Cripps, E. (2013), *Climate Change and the Moral Agent: Individual Duties in an Interdependent World*, Oxford University Press, Oxford.

Dasgupta, P. (2007), "Commentary: *The Stern Review's Economics of Climate Change*", *National Institute Economic Review*, vol. 199: 4–7.

Diamond, J. (1987), "The worst mistake in the history of the human race", *Discover Magazine*, May: 64–6.

Dobson, A. (2003), *Citizenship and the Environment*, Oxford: Oxford University Press.

Gardiner, S. M. (2004), "Ethics and global climate change", *Ethics*, vol. 114: 555–600.

Godard, O. (2008), "Climate modelling for policy-making: how to represent freedom of choice and concern for future generations?", *Interdisciplinary Science Review*, vol. 33: 51–69.

Gutwald, R., Leßmann, O., Masson, T. and Rauschmayer, F. (2011), "The capability approach to intergenerational justice: a survey", *UFZ Discussion Papers 8/2011 – GeNECA 4*, Helmholtz Centre for Environmental Research – UFZ.

Harman, E. (2004), "Can we harm and benefit in creating?", *Philosophical Perspectives*, vol. 18: 89–113.

Holland, A. (1995), "The assumptions of cost–benefit analysis: a philosopher's view", in K. G. Willis and J. T. Corkindale (eds), *Environmental Valuation: New Perspectives*, Wallingford: CAB International.

Holland, A. (1999), "Sustainability: should we start from here?", in A. Dobson (ed.), *Fairness and Futurity: Essays on Environmental Sustainability and Social Justice*, Oxford: Oxford University Press, pp. 46–68.

IPCC (2013), "Summary for policymakers", in IPCC, *Climate Change 2013: The Physical Science Basis. Contribution of Working Group I to the Fifth Assessment Report of the Intergovernmental Panel on Climate Change*, Cambridge and New York: Cambridge University Press, pp. 3–29.

IPCC (2014a), "Summary for policymakers", in IPCC, *Climate Change 2014: Impacts, Adaptation, and Vulnerability. Part A: Global and Sectoral Aspects. Contribution of Working Group II to the Fifth Assessment Report of the Intergovernmental Panel on Climate Change*, Cambridge and New York: Cambridge University Press, pp. 1–32.

IPCC (2014b), "Summary for policymakers", in IPCC, *Climate Change (2014), Mitigation of Climate Change. Contribution of Working Group III to the Fifth Assessment Report of the Intergovernmental Panel on Climate Change*, Cambridge and New York: Cambridge University Press, pp. 1–31.

Larsen, C. S. (2006), "The agricultural revolution as environmental catastrophe: implications for health and lifestyle in the Holocene", *Quaternary International*, vol. 150: 12–20.

Lemos, R. M. (1986), *Rights, Goods, and Democracy*, Newark: University of Delaware Press.

Lind, R. C. (1982), "A primer on the major issues relating to the discount rate for evaluating national energy options", in R. C. Lind, K. J. Arrow, G. R. Corey, P. Dasgupta, A. K. Sen, T. Stauffer, J. E. Stiglitz, J. A. Stockfisch and R. Wilson (eds), *Discounting for Time and Risk in Energy Policy*, Washington: Resources for the Future, pp. 21–94.

Mazor, J. (2010), "Liberal justice, future people, and natural resource conservation", *Philosophy & Public Affairs*, vol. 38: 380–408.

Meyer, L. H. (2003), "Past and future: the case for a threshold notion of harm", in L. H. Meyer, S. L. Paulson and T. W. Pogge (eds), *Rights, Culture, and the Law: Themes from the Legal Political Philosophy of Joseph Raz*, Oxford: Oxford University Press, pp. 143–59.

Neumayer, E. (1998), "Preserving natural capital in a world of uncertainty and scarce financial resources", *International Journal of Sustainable Development and World Ecology*, vol. 5: 27–42.

Neumayer, E. (1999), "Global warming: discounting is not the issue, but substitutability is", *Energy Policy*, vol. 27: 33–43.

Neumayer, E. (2007), "A missed opportunity: *The Stern Review* on climate change fails to tackle the issue of non-substitutable loss of natural capital", *Global Environmental Change*, vol. 17: 297–301.

Neumayer, E. (2013), *Weak versus Strong Sustainability: Exploring the Limits of Two Opposing Paradigms*, 4th edn, Cheltenham: Edward Elgar.

Nordhaus, W. (2008), *A Question of Balance: Weighing the Options on Global Warming Policies*, New Haven: Yale University Press.

Norton, B. (1999), "Ecology and opportunity: intergenerational equity and sustainable options", in A. Dobson (ed.), *Fairness and Futurity: Essays on Environmental Sustainability and Social Justice*, Oxford: Oxford University Press, pp. 118–50.

Norton, B. G. and Toman, M. (1997), "Sustainability: ecological and economic perspectives", *Land Economics*, vol. 73: 553–68.

O'Neill, J. (2014), "Sustainability", in D. Moellendorf and H. Widdows (eds), *The Routledge Handbook of Global Ethics*, Abingdon: Routledge, pp. 401–15.

Parfit, D. (1984) *Reasons and Persons*, Oxford: Clarendon Press.

Perrings, C. (1994), "Biotic diversity, sustainable development, and natural capital", in A. Jansson, M. Hammer, C. Folke and R. Costanza (eds), *Investing in Natural Capital: The Ecological Economics Approach to Sustainability*, Washington: Island Press, pp. 92–112.

Pezzey, J. (1992), "Sustainability: an interdisciplinary guide", *Environmental Values*, vol. 1(4): 321–62.

Ramsey, F. P. (1928), "A mathematical theory of saving", *Economic Journal*, vol. 38(152): 543–59.

Robinson, J. (2004), "Squaring the circle? Some thoughts on the idea of sustainable development", *Ecological Economics*, vol. 48: 369–84.

Sen, A. (1984), *Resources, Values, and Development*, Oxford: Basil Blackwell.

Sen, A. (1985), *Commodities and Capabilities*, Amsterdam: North-Holland.

Shiffrin, S. (2012), "Harm and its moral significance", *Legal Theory*, vol. 18: 357–98.

Solow, R. M. (1974), "Intergenerational equity and exhaustible resources", *The Review of Economic Studies*, Symposium on the Economics of Exhaustible Resources, 41: 29–45.

Spash, C. L. (1993), "Economics, ethics, and long-term environmental damages", *Environmental Ethics*, vol. 15: 117–32.

Stern, N. (2007), *The Economics of Climate Change: The Stern Review*, Cambridge: Cambridge University Press.

Tremmel, J. C. (2009), *A Theory of Intergenerational Justice*, Abingdon: Earthscan.

Van Liedekerke, L. (2004), "Discounting the future: John Rawls and Derek Parfit's critique of the discount rate", *Ethical Perspectives*, vol. 11: 72–83.

Waldron, J. (1987), "Theoretical foundations of liberalism", *The Philosophical Quarterly*, vol. 37(147): 127–50.

Weikard, H.-P. (1999), *Wahlfreiheit für zukünftige Generationen: Neue Grundlagen für eine Ressourcenökonomik*, Marburg: Metropolis-Verlag.

Weitzman, M. (2012), "The Ramsey discounting formula for a hidden-state stochastic growth process", *Environmental & Resource Economics*, vol. 53: 309–21.

WCED (1987) *Our Common Future* (The Brundtland Report), World Commission on the Environment and Development, Oxford: Oxford University Press.

8 Dimensions of climate disadvantage[1]

John O'Neill

Introduction

Climate change will result in an increased frequency and intensity of extreme weather events such as droughts, heatwaves and floods. These events cause death, ill-health, hunger, displacement and social dislocation. Lives and livelihoods are put at risk and lost. These impacts on life and well-being will be unevenly distributed. Drought, heatwave and floods are not new. Neither are the questions of justice raised by the uneven impacts of these events (Blaikie *et al.*, 1994; Klinenberg, 2002). Floods, heatwaves and droughts have a long history quite independent of human-induced climate change. However, with climate change their frequency and intensity will increase. This chapter will address questions concerned with the identification of those individuals and communities who will be most disadvantaged by climate change. Doing so matters for climate adaptation policy since it has implications for how responses can be best focused on those who need them most. Identification of climate disadvantage also matters for the framing of climate justice. It turns out that within a society, those most disadvantaged by climate impacts are also typically among those who are least responsible for the emissions of greenhouse gases (GHGs), have least voice and power in framing and shaping decisions, and are often most adversely affected by policy responses to climate change. These different dimensions of inequality produce compounded injustices.

This chapter defends a particular multi-dimensional approach to climate disadvantage. Both the dimensions of well-being that are put at risk by climate change and the personal, environmental and social factors that determine how badly different groups are affected by climate change are plural. One important consequence of looking at climate disadvantage in this multi-dimensional way is to refocus considerations of justice and climate change to include questions of class, inequality, gender and ethnicity that are lost in much of the standard academic and policy discussion on climate change that focus only or primarily on maldistributions across nations and generations.

Dimensions of climate injustice

The focus of much academic and policy debate on climate change has been on the international and intergenerational dimensions of responsibility for and the impacts of climate change. There are good reasons for this. Intergenerationally, the contrast between those who are responsible for and benefit from emissions of greenhouse gases and those who will be adversely affected by them is stark. The adverse effects of current emissions will fall most heavily on future generations. Those generations will bear no responsibility for those emissions. Globally there is similarly a divergence of responsibility, benefits and harms. Both historical and current responsibility for the emissions of greenhouse gases lies with the richer industrialised countries. The 2014 IPCC report notes: 'median per capita GHG emissions (1.4 tCO2eq/cap/yr) for the group of low-income countries are around nine times lower than median per capita GHG emissions (13 tCO2eq/cap/yr) of high-income Countries' (IPCC, 2014a: 46). At the same time, the negative impacts will fall disproportionately on people in low-income countries. The global and intergenerational dimensions of climate change are important.

However, while the international and intergenerational dimensions of climate change are important, the use of generations and nations as the foci of analysis can hide the significance of other dimensions of inequality across class, income, gender and ethnicity. For example, while international negotiations tend to use national emissions as the unit of analysis, this can disguise the fact that differences across income and class within countries matter to emissions through consumption. Differences in median per capita emissions between countries are consistent with large differences of emissions within countries according to income and wealth. The IPCC notes: 'There are substantial variations in per capita GHG emissions within country income groups with emissions at the 90th percentile level more than double those at the 10th percentile level' (IPCC, 2014a: 46). In the UK, for example, those in the highest income decile are responsible for well over twice as many emissions through consumption as those in the lowest income decile. The differences are particularly marked for transport where those in the highest decile have 4.5 times the emissions of those in the lowest decile, and in consumables and services where they have over 3.5 times the emissions (Gough *et al.* 2011; Gough, 2013). The differences are less marked for food and domestic energy where the ratio of highest to lowest income deciles is 1.8. Responsibilities are then significantly correlated with income, the higher the income, the higher the emissions.

However, when it comes to policy responses to climate change, those with the lowest income who are least responsible for climate change can face the highest policy burdens. This is in part due to the use of market mechanisms that respond to climate change through raising the price of carbon emissions or energy. While total emissions are correlated positively with income, when it comes to emissions per unit of income the relationship is reversed. Those on lower incomes have higher emissions per unit of income. For example, if one considers emissions per £ in the UK, the lowest income decile emits four times as much per £ as the highest, where this is greatest for energy and food (six times greater) and three times greater for consumer goods and 2.3 times great transport (Gough 2013: 205). Policies that rely upon raising the general price of emissions have the heaviest impact on those who contribute least to climate change and the lightest on those who contribute most. Moreover those impacts are worst in the consumption of basic goods such as food and household energy. Both responsibilities for and the impacts of policy responses to emissions of greenhouse gases are unevenly distributed. Finally, as I show in following sections of this chapter, the impacts of climate change on human well-being will tend to fall heaviest on those already least advantaged within any country.

Similar points apply across generations. Consider one standard argument for discounting. Economic models of future impacts of climate change defend discounting on the grounds that growth will mean that average per capita consumption in the future will be greater than that of current generations. Since those in the future will on average be richer, additional units of wealth will be worth less to them. We should discount future consumption accordingly.[2] But there are a number of problems with the assumption that future average per capita consumption will be higher. Given that emissions are closely correlated with growth and hence that growth itself in the near term will lead to more serious climate impacts in the longer term, the assumption that continuing growth will mean that average per capita consumption will be higher in the future is open to serious question. Short- and medium-term growth could well lead to falls in consumption in the longer term. However, even if average per capita consumption is higher it does not follow that all of those in the future will be better off. Average consumption can rise in conditions in which in the future the better off are richer than those in the present and the worse off are poorer. Higher average per capita consumption may entail that some individuals in the future will be much better off than any individuals in current generations in the sense that they will be wealthier. That wealth may allow them to protect themselves from the worst effects of climate change. However, that will not be true of all individuals. Average per capita consumption is not what matters for determining justice over time but rather what happens to the worst off. Justice requires a disaggregation of impacts within generations, both current and future, and not simply across generations. Given that climate change will have its largest negative impacts on the lives and livelihoods of the poorest, there are good reasons to think that, unless wide social and economic inequalities are addressed, the disaggregated story will be one in which a large portion of people in the future will be worse off. Hence, a positive discount rate on the basis that future generations on average will be richer is not justified. It is not averages that matter for considerations of justice.

None of this is to argue that the international and intergenerational dimensions of climate change do not matter. In terms of identifying differential responsibilities for and impacts of climate change they do matter. However, any such analysis needs to be wary of simple averaging across those within countries and generations. Disaggregation is required within those populations.

In disaggregating, other dimensions of climate inequality come to the fore notably across class, wealth and income. Internal inequalities in wealth and income matter. However, these are not all that matter for reasons that Sen gives in developing the capabilities approach to injustice. The same levels of income can have different outcomes for how well people can live their lives depending on personal, environmental and social facts about persons (Sen, 2009: chapter 12). Characterising and measuring the adverse impacts of climate change requires further disaggregation beyond wealth and income, important though these are. The points that Sen makes about the conversion of resources into different outcomes for well-being can also be made of the impact of events such as flood and heatwave. Personal, environmental and social factors can lead to the same climate-related event having very different outcomes for well-being. Age, health and gender, the physical environments in which individuals live, social networks and social dislocation, amongst other factors, will make a difference to how badly affected individuals and communities are by climate-related events. In the following I will develop this approach to climate disadvantage and outline briefly its use in the identification of climate disadvantage in the UK. I then consider both potential problems and benefits associated with the use of multi-dimensional measures of climate disadvantage. In the final section I return briefly to consideration of the implications of the framework for cross generational dimensions of climate change.

Mapping climate disadvantage

Whose lives and well-being will be most adversely affected by climate change related hazards such as floods, heatwaves and droughts? One part of the answer to that question will concern the distribution of exposure to the hazards. There exist both global and local variations in the frequency and intensity of exposure to climate related hazards. For example, globally more frequent and intense drought is likely in West Africa and the Mediterranean and less likely in central North America and northwest Australia (IPCC, 2014c: 1136). Similarly differential likelihoods of exposure exist within countries. Those who live in urban areas prone to urban heat island effects are more likely to suffer the effects of heatwaves. Flooding can come in different types: rivers (fluvial), surface water (pluvial) and sea (tidal). Each will have particular patterns of distribution. The distribution of pluvial flooding in cities will depend on patterns of drainage. People whose homes or sources of livelihood are by sea or river are more likely to be badly affected than those whose homes and sources of livelihood are on higher ground.

One significant strand of argument on environmental justice has been concerned with the ways in which exposure to environmental hazards such as toxic waste and pollution reflects wider patterns of injustice associated with race and class (Bullard, 1994, 1996). Is climate change another hazard that is distributed like this? In the case of climate change there is some overlap between prior dimensions of inequality and the distribution of exposure. For example in

England those in lower incomes deciles are much more likely to be exposed to coastal flooding than those in the highest income deciles (Walker *et al.*, 2006: 58–9; Walker and Burningham, 2011: 121–2). However, the relationship between flooding and deprivation is not systematic. For example, with fluvial flooding there is very little variation across different income deciles for England as a whole (Walker *et al.*, 2006: 56–7; Walker and Burningham, 2011: 221). Indeed, for fluvial flooding in southeast England there is an inverse relationship between exposures to flooding and deprivation, with those in the higher income decile more likely to be living in river floodplains. Does this mean that in this region those with higher incomes turn out to be more likely to suffer from river-related climate disadvantage? It doesn't. Exposure to flooding is not all that matters to measuring disadvantage. What also matters is the vulnerability of different persons and communities to the hazard.

How disadvantaged a person or community are by climate-related hazards is a function not just of the frequency and degree of exposure to the hazard but also their vulnerability to that hazard. Vulnerability refers to how well individuals are able to cope with impacts that events like flood, drought and heatwave will have on their well-being, in particular with their ability to respond to and recover from events and prepare for future events (cf. Kelly and Adger, 2000 p. 328) The vulnerability of a person or population to exposure to a hazard is a matter of the degree and likelihood of exposure to a hazard impacts on life, livelihood and well-being. If an individual is more vulnerable to a hazard then he or she is more likely to suffer a serious loss of well-being or life as a result of exposure to that hazard. Climate disadvantage is a function both of the frequency and intensity of exposure to climate-related hazards and the vulnerability of individuals and communities to exposure to the hazard.

Vulnerability is a matter of how exposure to a hazard converts into a loss of well-being. This characterisation of vulnerability raises a number of prior questions that need to be addressed in considering the distribution of climate disadvantage:

- First, how is well-being to be characterised and measured? Many studies of vulnerability have focused on losses of life, health and income or livelihood. There are good reasons for this focus. These all matter for well-being. They are also relatively easily to measure. However, climate-related events such as flood and heatwaves bring much wider losses in well-being. For example they bring social dislocation and the loss of abilities to plan for the future. An adequate characterisation of vulnerability needs to be based on an account of well-being that is able to include the full range of losses in well-being.
- Second, what factors are involved in the conversion of exposure to hazards into a loss of well-being? Again an adequate characterisation of vulnerability will include the full range of factors involved in the conversion of exposure to a hazard into a loss of well-being. These will include personal factors – including biophysical features of the person such as age and health. They will

include properties of the environment, such as access to green space and cool places in a heatwave. Finally, and not least, they will include social factors. Poverty, social networks, social dislocation, levels of trust and fear in a community, the nature public institutions, distributions of power and voice, and a variety of other social factors will all affect how well a community or individual is able to cope with the impacts of floods and heatwaves.

- Third, how far is this vulnerability specific to a particular hazard such as flood or heatwave or how far is it an instance of a more general vulnerability to a variety of different events that impact on well-being? Some vulnerabilities are hazard-specific. People who live in houses that are designed to withstand floods will be less vulnerable than those who are not. However, many vulnerabilities to climate-related hazards are particular instances of more general vulnerabilities. For example, the absence of power and voice, poverty and social isolation will render individuals vulnerable not just to floods and heatwaves but to a much wider array of hazards. Climate disadvantage reflects and reveals wider disadvantage and injustice.

Characterising and measuring well-being

How should well-being be conceptualised and measured? I consider three answers to that question: resources; subjective well-being; and objective states (O'Neill, 2006, 2008; Robeyns and van der Veen, 2007; Stiglitz *et al.*, 2009).

Resources: One standard metric that is used for measuring well-being is the resources a person has at their disposal. The metric is an indirect measure. Resources are means to people's well-being. However, the argument goes, well-being is understood by an individual, the more resources they have the better for their well-being. The proponent of the resource index sometimes takes this to be an advantage to the index. A resource metric is not paternalistic. Resources are what enable a person to pursue whatever their conception of a good life is. The use of the resource metric in economics tends to be associated with a preference satisfaction account of well-being. Well-being consists in the satisfaction of preferences. Resources allow individuals to satisfy their preferences, whatever they happen to be. A resource index is widely used as an indirect metric of well-being. We have already noted in the debates on discounting an assumption is made that where average per capita consumption is higher people will be better off. A resource metric is also used by economists to identify the negative impacts of events such as floods and heatwaves, for example through their impact on incomes and property values. However, because resources are only a means to an end, not ends in themselves, there are good reasons we have already touched upon for rejecting a resource metric. As Sen notes, the same resources can have very different outcomes on how well a person can live (Sen, 2009: chapter 12).

Personal, environmental and social factors can mean that the same resources result in very different capabilities for leading a good life. An individual with a physical impairment can, due to lack of medical care, to the lay out of the physical environment, and to social attitudes, institutional structures and norms, have far fewer opportunities to lead a good life than a person without that impairment, even where they have the same initial resources. Correspondingly, in order to address the disadvantage for that person, account must be taken not just of their resources. but also those personal, environmental and social conversion factors – through medical interventions, changes to the physical environment and changes to social structures and norms (Wolff, 2002). As shown below, similar points about different points of response to disadvantage apply to climate adaptation policy.

Subjective well-being: Developments in hedonic psychology have seen the revival of subjective state accounts of well-being (Kahnemann *et al.* 1997, 1999; Frey 2010; Layard, 2005). Subjective state theories take well-being to consist in being in the appropriate psychological state. Hedonic theories of well-being are the paradigmatic example. Well-being is identified with happiness and happiness with pleasure and the absence of pain. Resources on this account are a means to an end. There can be a departure between increasing resources and consumption and increasing well-being. While the income a person has relative to others in a society is correlated with reported subjective happiness, beyond a certain point absolute growth in income and consumption is not (Easterlin, 1995; Frey and Stutzer, 2002; O'Neill, 2006, 2008). Given that this is the case, even if those in the future had higher average per capita income it would not follow that they would be better off as measured by subjective state metric.

Climate-related events such as floods do have a clear impact on subjective well-being. They bring increased levels of anxiety and depression and falls in self-reported life-satisfaction. (Ahern *et al.* 2005; Sekulova, 2013: chapter 4). Subjective well-being matters and is adversely affected by flood, drought and heatwave. However, there are problems with simply using a subjective state metric for measuring inequality and disadvantage. One problem is that of adaptation, for example mental states adapt to adverse situations: 'The utilitarian calculus based on happiness or desire-fulfilment can be deeply unfair to those who are persistently deprived, since our mental make-up and desires tend to adjust to circumstances, particular making life bearable in adverse situations' (Sen 2009: 282). A subjective well-being metric is liable to underestimate the well-being losses of the more deprived. The measurement of inequality requires more objective measures of well-being that are not subject to the problems of adaptation.

Second, there is in any case more to well-being than subjective states. As Kahneman, one of the main figures in the development of hedonic psychology, notes in a paper with Sudgen:

> human well-being may be thought to depend, not only on the sum of moment-by-moment affective experiences ... but also on other aspects of life, such as autonomy, freedom, achievement, and the development of deep interpersonal relationships, which cannot be decomposed into momentary affective experiences.
>
> (Kahneman and Sugden, 2005: 176)

The point is important if the full range of losses in well-being associated with climate-related events such as floods and heatwaves are to be captured. While events like floods do have a major impact on subjective well-being, losses in subjective well-being are not all that matters. Losses in other dimensions of well-being, for example losses in autonomy or the disruption of social relationships, matter in themselves and not simply as a means to subjective well-being.

Objective states – capabilities, functionings and needs: Subjective states matter, but they are not all that matter. What matters for people's well-being is not just what they feel but what they can be and can do in their lives. The two approaches to well-being that attempt to capture what individuals can be and do are those that appeal to needs (Wiggins, 1998, 2006; Doyal and Gough, 1991; Gough, 2015; O'Neill, 2010) and to capabilities (Sen, 1993, 1999, 2009; Nussbaum, 2000). The differences between them can be inflated (Wiggins, 2006, O'Neill, 2010). Here I will use a capabilities approach, but a needs-based approach would capture the same dimensions of well-being at stake. According to the capabilities approach well-being is a matter of having capabilities to achieve central human functionings. Functionings are 'the various things a person may value doing or being' (Sen, 1999: 75). Typical functionings might include being healthy, being well-nourished, being housed, being able to plan and make decisions about one's own life, having good social relations, having self-respect. Capabilities are 'substantive freedoms to achieve alternative functioning combinations' (Sen, 1999: 75).

A virtue of a focus on capabilities and functionings is that it is able to capture the full range of goods constitutive of well-being that climate-related events put at risk. Loss of life, damage to health, loss of resources and income, psychological states of anxiety and depression are all effects of flooding for example. However, they are only some of the functionings and capabilities that are put at risk by flooding. There are other wider losses that also matter. Consider for example the following observation based on interviews and diaries of people affected by social displacement from floods in Hull in the UK:

> The process of recovery is one that carries with it the challenge of adjusting to displacement (caravans, living upstairs, rented accommodation, living with family), managing the process of physical recovery (loss adjustors, insurance companies, builders, retailers), trying to maintain 'normality' in everyday life (work, school, child care, illness, deaths, births, celebrations) and trying to rebuild social life (adjust to a new home, new community relations, build trust in the future).
>
> (Whittle *et al.*, 2010: 3)

The observations are fairly typical of functionings lost or put at risk by floods. In addition to the effects on health, a feature of displacement is a loss of support from others and the normal routines of life, and with this the loss of ability to plan and make further choices. Individuals suffer a 'personal planning blight' (Wolff and De Shalit, 2007: 69). Life is put on hold.

For Sen and Nussbaum capabilities rather than achieved functionings should be the aim of policy. There are two arguments offered for this priority given to capabilities. The first is freedoms to realise functionings that matter for well-being as such – there is a difference in welfare between a person who is starving and a person who is fasting. The person who is fasting has a choice to eat, whereas the person who is starving does not. The second is a liberal argument that policy should respect individuals' freedom to make their own choices about their lives. However, the impact of disasters such as floods on achieved functionings shows that there are good reasons for thinking the simple priority of capabilities over achieved functionings cannot be sustained. Certain achieved functionings are a condition of being able to effectively exercise freedoms and choices at all. These would include, for example, social networks, secure housing and minimum levels of health. Having the support of others in social networks is both an achieved functioning and a condition of exercising capabilities. The point is of particular importance in considering the impact of floods, droughts and heatwaves, since these events put at risk some of the functionings that are a condition of the exercise of capabilities. There is also a second independent reason for a focus on functionings in identifying climate disadvantage. It is much more difficult to identify and measure capabilities than it is measure individuals' functionings. In practice, the capabilities approach typically measures different levels of achieved functionings rather than capabilities.

Vulnerability: from hazards to disadvantage

Just as resources differentially convert into gains in well-being so negative events such as floods, heatwaves and droughts will differentially convert into losses in well-being. Personal, environmental and social factors can mean that the same event can lead to very different losses in well-being. What factors are involved in the conversion of exposure to hazards into a loss of well-being?

Consider heatwaves. The impact of heatwaves on life and well-being depends upon a variety of personal, environmental and social conversion factors. The personal conversion factors include age and health – the old and the very young and those with certain prior health conditions will be more sensitive to heat. Environmental factors are also clearly important. For example, those in urban conurbations without green spaces or access to cool buildings will suffer enhanced exposure to heatwaves. However, there are also a variety of social factors involved in the loss of life and well-being. Klinenberg (2002) in his classic study of the Chicago heatwave notes that social isolation, fear of crime and neighbourhood decline all had major impacts on death rates. Old people died alone, in rooms with windows closed and doors locked, fearful of crime and without social connections of support and without public cool spaces to which they could move. This unequal pattern of deaths in heatwaves reflected and revealed wider patterns of social deprivation and disadvantage:

> [E]xtreme exogenous factors such as the climate have become disastrous partly because the emerging isolation and privatization, the extreme social and economic inequalities, and the concentrated zones of affluence and poverty pervasive in contemporary cities create hazards for vulnerable residents in all seasons.... [T]he event expressed and exposed conditions that are always present but difficult to perceive.
>
> (Klinenberg, 2002: 230)

Similar points apply to floods. Personal factors such as age and health again will affect who is most adversely impacted. So also do environmental factors such as the patterns of drainage in cities or the design and elevation of buildings in which people live and work. However, there are also a variety of social factors that affect the degree to which people's well-being is affected. Those on low incomes are less able to make their homes resilient to floods, less able to take up insurance, are more likely to be displaced for long periods in inadequate temporary accommodation that makes it difficult to sustain supporting social networks or to maintain the capabilities to plan and shape their lives. Social networks are central to how well individuals and communities are able to respond and recover from floods (Whittle *et al.*, 2010). As with heatwaves, patterns of vulnerability to floods often reveal and reflect wider patterns of deprivation and disadvantage. Inequality in income and health and the deterioration of social networks of support are sources of vulnerabilities to a wider set of negative impacts on life.

A point to note here is that several of the conversion factors are also themselves functionings that are important to well-being. Social networks and health both matter in themselves and are central to maintaining other functionings. They are what Wolff and de Shalit (2007: 121–5) usefully term 'fertile functionings' and their loss 'corrosive disadvantages'. Their loss is a particularly damaging form of vulnerability since it brings other vulnerabilities in its wake. A particularly important fertile functioning is voice and power. Those with voice and social power are often better able to call on and mobilise resources in response and in recovery. Those without may be less able to do so even where their actual and potential losses in well-being are greater.

The examples used in this section are based primarily on research in the UK on climate disadvantage (Lindley *et al.*, 2011; Lindley and O'Neill, 2013; ClimateJust, 2015). While some of the losses to well-being and some of the conversion factors will be true generally, in different contexts different dimensions of well-being and different conversion factors will be more salient. For example, the seriousness and gravity of drought and flood will be greater in conditions of subsistence agriculture where life itself is dependent upon livelihoods that are put at risk (IPCC, 2014b: chapters 9 and 13). Problems of social dislocation and the loss of ways of life are at stake where the very existence of some island communities is threatened by rising sea levels (IPCC, 2014c: chapter 29). What conversion factors will be salient will also be different in different contexts. As the IPCC notes in developing a multi-dimensional approach to vulnerability and inequality, factors involved in vulnerability 'may be context-specific and clustered in diverse ways (e.g. class and ethnicity in one case, gender and age in another)' (IPCC, 2014b: 50). For example, where patterns of labour and livelihood and access to land and resources are marked by strong gender differences, gender will become more salient (IPCC, 2014b: 50, 808–9 and passim). Differences in both the dimensions of well-being and the factors that will be involved in loss of life and well-being require more detailed specification in different contexts. However, what emerges in all these different contexts is a relationship between many hazard-specific vulnerabilities and wider social and political inequality (IPCC, 2014b: 15). The virtue of understanding climate disadvantage across distinct dimensions of vulnerability is that it brings to fore this relationship between climate disadvantage and wider patters of inequality.

Multi-dimensional disadvantage

Climate disadvantage is a function both of the frequency and intensity of exposure to climate-related events such as floods and heatwaves, and of the vulnerability of individuals and communities to those events – to the degree and likelihood that the event will lead to a loss in well-being. Identifying and measuring climate disadvantage is a matter of bringing together exposure and vulnerability.

Is it possible to use this approach to identify geographical and social distributions of climate disadvantage? One way of doing so is to identify measures or proxy measures of the different conversion factors that lead from being affected by flood and heatwave to losses in well-being: personal conversion such as age and health; environmental conversion factors, such as the physical characteristics of housing and neighbourhoods; and social factors that determine how well individuals are able to prepare for, respond to and recover from floods and heatwaves, such as income, community networks, access to public spaces, access to medical services, local knowledge, abilities to plan and exercise autonomy. Mapping the distribution of vulnerability onto mappings of distribution of exposure to flood and heatwaves allows a mapping of the distribution of climate disadvantage (Figure 8.1).

There are clear limitations to an exercise of mapping like this (Lindley *et al.*, 2011: 29–30; ClimateJust, 2015). Some of these are practical. The metrics employed for different dimensions of vulnerability – personal, environmental and social – are imperfect. Some important conversion factors, such as degrees that individuals are able to plan and shape their lives, may have no metrics, direct or proxy. The mapping of vulnerability will be incomplete. While the metrics will be helpful in identifying some dimensions of vulnerability and targeting responses to those in greater need under those dimensions, they are not substitutes for judgement, local and practical knowledge or public deliberation.

In addition to these immediate practical problems, there are problems that might be raised with the use of a multi-dimensional space of disadvantage. Capabilities and functionings are plural. There is no single measure of gains and

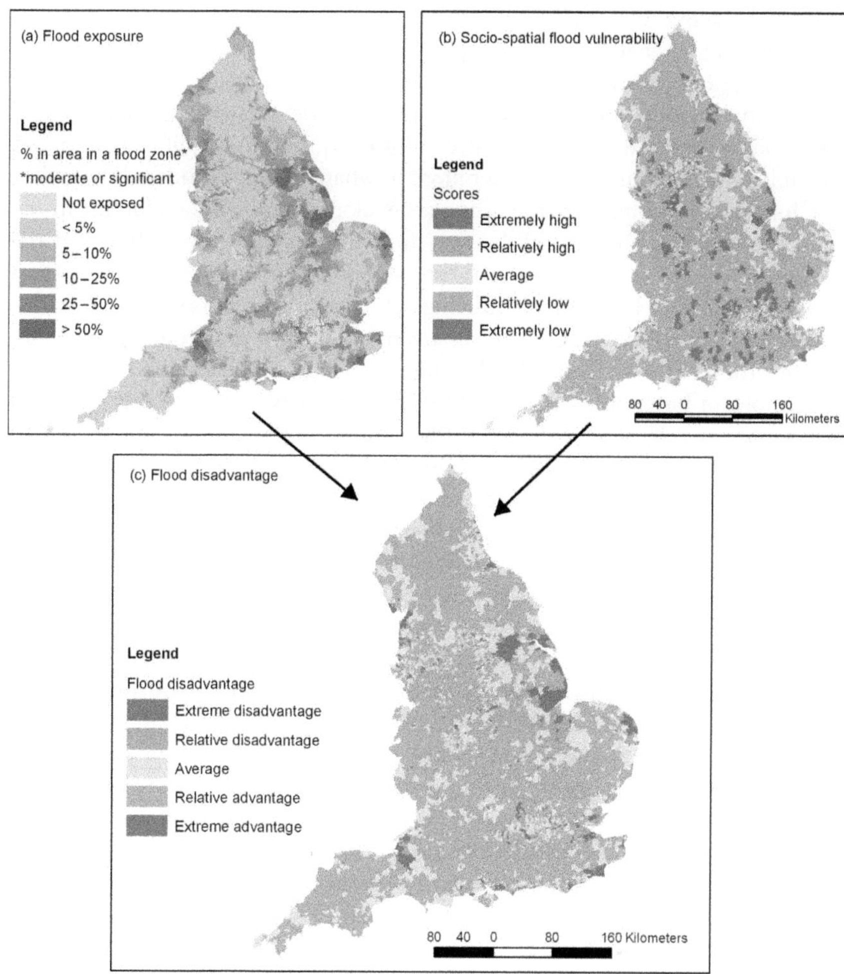

Figure 8.1 Mapping flood disadvantage (source: Lindley *et al.*, 2011: 56).

losses across different dimensions. Neither is there some trade-off schedule which would allow losses in one dimension of functionings to be compensated for by gains in others. Losses that take an individual below a minimal level of functioning in one dimension, for example that of social relationships, cannot be compensated for by gains in another, say improved nourishment. There is, as is said in popular parlance, no substitute for good friends.[3] Moreover, losses in functionings can matter in different ways: in their gravity, how seriously a person will be harmed; in their urgency, how rapidly action must be taken to respond to the harms; in their corrosiveness, how far their loss threatens other functionings (Wiggins, 1998; Wolff and de Shalit, 2007). We have then multiple functionings that matter in different ways.

The complexity of the multi-dimensional space of disadvantage is increased further by the existence of the different personal, environmental and social conversation factors that lead from exposure to flood, drought and heatwave to losses in various dimensions of well-being. Low income, social dislocation, age, health, the physical and social characteristics of neighbourhoods, and various other sources of vulnerability all matter. However, they do not all matter equally and judgements about which matter more in what context are difficult to make.

Climate disadvantage on the account developed here will be pluralist in the constituent dimensions of well-being – functionings and capabilities – in the dimensions along which losses in those dimensions matter, and in the factors that lead to the losses in well-being. A serious objection to this multi-dimensional approach to climate disadvantage is that it becomes difficult to identify those who are most disadvantaged. Indeed, given this multiplicity in dimensions of functioning and the different ways they matter, it may not even make sense to talk of a single most disadvantaged group. The question who is most disadvantaged invites the response: in what dimension of well-being and in what respect – gravity, urgency or corrosiveness? The approach developed here to climate disadvantage is not peculiar in this regard. Similar concerns have been raised more generally to capabilities approach, for example with respect to multi-dimensional measures of poverty (Alkire and Foster, 2011a, 2011b). In contrast the argument might run, a virtue of an approach that uses a single metric, for example a resource metric, is that the worst off can be identified.

In this chapter I consider two observations in response to this line of argument. The first is that, because different sources of vulnerability and well-being loss tend to cluster in the unequal societies in which we live, in practice the problem of identifying those with greater disadvantage is less acute than the theoretical objection might suggest. Groups on low income, in neighbourhoods with high levels of social dislocation and crime, with few green spaces or access to public facilities, or with high levels of ill-health will be disadvantaged over a number of different dimensions of vulnerability. One part of the reason for such clustering is that the certain disadvantages – ill-health, social isolation, poverty, reduced voice and power to shape decisions – are corrosive in the ways outlined earlier. The loss of corresponding functionings leads to losses in other functionings. Social vulnerabilities and losses in well-being cluster in ways that make identification of the most disadvantaged less difficult than might be thought.

The second observation is that the use of a single metric of disadvantage is not what is required for consideration of practical responses to disadvantages. They require rather understanding of the sources of vulnerability – the conversion factors – the different dimensions of well-being at risk and in what way their loss matters. If vulnerability in one neighbourhood is due primarily to the particular age profile of a community, it will require different kinds of response from one in which the vulnerability is due primarily to environmental factors – such as the physical nature of the neighbourhood – or to social factors such as community ties, poverty or the absence of local knowledge of risks within migrant communities. Where these different factors cluster, there is a need for co-ordination between different service agencies to best deliver responses. Moreover what matters in responses will change in different contexts. In preparing and recovering from floods or heatwaves the gravity and corrosiveness of losses will be of greater importance. In contrast, in responding to an emergency, the urgency of needs will become more salient. Differentiation between the different dimensions of climate disadvantage is what is required to plan responses and preparation.

Addressing disadvantage is a question of addressing the dimensions of well-being under threat and the different personal, social and environmental factors involved in the loss of well-being. The use of a single resource metric, in contrast, since it misses all the dimensions of well-being and the factors leading to a loss in well-being, makes for poorer responses to the problems of disadvantage. It cannot be used to specify responses that address the sources of disadvantage. For practical responses to disadvantage, a single ordering of disadvantage is rarely required or helpful. Practical reason requires a different kind of information – who needs what kinds of support. In practice the useful upshot of the mapping project was the information that was disaggregated across different dimensions of vulnerability. Multi-dimensional approaches to characterising and measuring climate disadvantage are better suited to the needs of practical reasoning.

Justice within and across generations

This chapter has been primarily concerned with mapping climate disadvantage within generations. In this final section I will consider the implications of the arguments for questions about justice and well-being across generations.

Standard economic approaches to future generations tend to employ a preference-based approach to well-being. Well-being is conceptualised in terms of preference satisfaction. The conceptualisation brings the concept of well-being under 'the measuring rod of money'. The strength of a person's preference for a marginal improvement in their goods is measured by their willingness to pay for that good. On the standard account, improving well-being is a matter of improving consumption. Growth in consumption improves human well-being. Consumption here is used in the specific market sense to refer to the acquisition of any goods and services for which a person can express a willingness to pay (Knights and O'Neill, 2015). As we saw earlier a standard assumption in the discounting literature is that, given that average per capita consumption is higher in the future, those in the future will be better off. Sustaining human well-being on this account is a matter of passing on capital that will deliver these consumption opportunities to those in the future. Weak and strong versions of sustainability are typically distinguished on the basis of how far delivering the relevant level of capital will be simply a matter of passing on some total amount of capital – human made or natural – or whether there is some critical level of natural capital that must be passed on and which cannot be substituted for by human-made capital. Passing on a level of capital is also typically what is taken to be required to insure that future generations are able to adapt to and cope with climate change. It will provide the stock of goods required for future generations to generate technological innovations and forms of physical defence that will allow them to live well in a world affected by climate change.

There are two central problems with this approach. The first is that total levels of consumption do not provide a good index for the provision of goods that matter for human well-being.[4] The mix of goods passed on matters, not simply the totals. A needs or capabilities based approach to well-being permits far less substitutability across different dimensions of well-being than a preference satisfaction account. Generally any objective state account of well-being which is pluralist about dimensions of well-being and claims that there exist minimal thresholds in those dimensions will be committed to limits in substitutability across dimensions of well-being. As we noted earlier it will not be possible to trade-off losses in one dimension of needs or functionings against gains in others. Losses that take an individual below a minimal level of functioning in one dimension, for example that of social relations, cannot be compensated for by gains in another, say housing. Losses in any dimension of well-being that take a person below a minimal threshold can only be properly addressed by the provision of goods in that dimension. A person who suffers from malnutrition requires specific objects of nutrition: better housing and education in themselves will not compensate for that loss.

Given the limits of substitutability across different dimensions of human functioning, insofar as intergenerational ethical concern is about maintaining or improving human welfare over generations, then it requires each generation to pass on a bundle of goods that is disaggregated across the different dimensions of human functioning. It requires the maintenance of the specific conditions and bundles of goods required for livelihood and good health, for social affiliation, for the development of capacities for practical reason, for engaging with the wider natural world and so on across other dimensions of functioning. Each dimension will require goods specific to that dimension. The capacities of reason require particular formal and informal institutions and goods for their development. The goods of social affiliation require cultural and physical conditions, including particular environments and physical places that are constitutive of good community. The bundle of goods to be passed on needs to be disaggregated. The mere aggregate provision of more goods and services as such is not what is important.

Second, what matters to future well-being are not simply the resources available and hazards that face people in the future, but how these will convert into gains and losses in well-being. In particular what matters is the kind of social world that is passed on to future generations. The point matters in particular in considering adaptation to climate change. Adaptation is not simply an apolitical technical problem concerned only with issues such as that of infrastructures required for defence against flood and drought. It has a strong political dimension concerned with the social dimensions of vulnerability. As we have seen many of those vulnerabilities are not hazard-specific. Rather they reflect wider patterns of inequality and social dislocation. Measures that address poverty, inequalities in wealth, power and voice, and the support of communities and neighbourhoods matter in themselves, but they are also central dimensions of adaptation policy. What matters for the well-being of people in the future is not, above certain threshold levels, primarily the consumption opportunities they have available, but rather the social and political world in which they live.

Climate change will increase the frequency and intensity of extreme weather events such as flood, drought and heatwaves. This chapter has argued that the impacts of these events need to be disaggregated across the full range of dimensions of well-being they threaten and the full range of personal, social and environmental factors that render individuals more or less vulnerable to them. What emerges from the process of doing so is that the impacts of climate change will both reflect and reveal wider patterns of injustice across dimensions such as class, gender and ethnicity which tend to be absent from much of the discussion of justice and climate change. Doing so also allows a better understanding of what justice requires between generations that has been, for good reason, central to the debates on climate change. The goods that are to be passed on to future generations need to be disaggregated themselves across different dimensions of well-being. The social, economic and political world in which future people live will matter to how climate disadvantaged they and their communities will be.

Notes

1 The arguments in this chapter draw heavily on research done as part of the project Justice, Vulnerability and Climate Change: An Integrated Framework, funded by the Joseph Rowntree Foundations and on parts of the subsequent report Lindley, S., O'Neill J., Kandeh, J., Lawson, N., Christian, R. and O'Neill, M. (eds) (2011) *Justice, Vulnerability and Climate Change: An Integrated Framework*, York: Joseph Rowntree Foundation. I would like to acknowledge the contributions of my co-researchers and co-authors in that project, Sarah Lindley, Richard Christian, Joseph Kandeh, Nigel Lawson, Martin O'Neill and Katharine Knox. The arguments also draw on work I did for the European Commission FP7 project Environmental Justice, Liability and Trade. I would particularly like to thank all the participants in the project, from whom I learned a great deal. I would particularly like to thank Joan Martinez-Alier, Beatriz Rodriguez-Labajos and Leah Temper for conversations on some of the topics discussed here. I would also like to thank Ian Gough for his comments and suggestions.

2 The argument is stated more formally in terms of the standard Ramsey formula for discounting future consumption (Stern, 2007: 46; Beckerman and Hepburn, 2007: 191):

$$\rho = \delta + \eta g$$

where ρ is the social discount rate for a project, δ is the pure time discount rate for utility or welfare, η is the elasticity of marginal utility with respect to consumption and g is the expected future growth rate of average per capita consumption. The value of η, eta, is a measure of the relative worth of consumption of some unit of consumption of the less well-off in comparison with the better-off. The *Stern Review* has $\eta = 1$ which means that £1.00 for one person A is worth 10 times more for poorer person B who has a tenth of the income of A. If η is given a higher value, the value of the same unit of good will be proportionally worth more to a person with lesser wealth. So if $\eta = 2$, £1.00 for one person A is worth 100 times more for another person B who has a tenth of the income of A. The value of η is correspondingly said to measure 'society's aversion to inequality of consumption' (Beckerman and Hepburn, 2007: 193). Much of the more recent debate on Stern has concerned the value he assumes for eta. Thus, for example, Dasgupta, while largely accepting Stern's view about the value to be put on δ, claims that the value he places on $\eta = 1$ is insufficiently egalitarian. The more egalitarian one is, so the argument goes, the higher will be the discount rate on consumption. This is true of only the assumption that the rate of growth of consumption, g, is positive and not negative. If growth rates are negative then we should value consumption in the future at a higher rate than it is today. The discount rate should be negative (Dasgupta, 2007: 10). However, if growth is positive so also should be the discount rate – the higher the growth rate, the higher the discount rate. The argument runs that if future average per capita consumption is higher we should discount.

3 This is not of course to deny that there are not important causal relations between losses in different dimensions of well-being as the existence of fertile functionings and corrosive disadvantages shows.

4 I develop this point in more detail in O'Neill, 2010, 2014.

Bibliography

Ahern, M., Kovats, R., Wilkinson, P., Few, R. and Matthies, F. (2005), 'Global health impacts of floods: epidemiologic evidence', *Epidemiologic Reviews*, vol. 27: 36–46.

Alkire, S. and Foster, J. (2011a), 'Counting and multidimensional poverty measurement', *Journal of Public Economics*, vol. 95: 476–87.

Alkire, S. and Foster, J. (2011b), 'Understandings and misunderstandings of multidimensional poverty measurement', *The Journal of Economic Inequality*, vol. 9: 289–314.

Beckerman, W. and Hepburn, C. (2007), 'Ethics of the discount rate in the *Stern Review on the Economics of Climate Change*', *World Economics*, vol. 8: 187–210.

Blaikie, M., Cannon, T., Davis, I., and Wisner, B. (1994), *At Risk: Natural Hazards, People's Vulnerability, and Disasters*, London: Routledge.

Bullard, R. (1994), *Dumping in Dixie: Race, Class and Environmental Quality*, Boulder: Westview.

Bullard, R. (1996), 'Environmental justice: it's more than waste facility siting', *Social Science Quarterly*, vol. 77: 493–9.

ClimateJust (2015) www.climatejust.org.uk/ (accessed 7 June 2016).

Dasgupta, P. (2007), 'Comments on the *Stern Review's Economics of Climate Change*', *National Institute Economic Review*, vol. 199: 4–7.

Doyal, L. and Gough, I. (1991), *A Theory of Human Need*, London: Macmillan.

Easterlin, R. (1974), 'Does economic growth improve the human lot? Some empirical evidence', in P. A. David and M. W. Reder (eds), *Nations and Households in Economic Growth: Essays in Honor of Moses Abraowitz*, London: Academic Press.

Easterlin, R. (1995), 'Will raising the incomes of all increase the happiness of all?' *Journal of Economic Behavior and Organization* 27: 35–47

Frey, B. (2010), *Happiness: A Revolution in Economics*, Cambridge MA: MIT Press.

Frey, B. and Stutzer, A. (2002), 'What can economists learn from happiness research?' *Journal of Economic Literature*, 40: 402–35

Gough, I. (2013), 'Carbon mitigation policies, distributional dilemmas and social policies', *Journal of Social Policy*, vol. 42: 191–213.

Gough, I. (2015), 'Climate change and sustainable welfare: the centrality of human needs', *Cambridge Journal of Economics*, vol. 39(5): 1191–214.

Gough, I., Abdallah, S., Johnson, V., Ryan-Collins, J. and Smith, C. (2011), *The Distribution of Total Embodied Greenhouse Gas Emissions by Households in the UK, and Some Implications for Social Policy*, CASE Paper No. 152, London: Centre for the Analysis of Social Exclusion, London School of Economics.

IPCC (2014a), *Climate Change 2014: Mitigation of Climate Change. Contribution of Working Group III to the Fifth Assessment Report of the Intergovernmental Panel on Climate Change*, Cambridge and New York: Cambridge University Press.

IPCC (2014b), *Climate Change 2014: Impacts, Adaptation, and Vulnerability. Part A:Global and Sectoral Aspects. Contribution of Working Group I. I. to the Fifth Assessment Report of the Intergovernmental Panel on Climate Change*, Cambridge and New York: Cambridge University Press.

IPCC (2014c), *Climate Change 2014: Impacts, Adaptation, and Vulnerability. Part B: Regional Aspects. Contribution of Working Group II to the Fifth Assessment Report of the Intergovernmental Panel on Climate Change*, Cambridge and New York: Cambridge University Press.

Kahneman D. and Sugden, R. (2005), 'Experienced utility as a standard of policy evaluation', *Environmental & Resource Economics*, vol. 32: 161–81.

Kahneman, D., Wakker, P. and Sarin, R. (1997), 'Back to Bentham? Explorations of experienced utility', *The Quarterly Journal of Economics*, vol. 112: 375–405.

Kahneman, D., Diener E. and Schwarz N. (eds) (1999), *Well-Being: Foundations of Hedonic Psychology*, New York: Russell Sage Foundation Press.

Kelly, M. and Adger, W. N. (2000), 'Theory and practice in assessing vulnerability to climate change and facilitating adaptation', *Climatic Change*, vol. 47(4): 325–52.

Klinenberg, E. (2002), *Heat Wave: A Social Autopsy of Disaster in Chicago*, Chicago: University of Chicago Press.

Knights, P. and O'Neill, J. (2015), 'Consumption and well-being', in T. Gabrielson, C. Hall, J. M. Meyer and D. Schlosberg (eds), *Oxford Handbook of Environmental Political Theory*, Oxford: Oxford University Press.

Layard, R. (2005), *Happiness: Lessons for a New Science*, London: Allen Lane.

Lindley, S. and O'Neill, J. (2013), *Flood Disadvantage in Scotland: Mapping the Potential Losses in Well-being*, Edinburgh: Scottish Government Social Research, Available at: www.scotland.gov.uk/Resource/0043/00436842.pdf (accessed 27 May 2016).

Lindley, S., O'Neill, J., Kandeh, J., Lawson, N., Christian, R. and O'Neill, M. (2011), *Climate Change, Justice and Vulnerability*, York: Joseph Rowntree Foundation, available at: www.jrf.org.uk/sites/files/jrf/climate-change-social-vulnerability-full.pdf (accessed 27 May 2016).

Nussbaum, M. (2000), *Women and Human Development: The Capabilities Approach*, Cambridge: Cambridge University Press.

O'Neill. J. (2006), 'Citizenship, well-being and sustainability: Epicurus or Aristotle?', *Analyse & Kritik*, vol. 28: 158–72.

O'Neill, J. (2008), 'Happiness and the good life', *Environmental Values*, vol. 17: 125–44.

O'Neill, J. (2010), 'The overshadowing of need', in F. Rauschmayer, I. Omann and J. Frühmann (eds), *Sustainable Development: Capabilities, Needs, and Well-Being*, Abingdon: Routledge.

O'Neill, J. (2014), 'Sustainability', in D. Moellendorf and H. Widdows (eds), *The Routledge Handbook of Global Ethics*, Abingdon: Routledge.

Pezzey, J. (1992), 'Sustainability: an interdisciplinary guide', *Environmental Values* 1(4): 321–62.

Robeyns, I. and van der Veen, R. J. (2007), *Sustainable Quality of life: Conceptual Analysis for a Policy-relevant Empirical Specification*, Bilthoven and Amsterdam: Netherlands Environmental Assessment Agency and University of Amsterdam, available at: www.mnp.nl (accessed 27 May 2016).

Sekulova, F. (2013), *On the Economics of Happiness and Climate Change*, PhD Thesis, Autonomous University of Barcelona.

Sen, A. (1993), 'Capability and well-being', in M. Nussbaum and A. Sen (eds), *The Quality of Life*, Oxford: Clarendon Press.

Sen, A. (1999), *Development as Freedom*, Oxford: Oxford University Press.

Sen, A. (2009), *The Idea of Justice*, London: Penguin.

Stern, N. H. (2007), *The Economics of Climate Change: The Stern Review*, Cambridge and New York: Cambridge University Press.

Stiglitz, J., Sen, A. and Fitoussi, J. (2009), *Report of the Commission on the Measurement of Economic Performance and Social Progress*, available at: www.insee.fr/fr/publications-et-services/default.asp?page=dossiers_web/stiglitz/documents-commission.htm (accessed 27 May 2016).

Walker, G. and Burningham, K. (2011), 'Flood risk, vulnerability and environmental justice: Evidence and evaluation of inequality in a UK context', *Critical Social Policy*, vol. 31: 216–40.

Walker, G., Burningham, K., Fielding, J., Smith, G., Thrush, D. and Fay, H. (2006), *Addressing Environmental Inequalities: Flood Risk*, Bristol: Environment Agency.

Whittle, R., Medd, W., Deeming, H., Kashefi, E., Mort, M., Twigger Ross, C., Walker, G. and Watson, N. (2010), *After the rain: learning the lessons from flood recovery in Hull*, final project report for 'Flood, Vulnerability and Urban Resilience: a real-time study of local recovery following the floods of June 2007 in Hull', Lancaster University, Lancaster.

Wiggins, D. (1998), 'The claims of need', in D. Wiggins, *Needs, Values, Truth*, 3rd edn, Oxford: Clarendon Press.

Wiggins, D. (2006), 'An idea we cannot do without', in S. Reader (ed.), *The Philosophy of Need*, Cambridge: Cambridge University Press, pp. 25–50.

Wolff, J. (2002), 'Addressing disadvantage and the human good', *Journal of Applied Philosophy*, vol. 19: 207–18.

Wolff, J. and de Shalit, A. (2007), *Disadvantage*, Oxford: Oxford University Press.

9 Moral asymmetries in economic evaluations of climate change

The challenge of assessing diverse effects[1]

Blake B. Francis

Introduction

Combatting climate change will require mitigation policies that abate greenhouse gas emissions as well as adaptation policies that buffer against the impacts. One of the problems that decision makers face concerns the complexity involved in assessing policy options – comparing, on the one hand, potential gains in agricultural productivity, biodiversity, and sea level stability from mitigation policy against the risk of higher energy/transportation prices, lower economic growth rates, lost employment opportunities and reduced competition in certain markets. Economic methods present a solution: they're designed to "measure diverse benefits and harms ... to arrive at overall judgments about value" (IPCC 2014b: 24).[2] For instance, cost–benefit analysis (CBA) measures total costs of a policy against benefits from reduced climatic changes on a monetary scale and sums them. A policy is justified when the result is positive and the benefits outweigh the costs.

Despite presenting an elegant way to resolve the challenge of diverse effects, economic methods invite serious criticisms. Economics "cannot account for all ethical principles" nor can it "take account of justice and rights" (IPCC 2014b: 24).[3] Indeed, philosopher Simon Caney argues that aggregation should be suspended in assessments that compare potential human rights violations to economic productivity and general well-being (Caney 2010). This chapter argues that we would be too quick to restrict or rule out the application of aggregative methods in assessing climate change policy, and offers an alternative diagnosis of aggregative economic methods based on the differences or "asymmetries" in the moral significance of "harms" and "benefits" appropriately defined (§2). While traditional economic methods fail to accommodate the moral difference between harms and benefits, it is possible to design aggregation methods to be more morally sensitive by assigning greater weight to certain harms or by creating aggregation functions that represent the moral asymmetries between diverse effects (§3 and §4).

Harm, benefit, and asymmetry

a Suffering harm

A fully adequate account of harm has yet to be developed. The most influential has been that of Joel Feinberg. In *Harm To Others*, Feinberg's aim is to give an account of wrongful harm – the sense of harm required to justify coercive punishment under criminal law. Feinberg's concept of wrongful harm can be roughly described as follows: Person A, wrongfully harms Person B, if A causes B to *suffer harm* in a way that violates B's rights (Feinberg 1984). The concept of wrongful harm contains a more broad, basic or fundamental notion of "suffering harm," which Feinberg understands in terms of having one's interests set back. A fundamental difference between wrongful harm and suffering harm is that freak acts of nature can cause a person to suffer harm, but *only* other people can inflict wrongful harms. What separates suffering harm from wrongful harm is that suffering harm doesn't have an "essential moral charge" in the way that wrongful harm does. Suffering harm is more like "killing." Killing isn't always wrong, unlike murder, which has a built in moral charge (Shiffrin 1999). When people suffer harm or are at risk of suffering harm, questions are raised about the moral status of the actions and events that brought about the harm and/or about what should be done to prevent, reduce, or alleviate it.

A central debate over the nature of harm focuses on the question of what it is to suffer harm.[4] Suffering harm is very important given that a goal of most governments is to reduce it. But what counts as suffering harm? If suffering harm could include *any* loss, including mere offense, disgust, annoyance, and minor hurts, then the government mandate to reduce harm would oppressively (and absurdly) extend to most corners of human life as public safety organizations turn their attention to correcting bad taste and rude behavior as well as reducing the number of toes stubbed per year. Moreover, the importance of the goal of reducing harm would come under suspicion, for reducing dissatisfaction and hurt feelings is simply lower on the priority list than reducing highway deaths and issuing chemical safety regulations.[5] So, an account of suffering harm needs to do (at least) two things:

- First, it needs to distinguish between suffering harm and mere loss.
- Second, it needs to do so in a way that captures harm's priority.

Rather than take space to attempt to defend a complete account of harm, I'll appeal instead to the considerable amount of overlap among different accounts of suffering harm. Shiffrin (2012: 5) suggests a provisional list of what accounts of harm should include: "physical injuries, many physical disabilities, many mental disabilities, some material inabilities, incidents of pain, the failure or ruin of certain sorts of important projects and relationships, some losses, and [some instances of] death."[6] Appealing to this list, however, won't provide a full picture of which effects of climate change involve harm and which don't. And for that matter, it won't allow for the settling of hard questions such as whether and how to characterize certain instances of theft, blocked opportunities, and death as harms.[7]

b *Benefit*

In a generic sense of the term, "benefit" refers simply to any advance in a person's interests broadly conceived. It refers to both windfalls and rescues, to both sustenance for the starving and pleasure for the gourmand, to life-saving medical treatment and to cosmetic plastic surgery. There are several different senses of benefit that ought to be distinguished. (See Feinberg 1984: Chapter 4). Feinberg argues that people are prone to equivocate between two importantly different senses of "benefit." The first sense includes what we'll call "gratuitous benefit." As the name suggests, gratuitous benefits are those bestowed to beneficiaries who have no entitlement to them by benefactors who are under no expectation of bestowing them. Receiving a windfall from a stranger out of the goodness of their heart or being given a gift out of the blue or doing someone else a favor are examples of gratuitous benefits. People can fail to give you such a benefit without having an effect on your well-being, even if your well-being would have been enhanced by the bestowal compared to a relevant baseline. Failing to give you a gift out of the blue leaves you just exactly where you are well-being-wise.

The second sense of benefit involves the prevention of harm. Since we haven't considered a complete account of harm, we don't know precisely what counts as a harm prevention. However, this sense of benefit can be adequately described using the list of core harms provisionally offered by Shiffrin (2012). Very provisionally, a harm prevention is the reduction, prevention, or alleviation of suffering harm: "physical injuries, many physical disabilities, many mental disabilities, some material inabilities, incidents of pain, the failure or ruin of certain sorts of important projects and relationships, some losses, and [some instances of] death" (Shiffrin 2012: 5). A life-saving rescue involves benefit in the harm-prevention sense, and so does giving money or food to the starving or otherwise needy. Reducing a person's harm by providing them with medical care or calling an ambulance count as "harm preventions" in the sense intended here. Warning someone that they are or will soon be in harm's way is another example. Benefit in the harm-prevention sense is referred to as "harm prevention" throughout this chapter.

c *Asymmetry*

The problem of equivocation between the two senses of "benefit" presents an opportunity to identify an asymmetry between preventing harm and bestowing benefits. Feinberg identifies several instances of equivocation in legal and moral arguments about Bad Samaritan Laws, which legally require the performance of easy rescues of people who are in peril. Consider the "Enforced Benevolence Argument," which holds that Bad Samaritan Laws have the absurd and illiberal implication of making charity mandatory. The argument holds that because the failure to prevent harm is merely a failure to (gratuitously) benefit, the victim has no more claim to an easy rescue than a stranger has to a charitable gift. James Barr Ames argued in 1908:

> however revolting the conduct of man who declined to interfere, he was in no way responsible for the perilous situation; he did not increase the jeopardy; *he simply failed to confer a benefit upon a stranger*. As the law stands today, there would be no legal liability, either civilly or criminally in … these cases. *The law does not compel active benevolence* between man and man. It is left to one's conscience whether he shall be a good Samaritan or not.
>
> (Cited in Feinberg 1984: 135; emphasis is Feinberg's)

Feinberg points out that Ames would equate rescuing another person with bestowing a windfall profit or walking up to a stranger on the street and giving him a $100 bill.

Feinberg argues that the Enforced Benevolence Argument equivocates between benefit in the harm prevention sense and benefit in the gratuitous sense, obscuring an important moral difference between bestowing benefits and preventing harm. Rescuing a child from drowning in a puddle is not *a mere benefit*, because encountering a child facing utter disaster presents very strong reasons for coming to their aid. Preventing death and injury is more morally important than giving cash to a decently well-off stranger. The moral significance of preventing harm is that one has very strong reason to do so when it can be done easily or without harm to the rescuer.

There are different ways to understand what we are calling the moral asymmetry between harm and benefit. For Feinberg, the moral asymmetry tracks the duties people have. The clarity and stringency of the moral duty to rescue declines along with the severity of the harm:

> As we … weaken the severity or probability of the threatened harm, the model of gratuity begins to take on plausibility. One stranger has a clear moral duty to make an easy rescue of another threatened with death, or to notify policy or an ambulance when he perceives another under attack …, but he has a less stringent duty, or no duty at all, to walk to the corner drugstore to buy a Band-Aid for a stranger who has just cut his finger and finds the interruption of his activities inconvenient.
>
> (Feinberg 1984: 141)

As I interpret him, Feinberg would consider the provision of a Band-Aid for a stranger who has inconveniently nicked his finger a gratuitous benefit, which the passerby has no *duty* to provide. Providing the benefit would be considerate and kind but is beyond moral requirement. It will be difficult or impossible to pinpoint precisely when the severity of an injury gives rise to a duty to easy rescue, or of what strength. Despite the availability of hard cases, the difference between a nick and a gash, between inconvenience and jeopardy, is clear enough to see the asymmetry.

Shiffrin's view in contrast understands the moral asymmetry between harm and benefit in terms of the strength of the moral pull that harm and harm prevention have on us compared to the bestowal or loss of what she calls "pure benefits" – any benefit that doesn't involve the prevention of harm of which gratuitous benefits are a class. She describes the phenomena as "the strength of our asymmetrical reactions" (Shiffrin 1999: 122). Examples of pure benefits will include benefits that one has a duty to provide. For example, the special relationship between parents and child gives the parents certain duties, including, perhaps, duties to give birthday gifts and duties to aid the child in securing educational opportunities even beyond those required for a decent life. We generally have strong reasons to avoid harming or to prevent harm. However, it is not always the case that benefits – in Shiffrin's sense – present us with weaker reasons relative to harms. At some point, the moral significance of harm can be overridden by important and life-enhancing pure benefits. Some pure benefits are of incredible importance either because they matter so much to people's way or quality of life, or because of the entitlements people have to the benefits stemming from promises made or from special relationships.[8]

Whether we adopt Shiffrin's or Feinberg's account of the moral asymmetry, it is plausible that such asymmetry exists. Our moral reasons to prevent harm are generally – but not always–much stronger than our moral reasons to provide (pure or gratuitous) benefits.

d Harm benefit asymmetry in climate change

Now that we have established at least a provisional account of harm, benefit, and their moral asymmetry on the table, let us consider how this asymmetry arises in the context of climate change. In order to draw out the asymmetry, we begin with an over-simplified and hypothetical proposal for an aggressive tax on carbon emissions. The Aggressive Carbon Tax would increase the cost of fossil fuels in an effort to restrict fossil fuel use, utilizing market forces to help invigorate a market in renewable energies, and to ultimately reduce climate change.[9] For the sake of demonstration and simplicity, we'll consider just a small slice of the larger puzzle. Compare the lost profits to an oil company from the carbon tax today to the reduction of climate change impacts on a coastal city in Bangladesh in the future.

Many of the impacts of climate change on coastal Bangladesh involve harms and many of the impacts of the Aggressive Carbon Tax on the oil company involve failures to gratuitously benefit. However, it is important to keep in mind that there are harms and gratuitous benefits on both sides of the equation. For example, lower- and middle-class consumers may suffer harm, if fuel prices increase.

To begin, the coastal impacts of climate change expected in Bangladesh from sea level rise and hurricanes involve very serious harms to many people:

> Most countries in South, Southeast, and East Asia are particularly vulnerable to sea level rise due to rapid economic growth and coastward migration of people into urban coastal areas together with high rates of anthropogenic subsidence [the lowering of land surface elevation] in deltas where many of the densely populated areas are located.
>
> (IPCC 2014a: 382)

These impacts could be particularly severe due to both socio-economic drivers and Bangladesh's inability to afford the costs of adaptation. Bangladesh faces a US$25 billion adaptation deficit when it comes specifically to hurricanes (IPCC 2014a).

Coastal impacts from climate change could have a variety of effects on food production, basic power, water and transportation infrastructure, and health. In addition, the growing level of exposure could lead to the displacement of human settlements and forced migration. Food production is threatened because of seawater intrusion into agricultural lands and because of the effects of climate change on fisheries. Mortality, morbidity, and bodily injuries are expected as a result of hurricanes as well as flooding events. Sea level rise is predicted to lead to an increase in disease vectors (IPCC 2014a: 383). The Bangladeshis face a litany of bad health effects, bodily injury and death from climate change impacts. In short, coastal Bangladeshis stand to lose their lives, health, homes, businesses, agricultural lands, and places of cultural significance to flooding and storm surges. Most of these impacts involve bad conditions on the provisional list of harms that any theory of harm would identify as harms – at least in some respect.

The effects of the Aggressive Carbon Tax on the oil company could result in lost profits, pay cuts, and lay-offs as well as price increases for consumers. In the extreme case, it could put the company out of business. Losses to stakeholders in the oil company involve a mix of harms and failures to benefit, but those failures to benefit are not particularly morally serious.

First, are stakeholders of the oil company put in a condition of harm by the imposition of the Aggressive Carbon Tax? The effects of the carbon tax will certainly negatively impact some people. Employees of the oil company could face pay cuts or lay-offs. Depending on employment opportunities and the social safety nets of the country they live in, they could be pushed into destitution. Increased fuel prices have a range of effects on the lives of consumers. Increasing the cost of fuel makes it more expensive to cook food, to heat homes, and to get to work. This could have a dire impact on the lives of the poor and the middle classes who will have to reevaluate their household budgets and will possibly face hard tradeoffs between buying food and heating their homes. Increased fuel costs will also affect consumers' abilities to participate in activities that enhance their lives, because recreation and travel may become more expensive and have even greater opportunity costs.[10]

At the same time, however, the Aggressive Carbon Tax could open up markets in renewable energy and energy efficiency resulting in lowered energy prices and/or job creation in alternative energy markets. The extent of the harms and benefits of the policy is uncertain economically and politically, and in terms of innovation, learning, and technological change. Another co-benefit of the policy involves the reduction of pollution in urban areas, reducing harms and saving costs of pollution-related health issues (see Thompson *et al.* 2014: 921). The annual cost of air pollution from the energy production sector in the US in 2011 was estimated at US$131 billion (Jaramillo and Muller 2016).

As is often the case, the loss of profit to the oil company from taxes involves a mixed bag of harms and failures to benefit. Many of the effects of the carbon tax involve failures to gratuitously or purely benefit, losses that do not involve suffering harm. Some losses in income affect one's ability to purchase luxury items without affecting basic needs. Accordingly, some losses suffered by members of the oil company's management, CEOs, employees, and consumers from pay cuts, lay-offs, and price hikes involve failures to benefit. Because of the moral asymmetry between harms and benefits, those losses that involve *failures to benefit* do not matter morally in the same way that the *harms* from the Aggressive Carbon Tax and the *harms* from climate change do.

Do the benefits outweigh the harms? This depends upon consideration of any special reasons for protecting the benefits at stake. Some might argue that some or *all* losses to the oil company from the Aggressive Carbon Tax are morally important because they violate the entitlements of the stakeholders. There are several ways to argue for this conclusion. Some have argued that certain companies in developing countries have a right to carry on with their business-as-usual emissions. These so-called "grandfathering arguments" appeal, at least in spirit, to John Locke and Robert Nozick. Such a perspective contends that established companies have a "right to prolong current emissions levels into the future and that such 'squatters' rights' can be derived from common law doctrine of 'adverse possession'" (Neumayer quoted in Bovens 2011: 125).[11] However, both Locke and Nozick argued that just property appropriation is limited to circumstances in which the situation of others is not worsened (Nozick 1974). So just because a company may have been operating under an assumption of infinite atmospheric capacity to store emissions doesn't provide them a special entitlement to continue business as usual once discovering that continued emissions worsen the situation of others. The relevant question, then, is at what point do the company's emissions worsen the situation of others – and compared to what baseline?

Also, it is worth noting that there are several historical examples in which government regulation, technological change, or market fluctuation caused some companies to flourish and other companies to fail. Consider the change from wood fuels to coal in the early part of the industrial revolution; the environmental scarcities that drove the change from whale oil to kerosene for lighting lamps in the nineteenth century; and the failure of companies that mined and sold asbestos before it was banned by the US government in 1989.[12] It seems hyperbolic to say that these company's stakeholders had an entitlement to hold the social, environmental, and technological context static so that they could continue to operate business as usual. These changes are part of the risk that companies take on when doing business in conditions of environmental scarcity, governments committed to public safety, and technological innovation.

A second argument to the conclusion that the carbon tax violates the entitlements of the oil company's stakeholders is inspired by classical liberal arguments offered by Milton Friedman (1962) and F. A. Hayek (1960), among others. It could be argued that the carbon tax is illegitimate because it is an untoward restriction on the economic liberties of the oil company's stakeholders. But Hayek allows for government regulation that impinges economic liberties in emergency circumstances (Hayek 1960: 130). So the question becomes: Is climate change a *great enough* emergency to justify market regulation? It is in principle possible that no entitlements are violated if the carbon tax is justified as an emergency prevention measure.

If the oil company is not entitled to the lost profits or the natural resources that keep them in business, then many of the losses to the company's stakeholders from the carbon tax policy involve a failure to receive a benefit, which shouldn't merit consideration in the same way that harms do. The impacts to the Bangladeshis and possibly to those made destitute by the Aggressive Carbon Tax count as harms. This being the case, there is an asymmetry in the moral significance of the effects of the Aggressive Carbon Tax: we have stronger reasons to prevent the harms than to prevent the failure to receive mere benefits.

Aggregating harms and benefits?

Traditional cost–benefit analysis doesn't differentiate between preventing harm or harming, and gratuitously benefiting or failing to gratuitously benefit. The trouble with economic methods is that the costs and benefits are quite generic, in the sense that costs are identified with any setback and benefits are identified with *any* advance in well-being. This generic sense of cost and benefit is presented in the climate change economics literature as a good way of measuring and comparing diverse effects. This generic treatment assumes that costs and benefits are symmetrical: a benefit is just a cost with a positive valence and vice versa. Costs and benefits can be understood simply as downward and upward movements along a scale of well-being. Equal movements along the scale are equivalent to each other whether or not one increase involves a large cash gift and the other involves rescuing a drowning child. The moral asymmetry between gratuitous benefit and the prevention harm suggests that these equal movements along a scale should be treated differently, because the reasons in favor of rescuing the child are stronger than the reasons to give the gift.

The problem with this result *isn't* that there is something morally suspect about the claim that monetary gains can cancel out malnutrition, morbidity, and death. See below for an argument that it is at least possible that trade-offs can be made between economic productivity and human health (e.g., when the economic loss is certain and the gains in human health are chancy, or when the economic loss is severe and couldn't be prevented in any other way). The problem with CBA *isn't* that it aggregates. In its generic understanding of costs and benefits, CBA occludes the moral judgment that harms and their prevention matter more than gratuitous benefit.

However, it is possible to aggregate in a way that is more morally sensitive. One way of doing so simply adjusts the weight given to certain harms. Before defending this possibility against objections, we'll sketch the general strategy of "asymmetrical aggregation."

Just as there are different ways of spelling out the details of what makes harm morally significant, several different methods of aggregation could be recommended that take account of harm. Among other ways, moral differences between harm and benefit could be factored into the analysis: (i) by amending the shape of the aggregation function, (ii) by applying moral weights to harm and the prevention of harm, (ii) by measuring and aggregating different effects on disparate scales. We'll consider each in turn:

i Aggregation functions take different shapes. Continuous functions, like the function that describes diminishing marginal utility, are represented by curves without any breaks. It is also possible to create functions that are continuous, but "kinked." The kink results from the point beyond which the shape of the curve changes. For example, a recent suggestion made in the context of legal economics is to build thresholds into the aggregation function, which designate levels of social benefits important enough to override some amount of harm to others (Zamir and Medina 2010).[13]

ii More weight could be given to people who experience more harm, similar to the way that prioritarians assign greater weight to the well-being of the worst off (Parfit 1995). For example, harms and benefits could be plotted on a continuous concave function, which assigns more weight the more serious the harm or benefit.

iii If harms and benefits are asymmetrical in a way that makes it difficult to measure them along the same scale, they may require measurement on disparate scales (Satz *et al.* 2013). A harm scale could measure differences in the extent or severity of harms regardless of their cause, assigning, for example, greater measure to harms from an earthquake than to harms from cut fingers. A benefit scale can be used to measure the magnitude of gratuitous and other pure benefits, assigning, for example, greater measure to important education benefits than to an extra piece of candy. The dimensions of harm and benefit are aggregated using different functions. This approach involves a level of disaggregation in the sense that it separates out component parts of the total outcome. It is important to emphasize that informative comparisons can be made across the disparate scales. People can rank the relative importance of marginal changes of different sizes along the scales. For example, a large marginal change on the benefit scale may rank higher than a tiny marginal change on the harm scale.

a An objection: getting the numbers right

An important objection to morally sensitive aggregation in defense of more traditional CBA should now be considered. Take the suggestion for assigning greater moral weight the more serious the harm (ii). Aiding the seriously injured should get more weight than a scratched finger, as Feinberg points out in comparing the strength of the claims on others. Barbara Fried considers a similar argument for a continuous aggregation function that applies greater weight the more serious the harm.[14] She offers this objection:

> If the argument is that serious harms are, well, a lot more serious, that obvious truth should be reflected in the subjective disutility that individuals assign to serious and trivial harms respectively. That is to say, a properly done cost/benefit calculus based on subjective preferences would normally assume steeply increasing marginal disutility as one moves up the scale of harms.
>
> (Fried 2012: 63)[15]

Fried's point here is *not* that there aren't asymmetries between harms and benefits, but that those asymmetries would already be captured when measuring well-being. In other words, if you just get the numbers right in the first place, the difference in moral significance is captured and plain old addition will do. Indeed, many of the intuitive problems that come up in discussing the harm/benefit asymmetry can be assuaged by getting the numbers right. We can explain to a large extent why we care less about the billionaire's loss or gain of $1,000 than we care about broken arms just by getting the numbers right. The broken arm matters more, because it has a greater effect on the well-being of the injured party than the loss or gain of $1,000 to the billionaire. For that matter, we can learn a lot about the effects of different climate polices if we get the numbers right for the oil company's lost profit and the losses from a future hurricane in Bangladesh. This is especially so if getting the numbers right involves correcting discrepancies in non-market damage estimates of disasters that affect poor regions.

Fried is correct that getting the numbers right can take us a long way. However, there are crucial problems with using subjective preferences as a metric for doing so, as is the practice among many economists. An obvious problem is that people sometimes prefer bizarre, monstrous, and trivial things that would be better left out of the calculus applied to public policies.[16] A less obvious problem is that people's preferences don't necessarily track the claims they have on others for assistance. Thomas Scanlon (1975: 659) gives the example of a religious devotee who, in the face of starvation, would give up food in order to build a monument to his god. Scanlon argues that the devotee's urgent need for food generates a stronger claim on those who have a duty to assist him regardless of the strength of his preferences for monument building.

Further, such an all-encompassing understanding of economic welfare as preference satisfaction has absurd implications for identifying and correcting externalities. Externalities are goods and bads imposed on others that are not captured by market prices paid by consumers. For example, if pollution from a waterworks project in an upstream community threatens the community downstream, a negative externality is created. Similarly, climate change is considered to be a negative externality produced by markets in fossil fuels: "Those who produce greenhouse gas emissions are ... imposing costs on the world and on future generations, but they do not face directly, neither via markets nor in other ways, the full consequences of the costs of their actions" (Stern 2007: 27). The externalities that economists (rightly) care about involve negative externalities like pollution and other effects that impose *important* costs on people.

However, if welfare is just whatever people value, then there are many more negative externalities to consider, many of which would lead to absurd social policy. For example, if someone is offended by a Rastafarian's uncombed hair, there's an externality to correct (Herzog 2000). If people in same sex relationships offend members of the Westboro Baptist Church, there's another externality to correct. If climate change deniers would prefer not hearing about carbon dioxide emissions, there's another externality to correct. In fact, depending on the number offended and the degree of their offense, quite a bit of economic welfare understood in terms of people's preferences is at stake in these negative externalities. Should these inefficiencies be corrected? Should a Rastafarian or a gay couple be required to pay compensation to the offended to correct the externality? Of course not.

Importantly, economists do not identify externalities when people have preferences about each other's preferences, and they do so often for implicit and perfectly sensible ethical reasons: "they identify externalities in ways closely tracing the traditional harm principle of liberal theory" (Herzog 2000: 912). Feinberg understands the harm principle to be a type of "liberty limiting principle," which identifies harms and acts of harm to be a valid reason to exercise the coercive power of the state by instituting criminal statutes, taxation, licensure, etc. In identifying externalities, economists implicitly or explicitly distinguish between "harms," "unjustifiable intrusions on others' interests," and hurts, "ways of bugging [others] that, however painful, don't give them any legitimate claim against us" (Herzog 2000: 913). Indeed, *The Stern Review* suggests that economists capture concerns about preventing harm by correcting externalities:

> Protection from harm is ... expressed in many legal structures round the world in terms of legal responsibility for damage to the property or well-being of others. This is often applied whether or not the individual or firm was knowingly doing harm. A clear example is asbestos, whose use was not prohibited when it was placed in buildings with the worthy purpose of protecting against the spread of fire. Nevertheless insurance companies are still today paying large sums as compensation for its consequences.... This version of the "polluter pays" principle that is derived from notions of rights ... also arises from an efficiency perspective within the standard economic framework.
>
> (Stern 2007: 47, see also 27–31)

Such a principle arises from an economic framework designed to correct for externalities. If externalities are considered to involve harms imposed on others, then this requires differentiating between harm and mere dissatisfaction. Some method other than preference satisfaction will be needed. This is because well-being at least as it appears to be understood in the context of externalities is an *evaluative* notion; it can't be read directly off of what people prefer (Herzog 2000).[17]

A qualified defense of aggregation

a Human rights and lexical priority

The morally sensitive aggregation strategy is subject to a serious objection even if it can get the numbers right. The three strategies for including harm's moral significance in aggregation suggested above will most likely result in different answers than conventional cost–benefit analysis, but they still involve *aggregation*. Aggregation in any form is objectionable because it allows harms to some to be offset by benefits to others. Simon Caney makes a version of this objection against CBA in the context of climate change. He says:

> In virtue of its aggregative nature, a cost–benefit approach is concerned only with the total amount of utility, and therefore the total wealth of current and future generations, and it is indifferent to the plight of the very severely disadvantaged if their disutility is outweighed by the utility of others.
>
> (Caney 2010: 170)

For these and other reasons, Caney argues that a human rights approach to assessing climate change has several advantages over CBA and, most likely, other aggregative approaches. Caney argues that human-caused climate change violates the human rights to life, health, and subsistence, and that the aim of climate change policy is to stop violating peoples' human rights as much as possible. According to Caney's ecumenical understanding of human rights, a human right is a basic entitlement that each and every person possesses in virtue of their humanity and independently from social conventions and social practices (Caney 2010). Caney argues that, when it comes to a conflict between violating a person's human right and other values, such as economic efficiency or promoting well-being, human rights *generally* take lexical priority.[18] Lexical priority means that human rights "trump" other values. Or more formally, A trumps B when *any* amount of A is more valuable than *any* amount of B (Satz *et al.* 2013; see also Raz 1986; Griffin 1986). Any number of human rights under threat is more valuable than any amount of, for example, economic efficiency or total well-being. The lexical priority of human rights requires doing everything we can to *not* violate human rights or "create threats" to human rights, and it requires that we promote other values only when doing so doesn't threaten human rights (Caney 2010: 176 n.38).[19]

Because of the lexical priority that Caney gives to human rights, balancing threats to human rights against economic productivity above the human rights threshold is not a matter of getting the numbers right. This is because no amount of mere economic productivity can outweigh the disvalue of even a single human rights violation.

In response to Caney, the following is a qualified defense of aggregation. First, the argument is that Caney's assignment of lexical priority to human rights is problematic. We will then discuss a qualification regarding when aggregation should be suspended or supplemented.

The problem with methods that are of aggregative character, on one reading of Caney's view, is that some harms – the ones that involve human rights violations – are incommensurable with other harms and benefits. Lexical priority is a weak form of incommensurability. If A is lexically prior to B, they can't be aggregated through addition, because no amount of B can offset any amount of A. One strategy for defending aggregation is to deny lexical priority. We'll start by denying the lexical priority of life and health over other goods.

To borrow an example from James Griffin (1977: 44), a person will probably not agree to have his arms and legs cut off in exchange for any number of delicious desserts. But this does not imply that there is a general priority rule about sacrificing body parts for gustatory pleasures (i.e., body parts trump desserts). It is unlikely that a person would make such a tradeoff. But this is because some goods, like desserts, become less and less valuable the more they're consumed in quick succession. Their value ranges across a series of infinitely diminishing amounts, which add up to a small finite number.[20] This, Griffin thinks, is a very loose sense of incommensurability: "Some values, because they diminish, sometimes to nothing, can never be added in a way that will make them equal to certain other values" (Griffin 1977: 45). This however, doesn't establish the computational break down implied by trumping. Indeed, Griffin suggests he'd give his pinky for a moderate number of incredibly fancy bottles of wine (Griffin 1977: 45). Similar things can be said about lives and other values. Free solo mountain climbers are willing to risk their lives for their sport, and some may even trade exhilaration for a shorter life.

But Griffin's examples have to do with the satisfaction of individuals' desires when it comes to trading off the risk of bodily harm for pleasure or excitement. Caney's claim about lexical priority concerns tradeoffs that governments make when setting policy. Examples from public policy suggest that the priority rule doesn't always hold – despite the fact that public policies very often express commitment to protect people's lives and health. Governments and medical doctors make tradeoffs between lives and money every time they decide to spend money on recreation or quality-of-life enhancements instead of saving lives. For example, a government may choose to allocate resources to expanding the trail system in a public park when it could have spent that money on improving highway safety (Harel and Porat 2011). Also, raising the speed limit is sometimes justified even though it will most likely result in more deaths. Governments routinely choose between safety and saving money for use on projects that have nothing to do with safety, accepting that some will suffer harms. Griffin puts the point this way:

> We seem willing to exchange length of life for beauty, convenience, excitement. *One* person is willing to accept an exchange of quantity for quality in his own life, and we expect governments to accept such an exchange in taking decisions that affect *many* people. We should not like the government to spend so much money on life-saving schemes (road improvements X-ray screening, certain medical research) that life-enhancing schemes (other medical research, education, art, housing) are abandoned.
>
> (Griffin 1977: 54)

But in choosing to spend less money on saving lives than on life-enhancement through recreation or comfort or convenience, do governments and hospitals *create threats to human rights*? Caney would have to say they do:

> Humans can violate the three human rights in two different ways. The first (and most obvious) route is for humans to emit high levels of greenhouse gases and to destroy carbon sinks, which will in turn produce high temperatures, increased precipitation, and severe weather events. The second route is for humans to design social and political institutions that leave people vulnerable to the physical impacts of climate change. Suppose that climate change were nonanthropogenic (and so route 1 was inapplicable), but politicians could implement an effective program of adaptation and design institutions that would safeguard the vital interests of people in life, health, and subsistence but chose not to do so. They could then be said to violate the human rights of others to life, health, and subsistence because they would be acting in such a way as to create threats to life, health, and subsistence.
>
> (Caney 2010: 176 n.38)

It is true that legislators and hospital directors *could* implement policies that safeguarded all (or at least more of) the vital interests of people in life, health, and subsistence, if they spent more money on safety and lifesaving. This implies that when governments choose to fund recreation instead of the life-saving policy, they are threatening human rights in a way that is morally suspicious. But if this were the case, much of what twenty-first-century governments do would be suspect, because finite resources require making decisions about whether to spend money to prevent death and injury or to spend money to improve people's lives. Because a government could save more lives by instituting 30 mph speed limits on the freeway, it seems that the government is threatening human rights when it opts instead for the convenience of 65 mph. If this is the case, it is highly plausible that some threats to human rights are worth imposing for the sake of convenience, comfort, excitement, beauty, and quality of life. If that is the case, the lexical priority of human rights over other values is put into question. Morally significant aggregation that differentiates between harm (or for that matter threats to human rights) and benefits (or effects less important than threats to human rights) could help policymakers to form judgments about when imposing harm is justified, when it is excusable, and when it is impermissible.

b *A qualification: what do the numbers mean?*

Although it has been argued here that it is possible to conduct aggregation over effects that are harm/benefit asymmetrical, there remains a serious practical limitation to aggregation: it obscures important information. Consider what we can learn about vulnerability to climate change from the estimates of the total damage from two storms: Super Storm Sandy, which swept the Caribbean and the east coast of North America in 2012, and Hurricane Nargis in Myanmar in 2008. The total damage estimate of Super Storm Sandy in the US was $71 billion.[21] The total damage estimate of Nargis was just over $10 billion, making it the most destructive hurricane to hit the Indian Ocean to date.[22] Based on these numbers – which should be compared very cautiously – Sandy resulted in greater net damages than Nargis by a large factor.[23]

However, the damage assessment looks considerably different when you disaggregate and consider the numbers of lives lost. A total of 222 people died as a result of Super Storm Sandy (NOAA 2013), whereas 138,000 people died in Hurricane Nargis (CRED 2009; IPCC 2012). The amount of damage from property and infrastructure loss makes up a huge portion of the damages from Sandy – in part because property values are exponentially higher in the US than in Myanmar. Estimated damages from Nargis represent the loss of hundreds of thousands of lives.[24] The proposals here for asymmetrical aggregation would do a better job of treating the differences in the extent of the damages in the two cases by treating the loss of life and harmful forms of property damage asymmetrically. However, even when aggregation is perfectly possible and appropriate, supplementing the net figures with disaggregated information about what makes up the net figure is called for in order to make *what the numbers mean* explicit.

There are three reasons for including additional information alongside the results of aggregation functions. First, disaggregated information may be more relevant to the *goals* of a given policy. The aim of the policy may not be net savings in monetized damages, but saving lives, reducing low-income property damage, or improving overall human well-being. Second, disaggregated information is required for *transparency* about value assumptions.[25] This is especially important in contexts of disagreement. People disagree about the value of culturally significant places and buildings, the value of ecosystems, and the value of a human life. Fine-grained detail is helpful for healthy deliberation about these matters, especially when people may disagree with the value assumptions built into the aggregation function. Third, policymakers are in a position to make a moral judgment about how resources should be distributed, and this will require considering more than the net damages. The relative importance of *other moral factors* like distribution, vulnerability, and fairness, need to be considered explicitly by the people making decisions.[26] When comparing the two hurricanes, for example, the moral issues of global inequality and protection of the vulnerable come into clear focus once the numbers are disaggregated. Disaggregation helps to make the stakes explicit in a way that net figures can obscure.

Conclusion

The aim in this chapter has been to demonstrate a different way of identifying the limitations of climate economics that does not rule out aggregation. The motivation for doing so is belief that there is plenty of conceptual space for a view in climate change ethics that is both friendly to aggregative economic methods and which takes seriously morally significant factors such as suffering harm. We have seen the modest point that there is moral asymmetry in the climate change context that could be aggregated in a way that is morally sensitive, and explored the practical limits to aggregation due to the informational constraints of aggregate figures. Even where measurement and aggregation is helpful, aggregation obscures important information about value assumptions and the moral significance of the effects in question.

Notes

1 Earlier versions of this chapter were presented at The Ethical Underpinnings of Climate Economics, University of Helsinki November 2014 and at the Conceptual Analyses in Environmental Philosophy session at the Pacific meeting of the American Philosophical Association April 2015. For helpful comments on various drafts of this chapter thanks to: Ariel Mendez, Ben Miller, Sara Mrsny, Carlos Nuñez, Duncan Purves, Mathew Rendall, Tamar Schapiro, and Debra Satz. Thanks also to John Broome, Josh Cohen, Chris Field, Peter Hawke, R. J. Leland, and Katy Meadows for helpful conversations about many of the ideas in this chapter.

2 Climate economists William Nordhaus and Nicolas Stern both emphasize the diversity of effects involved in climate change, which they measure in terms of the monetary value of the goods and services, where labor, savings, knowledge and natural resources generate goods and services. The Stern Review conceives of these goods and services broadly in terms of four dimensions: consumption, education, health, and the environment. (Stern 2007: 31). In *A Question of Balance*, Nordhaus emphasizes that climate change – as well as any other policy issue – requires the proper measurement of what he calls economic welfare. When properly measured, economic welfare includes "everything of value to people" (Nordhaus 2008: 4).

3 CBA doesn't take into consideration historical responsibility. For example, CBA would assign the loss of a Pacific island to sea level rise a relatively small value, which can easily be outweighed by other benefits regardless of whether the loss of the island results from wrongdoing (IPCC 2014b). Further, CBA cannot help us to identify *who* should get compensated for a wrong done. Second, economic methods have difficulty capturing the value of lost lives and other non-market values (e.g., species, ecosystems, works of art), which some argue can't be valued on a monetary scale. Third, CBA is too insensitive to the enormous economic inequalities present in the climate change policy context, including inequality across time. Finally, CBA

faces challenges when it comes to including the tiny uncertainties of enormous catastrophe from climate change in their analysis in part because calculations of expected utility often assume a normal or quadratic distribution of risk (See Weitzman 2009 and Nordhaus 2011).

4 There are several proposals on offer. "Comparative" accounts, like Feinberg's, define suffering harm in terms of having an interest set back compared to a relevant baseline (where an interest is a discrete aspect of a person's well-being). Other comparativists define harm in terms of setbacks only to certain core interests. For example, Stephen Perry argues that suffering harm involves the worsening of core interests compared to a historical baseline. What is included in the core set of interests is a matter of some debate (Perry 2003: 1306–7). The so called "non-comparative" accounts define suffering harm in terms of an objective list of evil conditions, where the items on the list can be given some unified justification for making it to the list (Shiffrin 1999, 2012; Harman 2004). Elizabeth Harman appeals to human functioning to identify what unifies conditions of harm, and Shiffrin's admittedly incomplete account understands harm in terms of what is in accord with a person's will. David Velleman raises an objection against Shiffrin's view: fixing what counts as a harm in terms of what a person would will adds a subjective dimension to harm that could open up what can count as a harm in a troubling way (Velleman 2008). There are many more accounts, each of which face difficult challenges in analyzing the concept of harm to exclude mere desire satisfaction while at the same time including important failings, like the failure to achieve precious life goals. For example, disagreement abounds about whether a set back to a genius that leaves her at average intelligence counts as suffering harm, or whether certain seriously offensive activities cause harm (e.g., protests at funerals).

5 Sometimes comparative accounts rule hurts and dissatisfactions out by identifying them as *di minimis* harms (Feinberg 1984: 51).

6 Some of the conditions on the list present problems for some accounts of harm either because their status varies with circumstance or because some of the conditions – death especially – present notorious puzzles of their own (Feinberg 1984). Comparative accounts of harm that identify whether a worsened condition is suffering harm by comparing that condition to a baseline, may not always identify the items on the list as suffering harm. This will depend on the location of the baseline. For example, if the baseline is defined historically, and a person has been in a disabled condition since birth, her being in a disabled condition is not a case of suffering harm. This strikes many as a problem for comparative accounts. But comparativists can deal with these issues by appealing to moralized baselines or by arguing – like Perry seems to – that the *concept* of suffering harm implies having your condition worsened by some action, omission, or event. The badness of being born disabled (when your parents are not to blame) is serious; it's just not a harm.

7 One disagreement in particular would affect judgments about harm in the climate change context. There is disagreement about whether causing harm to someone requires causing their condition to worsen all things considered. For example, Feinberg (1992) argues that if a benefit is bestowed at the same time as a person is also made worse off in some respect, the action is not an instance of harming if the net effect of the action is positive. Shiffrin disagrees. She thinks that being put in a bad condition harms no matter what benefit accompanies it.

8 There may not be much more than a semantic difference between the accounts, because the loss of pure benefits that Shiffrin would count as very important (breaking a promise or failing to give your child a birthday gift), Feinberg might count as harms, because they set back important interests.

9 I'm using the Aggressive Carbon Tax scenario to illustrate my point. I don't offer it as a proposal for a policy instrument, and I don't offer a defense of it. I consider it only to identify how harm/benefit asymmetries arise in the climate change context.

Fully evaluating the Aggressive Carbon Tax would be an incredibly complex project that would require taking into account the costs and feasibility of adaptation as well as comparing the costs and co-benefits of the tax to current generations to the reduced residual climate damages in the future, as well as any adverse effects involved.

10 Thanks to Sara Mrsny for discussing with me the importance of emphasizing the losses to middle class consumers.

11 See Bovens (2011) for discussion of this idea. See also Hans Peter-Weikard's "A Lockean approach to greenhouse gas emission rights" in this volume.

12 Thanks to Chris Field for pointing out these examples to me.

13 See also Daniel Halliday (2011).

14 Fried discusses a form of threshold deontology that is adopted by thinkers in the contractualist tradition. (Fried 2012: 62).

15 Fried also mentions other important objections to weighting harms, which I don't have space to consider in this paper. First, there is a very serious problem concerning how to figure out what harms weigh under any criteria. Second, she raises concern about paternalism and perfectionism in setting the relative weight of harm either according to what one thinks people will prefer in the future or what they ought to prefer (Fried 2012: 63). This point about paternalism draws on the connection between preferences and autonomy. If people's welfare turns out to be different from what they prefer, the threat of paternalism is live. However, this isn't obvious and a defense of understanding autonomy in terms of people's preferences is sorely needed (Herzog 2000: 914).

16 Another problem with preferences is that people disagree about the consequences of the policies that would combat climate change and about the consequences of the activities that cause climate change (Hausman and McPherson 2006: 285). People who are climate skeptics likely have no preferences at all regarding the predicted bad consequences of the fossil fuel regime, but they may have strong preferences concerning the opportunity costs of dedicating resources to combat climate change. Similarly, imagining the end of human life on Earth leads some to have incredibly strong preferences regarding the tiny chance of doom from even relatively low levels of climate change. However there are at least partial fixes for these issues within the preference satisfaction metric. Hausman and McPherson (2006) consider the argument that satisfying preferences doesn't justify "adhering to preferences that reflect mistaken beliefs" about the badness of a particular consequence. Instead, economics could consider only preferences for those consequences there is good reason to expect. But there are still problems, because preference-satisfaction is simply not the same as well-being, as the absurd consequences of equating harm to preference dissatisfaction involving mere hurt and offense indicate.

17 See also Hausman and McPherson,who argue against a theory of welfare based on "spruced-up" preferences that, "welfare is not the satisfaction of preferences, no matter how spruced up" (2009: 2).

18 Caney describes the lexical priority of human rights as "general," because he doesn't think human rights have *absolute* priority. In exceptional cases, violating human rights of the few may be required in order to protect the human rights of others (Caney 2010: 165, 174 n.12).

19 Because human rights pick out the most basic moral standard, Caney's human rights approach leaves room for other moral ideas and values, including economic efficiency, which can be considered once the threshold is achieved. So there's a space for economic methods in Caney's approach to climate change, but only for effects above the human rights threshold.

20 John Broome (2010) makes a similar argument.

21 Damage estimate for the USA (NJ, NY, CN), including post-tropical storm and landfall: 71,400,000,000 (unadjusted US$) (NOAA 2014).

22 The $10 billion figure was cited in Fritz *et al.* (2009). The Mynamar government also announced the $10 billion figure shortly after the disaster (Sputnik News 2008). However, the official disaster database lists damage estimates at an even lower figure (CRED 2009).

23 Calculating the economic costs of damages is highly complex. Most damage estimates sum the direct and indirect effects of a disaster, rather than relying on macroeconomic data about the disaster's effects on economic growth. Governments differ in their record keeping as well as in the way estimates are calculated. Because disasters are highly complex, estimates from different countries and different places will differ in the costs they include, and so are quite difficult to adjust and accurately compare. This is the case even when looking at databases specifically designed for cross-country analysis (Kousky 2012).

24 John Nolt (2015) argues that casualties should be used as a measure of climate change impacts. I think this is a step in the right direction. However, I don't think that the number of deaths alone is an adequate measure of harm. Very many people suffering bodily injuries could be quite a bit worse-off harm-wise than death.

25 See Schneider *et al.* (2000) for recommendations and a discussion of the importance of transparency about values for widening the range of possible policies in the face of uncertainty about climatic change.

26 See IPCC (2014b: 220) for a helpful discussion on Multi-Criteria Analysis.

Bibliography

Bovens, L. (2011), "A Lockean defense of grandfathering emission rights," in D. G. Arnold (ed.), *The Ethics of Global Climate Change*, Cambridge: Cambridge University Press.

Bradley, B. (2012), "Doing away with harm," *Philosophy and Phenomenological Research*, vol. 85: 390–412.

Broome, J. (2010), "No argument against the continuity of value: reply to Dorsey," *Utilitas*, vol. 22: 494–95.

Caney, S. (2010), "Climate change, human rights, and moral thresholds," in S. M. Gardiner, S. Caney, D. Jamieson, and H. Shue (eds), *Climate Ethics: Essential Readings*, Oxford: Oxford University Press.

CRED (2009), "EM-DAT The international disaster database," available at www.emdat.be/ (accessed 30 May 2016).

Feinberg, J. (1984), *Harm to Others*, Oxford: Oxford University Press.

Feinberg, J. (1992), "Wrongful life and the counterfactual element in harming," in J. Feinberg, *Freedom and Fullfillment*, Princeton: Princeton University Press, pp. 3–36.

Francis, B. (forthcoming), "Climate change and the moral significance of harm," Unpublished PhD thesis, Department of Philosophy, Stanford University.

Fried, B. H. (2012), "Can contractualism save us from aggregation," *Journal of Ethics*, vol. 16: 39–66.

Friedman, M. (1962), *Capitalism and Freedom*, Chicago: Chicago University Press.

Fritz, H., Blount, C. D., Thwin, S., Thu, M. K., and Chan, N. (2009), "Cyclone Nargis storm surge in Myanmar," *Nature Geoscience*, vol. 2: 448–9.

Griffin, J. (1977), "Are there incommensurable values?," *Philosophy & Public Affairs*, vol. 7: 39–59.

Griffin, J. (1986), *Well-being: Its Meaning, Measurement and Moral Importance*, Oxford: Clarendon Press.

Halliday, D. K. (2011), "Endowments, inequality and aggregation: An inquiry on the foundations and methods of distributive justice," Unpublished PhD thesis, Department of Philosophy, Stanford University.

Harel, A. and Porat, A. (2011), "Commensurability and agency: two yet-to-be-met challenges for law and economics," *Cornell Law Review*, vol. 96: 749.

Harman, E. (2004), "Can we harm and benefit in creating?," *Philosophical Perspectives* vol. 18: 89–113.

Hausman, D. M. and McPherson, M. S. (2006), *Economic Analysis, Moral Philosophy, and Public Policy*, Cambridge: Cambridge University Press.

Hausman, D. M. and McPherson, M. S. (2009), "Preference satisfaction and welfare economics," *Economics and Philosophy*, vol. 25: 1–25.

Hayek, F. A. (1960), *The Constitution of Liberty*, Chicago: University of Chicago Press.

Herzog, D. (2000), "Externalities and other parasites," *The University of Chicago Law Review*: 895–923.

IPCC (2012), "Managing the risks of extreme events and disasters to advance climate change adaptation," in IPCC, A *Special Report of Working Groups I and II of the International Panel on Climate Change*, Cambridge: Cambridge University Press.

IPCC (2014a), "Climate change 2014: Impacts, adaptation and vulnerability," in IPCC, *Contribution of Working Group II to the Fifth Assessment Report of the Intergovernmental Panel on Climate Change*, Cambridge: Cambridge University Press.

IPCC (2014b), "Climate Change 2014: Mitigation of climate change," in IPCC, *Contribution of Working Group III to the Fifth Assessment Report of the Intergovernmental Panel on Climate Change*, Cambridge: Cambridge University Press.

Jaramillo, P. and Muller, N. Z. (2016), "Air pollution emissions and damages from energy production in the U.S. 2002–2011," *Energy Policy*, vol. 90: 202–11.

Kousky, C. (2012), "Informing climate adaptation: a review of the economic costs of natural disasters, their determinants, and risk reduction options," *Resources for the Future*, Washington, DC.

NOAA (2013), "Service assessment: hurricane/post-tropical Cyclone Sandy." Available at: www.nws.noaa.gov/os/assessments/pdfs/Sandy13.pdf (accessed 27 May 2016).

NOAA (2014), "The thirty costliest mainland United States tropical cyclones 1900–2013." Available at: www.aoml.noaa.gov/hrd/tcfaq/costliesttable.html (accessed 27 May 2016).

Nolt, J. (2015), "Casualties as a moral measure of climate change," *Climatic Change*, vol. 130: 347–58.

Nordhaus, W. D. (2008), *A Question of Balance: Weighing the Options on Global Warming Policies*, New Haven: Yale University Press.

Nordhaus, W. D. (2011), "The economics of tail events with an application to climate change," *Review of Environmental Economics and Policy*, vol. 5: 240–57.

Nordhaus, W. D. (2013), *The Climate Casino: Risk, Uncertainty, and Economics for a Warming World*, New Haven: Yale University Press.

Nozick, R. (1974), *Anarchy State and Utopia*, New York: Basic Books.

Parfit, D. (1995), "Equality or priority? The Lindley lecture," University of Kansas, Department of Philosophy.

Perry, S. (2003), "Harm, history, and counterfactuals," *San Diego Law Review*, vol. 40: 1283.

Raz, J. (1986), *The Morality of Freedom*, Oxford: Oxford University Press.

Satz, D., Gould, R, K., Chan, K. M. A., Guerry, A., Norton, B., Satterfield, T., Halpern, B. S., Levine, J., Woodside, U., Hannahs, N., Basurto, X., and Klain, S. (2013), "The challenges of incorporating cultural ecosystem services into environmental assessment," AMBIO, vol. 42: 675–84.

Scanlon, T. M. (1975), "Preference and urgency," *The Journal of Philosophy*, vol. 72: 655–69.

Schneider, S. H., Kuntz-Duriseti, K. and Azar, C. (2000), "Costing non-linearities, surprises, and irreversible events," *Pacific and Asian Journal of Energy*, vol. 10: 81–106.

Shiffrin, S. V. (1999), "Wrongful life, procreative responsibility, and the significance of harm," *Legal Theory*, vol. 5: 117–48.

Shiffrin, S. V. (2012), "Harm and its moral significance," *Legal Theory*, vol. 18(3): 357–98.

Sputnik News (2008) "Cyclone Nargis costs Myanmar over $10 bln," *Sputnik International*. Available at: www.sputniknews.com/world/20080519/107755823.html (accessed 16 November 2015).

Stern, N. (2007), *The Economics of Climate Change: The Stern Review*, Cambridge and New York: Cambridge University Press.

Thompson, T. M., Rausch, S., Saari, R. K., and Selin, N. E. (2014), "A systems approach to evaluating the air quality co-benefits of US carbon policies," *Nature Climate Change*, vol. 4 (10): 917–23.

Velleman, D. J. (2008), "Persons in Prospect," *Philosophy and Public Affairs*, vol. 36: 221–66.

Weitzman, M. L. (2009), "On modeling and interpreting the economics of catastrophic climate change," *The Review of Economics and Statistics*, vol. 91: 1–19.

Zamir, E. and Medina, B. (2010), *Law, Economics, and Morality*, New York: Oxford University Press.

10 The ethical failures of climate economics

Clive L. Spash and Clemens Gattringer

Introduction

Discussions relating to the ethical underpinnings of economics and their implications for understanding human-induced climate change have typically been sustained at a superficial level of engagement due to the restrictions imposed by maintaining consistency with the tenets of mainstream economics. Belief in a Humean fact-value dichotomy is evident in the promotion of economics as a positive science and the persistence of regarding "efficiency" as an uncontroversial and value free objective. This distinction made by Hume as a passing remark, about not believing everything you read, was taken up as a major philosophical distinction. Hume's concern was that some authors drew unwarranted moral direction from factual/empirical claims to knowledge. Later this became taken as a prescriptive difference with the analytical/factual/empirical being seen as scientific while the normative/ethical/moral was seen as a distinct area of knowledge; the former supposedly could not direct human action while the latter could provide such direction. In economics this is enshrined in the split between positive and normative economics, in philosophy the analytical vs. normative, and more generally the division between science and politics.

Under such reasoning, discounting the future becomes merely ads aspect of empirical reality to be objectively observed in a positive economics. The logic of discounting is then enforced as part of resource efficiency as if this were not an ethical choice (e.g. Arrow *et al.* 1996). Even those who recognise the importance of ethics in economics wish to maintain an analytical economics separated from the ethics and fall back heavily on a narrow consequentialism (Stern 2014a). Thus, climate economists typically regard policy decisions as being made on the basis of weighing the costs of death and destruction against the benefits of increasing consumption, and deem this a necessary act of rational and efficient economic risk management (Stern 2006). Under the mainstream economic framing the imperative of growth cannot be questioned and is actually described as a means for controlling human induced climate change (GCEC 2014), rather than a fundamental cause of the problem in the first place.

None of this mainstream climate economics has gone without critique (Spash 1993, 1994a, b, 1996, 2002a, 2006, 2007a, b, c, d, e, 2008, 2010, 2011, 2014, 2015). The problems include the value loading of economic models, the reduction of strong uncertainty to risk management, ad hoc assumptions of cost–benefit analysis including the attribution of differential values of life to rich and poor, and the basic ethical narrowness of utilitarianism, especially in its preference version (Spash 2002a, 2007a, e). Yet, such issues have made no substantive impact on the practices of climate economists (such as Nordhaus, Pearce, Fankhauser, Velinga, Tol, Hope, Stern). Even those who note the problems and discuss some of the fundamental flaws in analysis, go on to defend the basic approach of mainstream economics. For example, Stern (2014a, b) repeatedly pours derision on the main climate-modelling methods and approaches (e.g. integrated assessment model, expected utility, discounting, cost–benefit), but he claims all such economics must be kept as part of the information set (note, all these were also employed in the Stern Review and its policy recommendations). We might speculate that commitment to the orthodoxy comes prior to undertaking critical science and clearing out redundant approaches and misleading information.

That the work of economists is fraught with problems is relevant to both the theoretical approaches taken and the policy recommendations made on the basis of economic analysis (e.g. internalising externalities, adjusting prices, implementing tradable permit markets). While economists claim their analysis of pollution problems, such as greenhouse gases (GHGs), is distinct from the policy instruments to be employed, in reality the two are heavily entwined. Indeed, mainstream economists are self-defining as those who favour market-based institutions to achieve efficiency and who promote them above all else. Decades of neoliberalisation in politics has impacted neoclassical economics, and its resource and environmental economic offshoot, so that the differences between the neoclassical and neoliberal have faded away (Fellner and Spash 2015). This is evident in the lack of any serious attention to planning and regulation as substantive and effective alternatives to price mechanisms and markets, and the failure to highlight the need to regulate international corporations, which operate as much as possible outside of the legal systems that are established and enforced primarily by nation states within their national jurisdictions.

In this chapter we explore some key ethical issues within climate economics and place them in the broader public policy context of a growth economy. More specifically five aspects are discussed:

- the notion of intergenerational ethics, and how future generations are included into economic models, with a debate centred on choosing the appropriate discount rate;
- the interregional context is raised as a central topic often neglected in economic debate, but one that has been highlighted by the environmental justice movement and is clearly central to concerns over equity in mitigation and the urgency attributed to impacts;

- the current international mindset of regarding development as economic growth is explored as a central presumption of mainstream economics and the international policy community. The implications – justifying business as usual while deliberately creating harm of the innocent – are far reaching;
- the issue of incommensurability is raised, in the context of compensation, and a distinction drawn between basic maintenance of living standards and liability for harm; and
- the way in which uncertainty is conceptualised as risk is seen to predetermine the ethics that are applied, allowing prevalence of a narrow consequentialist approach as rational management.

Intergenerational ethics

From the outset, economists addressing human induced climate change framed the issue as primarily an intergenerational problem (d'Arge *et al.* 1982). This led economists to focus on the equity of resource distribution and the necessity of transfers from the present to the relatively distant future to achieve compensation for the deliberate harm of the innocent (Spash 2002a; Spash and d'Arge 1989). This focus arose because GHG control costs were assumed to be incurred immediately any mitigation action was taken, while the benefits of that control (i.e. harm avoided) would accrue in the distant future. Economists, obsessed by optimisation and economic efficiency, then looked for the optimal allocation of costs and benefits in a model that both questioned current practice (emitting GHGs) but also justified its continuation (control costs exceed benefits).

The economic perspective recognises that business as usual means the damages from human-induced climate change are pushed onto as yet unborn generations, but does not condemn this as unethical in itself. The concern is limited to criticising the outcome as possibly inefficient as a means of maximising utility. Killing future people and destabilising the Earth's climatic system for too little economic gain in the present is a poor resource allocation decision. If it achieved the maximisation of expected aggregated net benefits, or social welfare, then that would be fine. What is required, according to this logic, are potential Pareto improvements where some gain (e.g. the already rich) and theoretically none would lose (i.e. if there was actual redistribution of the gains to the actual losers).

In order to make such claims operational in economics, time horizons must be bound and flows over time of welfare, or utility, weighted. Discounting provides a means by which economists can effectively write off future consequences as of little or no importance, compared to current ones, and do so without explicitly clarifying the ethical basis for their choice (e.g. Arrow *et al.* 1996). The ethics and economics of discounting are part of the theoretical approach to addressing resource allocation and making decisions within an economic consequentialist philosophy. This is linked to models which claim to optimise resource allocation on the basis of utility maximisation. Such models have been employed continuously from the start of the climate economics literature:

Nordhaus (1977) through Stern (2006) to the 2014 IPCC report of Working Group III on mitigation (Kolstad *et al.* 2014). The approach connects to economic welfare theory and assumes methodological individualism, whereby society is treated as an aggregate of individuals and well-being can be represented in a social welfare function (SWF). Yet, even a minute benefit that exists for an infinite time horizon would be infinite, dominate aggregation calculations and so destroy the economist's trade-off and net benefit analysis. This means, in addition to discounting, a fixed time horizon is always also required to avoid infinite values. Bounding the time frame appears logical, in the context of discounting, because future flows of welfare head asymptotically towards zero and, as a result, soon have so little weight as to effectively become insignificant.

In summary, the economic approach aims to aggregate social welfare overtime, using discounting, and cut off the long-term prospects that would make calculations meaningless. The foundational presumption for both discounting, and cut-off, is that future benefits and costs should have less weight in current decisions than those of the present. There are two main justifications for this:

- individuals are argued to have a time preference bias which means they want to consume things now, and not wait, and they prefer to push harms into the future. This preference utilitarian justification is criticised as leading to myopia, but remains central to the economic approach; and
- the presumption that economic growth will always be positive and increase the amount of consumption in the future. This makes the present generation the poorest in terms of aggregate social welfare.

Why then should the poorest (present generation) be required to transfer to the rich (future generation)? The argument is that investment in capital results in greater productivity which acts "as the minimum rate of return that is necessary to compensate for this adverse effect on the SWF of investing for the future" (Kolstad *et al.* 2014: 229). So, the economic logic is that the present needs to be rewarded (or compensated) for investing in the future (i.e. delaying consumption by creating capital) and capital growth will achieve this. Present growth rates are then aggregated and extrapolated, ignoring anomalies of non-growth periods, non-growing economies and the vast majority of human history where economies did not grow. A typical consumption growth rate adopted is 2 per cent.

Establishing what the social discount rate should be for public policy projects is highly contested within economics, but as a technical issue not an ethical one. A standard formula combines the pure rate of time preference and the declining marginal utility of income[1] to define the discount rate *r*:

$$r = \delta + \eta g$$

where δ (delta) is the rate of pure time preference, g (gamma) is the growth rate of per capita consumption, and η (eta) determines the effect of economic (consumption) growth on the discount rate. The term η is variously described as an inequality and/or risk aversion parameter. Inequality here refers to the assumption that the future will be consumption rich and the present is relatively consumption poor. Some argue the pure rate of time preference should be zero (e.g. Cline 1992); Stern (2006) used 0.1 per cent on the basis of potential planetary extinction; while the IPCC's Working Group III cite Weitzman as recommending 2 per cent (see Kolstad *et al.* 2014: Table 3.2).

An argument that has been employed by economists is that the social discount rate should be constructed on the basis of empirical observation (e.g. actual growth rates and time preferences). This was used to justify discounting by the IPCC in both its 3rd (Arrow *et al.* 1996) and 5th (Kolstad *et al.* 2014: 229) assessment reports. Economists who employ this argument believe that markets operate as perfectly as described in their microeconomic textbooks and discount rates are merely the price (or opportunity cost) of time. They may claim that all public projects should earn the market rate of return, and if they cannot they are not justified on the basis of efficient resource allocation. The implication is that there is a relevant, single, easily measurable rate that can be observed, rather than the reality of many rates existing in different countries and contexts that are conflated with the differential risks associated with alternative capital investments.

This naïve empiricist position is also indicative of the way in which economists claiming to be analytical divorce the implications of discounting from its full consequences and hide the implicit ethical position they adopt. Ethics is impossible to divorce from the discount rate chosen and is a good example of why the fact–value dichotomy, and the associated positive–normative distinction in economics, are illusions. That an ethical judgement is inevitably adopted whatever rate is chosen, and on whatever basis it is chosen to be justified, is generally ignored by economists (Spash 1993, 1994b). To make the point clear, Table 10.1 shows the full range of potential positions on the social discount rate and specifies alongside each the ethical implications.

While the preceding explanation should make clear that determining a discount rate denotes a fundamental ethical judgement, economists have a tradition of treating discounting as a technicality (Price 1993). They persist in the belief that some scientific approach is to be implemented that is value free. In practice the social discount rate employed in climate models and assessments is chosen arbitrarily and varies widely, along with its justification (Pindyck 2013). For example, Nordhaus (2007) has applied a discount rate of 4.3 per cent, Stern *et al.* (2006) used a rate of 1.4 per cent. The dominant convention in cost–benefit analysis has been to use relatively high (e.g. 5 to 10 per cent) discount rates.

The 5th assessment report by IPCC Working Group III presents a selected literature and some data in order to claim that: "An appropriate social risk-free discount rate for consumption is between one and three times the anticipated growth rate in real per capita consumption" (Kolstad *et al.* 2014: 211). That same report calculates and presents differential rates for a selection of countries (Kolstad *et al.* 2014: 231). China is attributed a rate of 15.20 per cent while, at

Table 10.1 Economic discount rates and intergenerational ethics

	Social discount rate	*Ethical implication*
1a Future Ignored	An infinite social discount rate	No moral obligations beyond the present exist
1b Future Ignored	A social discount rate high enough to effectively weight consequences for the next generation at zero	No moral obligations to the next generation exist
2a Present has Priority	The intergenerational social discount rate is set the same as the intratemporal rate (e.g. rate of return on capital) which is positive	Present and future persons are subject to the same rules regardless of consequences (e.g. procedural justice)
2b Present has Priority	The intergenerational social discount rate is greater than zero but less than the intratemporal rate	Moral obligations to the future exist, but the future is assigned less weight than the present
3 Present & Future are Equal	The social discount rate is zero	Moral standing (e.g. rights and interests) of future persons are the same as those of contemporary persons
4a Future has Priority	The intergenerational social discount rate is set the same as the intratemporal rate and economic growth is negative	Present and future persons are subject to the same rules regardless of consequences (e.g. procedural justice)
4b Future has Priority	A negative intergenerational social discount rate should be used	Moral obligations to the future exist, and the future is assigned more weight than the present

Source: adapted from Spash (1993, 1994b).

the opposite extreme, Zaire has –5.52 per cent. In terms of the consequences for action on climate change this would mean China can totally ignore future welfare and any damages because they have little weight in current decisions (i.e. after 30 years only representing 1 per cent of an equivalent cost or benefit today). Such countries with fast-growing consumption rates are meant to value the future less because the utility of consumption is declining. By contrast a country with a negative consumption growth rate would (on economic efficiency grounds) need to weigh future losses as more important than present gains, because future consumption is more valuable. Thus, given damages arise in the future, on this economic logic, growth economies, the high GHG emitters, should ignore GHG control while the non-growth economies, low GHG emitters, should undertake action.

The lie of the technical calculation argument, and its naïve empiricist approach, is that its advocates are never prepared to implement or even discuss such conclusions. Instead economists simply ignore zero and negative discount rates when economies are in recession, because this is not "normal". Economies that fail to perform as the economic growth modellers predict are regarded as just temporary anomalies. So, as the World Bank's development indicators show, while a variety of countries have in recent times recorded persistent negative growth rates (e.g. in the European Union alone 16 out of 28 countries over the period 2009–13 with all countries except Poland having one or more years of negative growth), these have not been allowed to influence the use of generic positive discount rates in all climate economics (and elsewhere). Neither do economists take into account the evidence for individuals holding negative time preference rates, whereby they bring forward harms and delay pleasures (Baer and Spash 2008). The conclusion is that economists choose to use positive discount rates because this fits their a priori theoretical commitments and ideological beliefs – that society should increase consumption – not any empirical reality.

In any case, deriving a discount rate from the observation of markets has little to do with protecting the long-term interests of society, not least because human preferences are an inadequate basis for guidance as to moral action (O'Neill 1993). The use of discounting ignores the need for precaution in the face of a highly uncertain future with irreversible catastrophic scenarios. None of this prevents the endless rhetorical debate of climate economists about discounting, which serves to distract from more substantive issues, including the ethical implications of their policy recommendations.

Interregional ethics

Impacts of human-induced climate change, such as weather anomalies in specific parts of the world, are already occurring according to the IPCC 5th Assessment Report (IPCC 2013). This makes evident that the focus on intergenerational ethics has become highly misleading, and that there are ethical concerns relating to shifting costs onto others across space as well as time. In fact, intratemporal distribution was always relevant to the economics of mitigation strategies (see d'Arge and Spash 1991), even if ignored by most economists and their models. The interregional ethical implications of human-induced climate change arise in two ways:

- the issue of who is seen to be responsible for GHG emissions, and so who should be undertaking mitigation measures; and
- how the consequences of climate change and ability to respond of those impacted are both differentially distributed across space as well as time.

On the mitigation issue the attribution of responsibility for control of GHGs has implications for who gets to burn fossil fuels, and so who gets to continue using the knowledge, technology and related infrastructure of the fossil fuel economy that has been constructed over the past 200 years. The failure to undertake any significant mitigation measures during the last quarter century has meant much hope is increasingly placed upon geoengineering, and similar technological miracles (biotechnology, carbon capture and storage), which claim that no systemic change is necessary and the continued use of fossil fuels is possible. Such techno-optimist positions rely on unproven future technological promises that have highly uncertain side effects. In addition, the much hyped carbon capture and storage has limited applicability, high costs and little impact on the required emissions reductions (e.g. see McGlade and Ekins 2015). There are no technologies available that can remove GHGs from the atmosphere after they have been released on the scale of current emissions, store them securely with low risk of failure, and do so at a resource and energy cost that makes any economic sense. That negates the argument for rich nations discharging their ethical responsibilities under human-induced climate change by investing in technology and passing on the results to others (e.g. GCEC 2014; Stern 2014b). This leaves the immediate issue as preventing GHG emissions from occurring in the first place and doing so with existing technology and knowledge.

The prospect for development, when defined as traditional fossil fuel-driven economic growth, is then highly constrained. This is a key issue of contention for countries wanting to follow the same path already taken by industrialised nation states. The nations of Europe and North America, as the first to industrialise, have had longer to burn fossil fuels and embody them in infrastructure, capital stock and military power that has enabled access to resources elsewhere. They have been responsible for the historical accumulation of GHGs that has created enhancement of the greenhouse effect. As other nations, such as Japan and Australia, industrialised they joined the club of GHG emitters. In recent times Brazil, Russia, India, China and South Africa (the BRICS nations) have become new major sources of accelerating emissions. China and India are presently heavily implicated in expansion of emissions from a massive build of coal-fired power stations, and this is set to continue, regardless of their claimed intended reductions (or independently determined national contributions) under the United Nations Framework Convention on Climate Change (UNFCCC) Conference of the Parties (COP) Paris Agreement in December 2015. The top six emitters of CO_2 in absolute terms, in 2014, were China (30 per cent), the United States of America (15 per cent), European Union (10 per cent), of which Germany contributed over one-fifth, India (7 per cent), Russia (5 per cent) and Japan (4 per cent), regions that together were responsible for 71 per cent of global emissions (Olivier *et al.* 2015). Meanwhile, there are 120 countries producing only 1 per cent of emissions (World Bank 2016). Clearly, the responsibility for producing GHGs differs extensively across nation states in correlation with industrialisation and mass consumerism, with many having little or no responsibility for human-induced climate change.

The position is even more stark when considering consumption inequity per capita because the vast majority of the world's population lack access to, and/or consumption of, the goods and services that are the products of the fossil fuel combustion economy. The largest per capita emissions come mainly from oil and shale oil producing nations and some small island states, but also in the top 20 or so are the USA, Canada, Australia (all in the 16–17 metric tons per capita range) and Russia (12.6 metric tons per capita). At the extremes are Qatar with 44.0 metric tons per capita compared to the low-income country average of 0.3 metric tons per capita (2011 figures from World Bank 2016). Again there is clearly gross inequity between countries based on industrialisation and resource extraction.

The basic issue here is that only a limited amount of GHGs can be emitted before exceeding atmospheric concentrations that threaten serious, significant, on-going and irreversible damages. For example, current proven reserves of fossil fuels represent at least three times the budget, in terms of carbon equivalent emissions, that can be used if the 50:50 chance of a 2°C target were being attempted (Spash 2016). Several questions then arise. An obvious one is on what basis should the GHG budget be allocated and who is required to leave their reserves untouched and in the ground? In addition, who gets to burn the fossil fuels that are extracted (e.g. industrial imperial China burning Australian coal), on what basis (e.g. purchasing power, military power, or fair share) and who must accept they cannot do so? Who then benefits from this combustion (e.g. North Americans and Europeans buying Chinese products or the world's poor)? The overarching problem here is that claims are being made for the importance of equity (e.g. the Paris Agreement) but what that means is left totally unclear, and, if left to business as usual – under the rhetoric of "more growth for all" – it will be a continuation of injustice.

One approach to equity is to divide the remaining GHG budget per capita, but this would not take into account the historical use. That is, some countries have already used far more than their "fair share" of all permissible emissions across time. So, an alternative is to allocate on the basis of historic emissions. However, this might backfire by allowing new fossil fuel combustion infrastructure and absolute additions to the atmospheric concentrations, for example as is now happening in China and India. Similarly, emissions would be encouraged to increase where little or none have occurred before and they might be more easily avoided due to lack of infrastructural lock-in. That is, the potential for non-fossil fuel development paths is too readily pushed aside in the scramble for rights to burn fossil fuels. At the same time, such a policy might fail to remove the global fossil fuel infrastructure where it already exists. The difficulty of addressing the latter problem is also a major political stumbling block for international policy. The modern industrial state has an accompanying military power that is in essence based upon fossil fuels for its ability to operate on a daily basis. Who will take away fossil fuel infrastructure from the USA, China, Russia, to name but a few military-industrial nation states?

Some aspects of dividing-up the remaining budget have been explored by Raupach *et al.* (2014) for a 2°C target. They contrast the positions of the USA, the EU, China and India with the Rest of the World (RoW). They pose three scenarios: business as usual, mixed and per capita with 37 per cent, 45 per cent and 53 per cent of the budget going to RoW under each option, respectively. The shift for the USA and the EU in the move from business as usual to per capita scenarios is to cut their budgets: the USA from 26 per cent to 4 per cent; the EU from 18 per cent to 7 per cent. When they add in the past cumulative emissions and those to which there is already a commitment, due to new infrastructure, the result is that the USA and China have already exceeded their allowance under their equity principle based on population.

Additional problems arise in deciding how to attribute budgets and emissions responsibility between production and consumption. Employing manufacturing production as the measure of emissions can allow Western mass consumer economies to push emissions responsibilities to industrially less-developed countries, while continuing the consumption of their products. For example, Bangladesh produces cheap clothing for Western countries and under a production approach would need to account for the related emissions, rather than the richer countries that buy the products. However, neither consumer nor manufacturing responsibility for emissions addresses resource extraction and supply so that nations such as Norway and Australia avoid responsibility for carbon emissions due to their oil and coal production respectively. Ethically this is like stating "I only made the gun, I didn't shoot anyone", while knowing the use intended.

In addition to the mitigation issue there is the inequitable spatial distribution of impacts and the variation in ability to adapt to those impacts. Specific changes in regional climates are expected to differ substantially from the expected global averages, and so the resulting costs will be distributed unevenly. Greater costs are generally expected for developing countries. Altered growing seasons, for instance, would undermine the economic basis of agriculturally based economies. Africa is regarded as most vulnerable due to widespread poverty and associated limited adaptation capabilities (Watson *et al.* 1997). The impacts of climate change are unevenly distributed and the beneficiaries of fossil fuel emissions are not the same as those who will be harmed by those emissions. For example, a country such as Bangladesh is expected to suffer substantially through rising sea levels, while also lacking the means to react to such changes compared to nations that have the power to command resources and have accumulated infrastructure.

In general, economics has pushed equity and distributional issues out of its analysis on the basis that this is a political (value) issue and not an efficiency (factual) one. Mainstream welfare economics then focuses on Pareto improvements assuming the initial distribution of wealth is given. Exchange and trade through markets is then meant to increase the overall level of welfare. The analysis fails to recognise that markets are just one institution amongst many that constitute societal organisation (Chang 2002). Establishing markets as the means for resource allocation also establishes the principles for obtaining resources and so what is deemed equitable. In separating distributional issues from allocative efficiency of resources, economics claims it is only undertaking analytical research and that the resulting work employs objective (value free) evaluations. However, the methodology makes ethical judgements implicitly, not least in its prioritisation of efficiency above other social goals and markets above other institutions.

One response to the problem of distribution in economics is the claim that economic growth will provide so much wealth that nobody need worry. Everybody who has so far been left out (the vast majority of the world's population) will benefit from economic growth. This has been used in the past to avoid redistribution within a country, minimum wages, progressive taxation, inheritance taxes and so on. Today the same argument is being employed to claim growth can both solve climate change and do so by providing gains so nobody need be worse off (i.e. Pareto efficiency). Thus Stern (2014b) argues that combining growth with technology will mean no need for difficult choices over burden sharing. He co-heads, with former Mexican President Felipe Calderón, an initiative to promote the ideology of growth in the context of human-induced climate change (GCEC 2014).

Climate ethics in a growth economy

Ecological economists have long pointed out the consequences of the growth economy subject to the laws of thermodynamics (Georgescu-Roegen 1971, 2009 [1975]; Martinez-Alier 1990). Prioritisation of affluence, based on material and energy throughput, means creating the same mass in terms of waste as the mass of resources that go into the production system (i.e. neither mass nor energy is created or destroyed). As fossil fuels are burnt CO_2 must be released and so there is a direct correlation of both with production and consumption in the modern fossil fuel-driven economy. Climate change is then an inevitable structural part of the current economic system. Economists, such as Stern (2014b: 419), who label this the biggest market failure ever, have not grasped the basic functioning of the economy in biophysical terms, nor the fact that, socially, costs are shifted as part of the functioning of the economy, not as some error of the price system (i.e. an externality). Kapp (1978) long ago criticised the inaccuracy and unreality of the externality conceptualisation as used by economists.

One result of this misconceptualisation is a strong presumption in the economic approaches to climate change that, subject to some price corrections, economic growth will continue and indeed that it is a priority that it does continue. The assumption that it will continue is the primary justification behind discounting. The fear that it might be stopped by climate change is a primary motivation in calls for action led by an elite of economists, financiers, bankers and political leaders (Spash 2014). The combination motivates mainstream economists to promote the growth economy as being ethical despite the apparent creation of unethical outcomes. That is, when growth and the drive for material affluence creates harms, the pro-growth economist feels the necessity to counter this by arguing the growth economy is the only way to create other more important good outcomes. This is the revelation of the consequentialist and utilitarian logic that is implicit in the ethics of mainstream economics.

Thus, the linking of growth to poverty alleviation has seen a revival (GCEC 2014), despite the infamous trickle-down effect having been discredited (OECD 2011). Recognition that the current economic system benefits a minority is nothing new (e.g. the writings of Gramsci in the 1920s and 1930s, see Hoare and Smith 1971), but consistently the opposite is claimed. So the message must be restated that there is nothing inherent in a growth economy that necessitates improving the lot of those at the bottom. Indeed, across the globe the exact opposite has proven to be the case in a system where subsistence wages are maintained for the majority, labour exploited and resources extracted for export leaving a degraded and polluted local environment. The resulting economic and societal organisation has been termed the "imperial mode of living" by Brand and Wissen (2013), because all those who benefit in terms of affluence do so at the cost of others (e.g. through appropriation of their environment, resources and ecological assimilative capacities). The beneficiaries accept, or more typically ignore, the harm their lifestyles create because this is the norm in the modern affluent society. Climate change is then the imposition of damages via a massive cost-shifting exercise which aims to benefit the capital accumulating economies and sectors, and those who obtain (mainly by luck of location and birth) sufficient purchasing power to actively engage in the hedonistic pleasures of the consumer society.

The debate around climate economics has increasingly been shifting ground from the implications of an environmental catastrophe to the meaning for the growth economy. Apologists for growth claim they are agnostic about it, as if the issue were irrelevant to the environmental crisis, because the goal is really welfare creation and growth just happens along the way while protecting the capital stock and rates of return (Jakob and Edenhofer 2014). Natural capital can then include everything to do with the environment and provide competitive rates of return so that all will be right with the world (for a critique of natural capital see Spash and Clayton 1997). Those who know the political importance of growth – for maintaining the existing social structure of which they are on top – are far more ready to attack anyone questioning growth (as Stern has done publicly, see Spash 2014). Regardless of differences, both these pro-growth and agnostic/apologist camps end up promoting growth as the only means for addressing poverty. The big success of the economic growth lobby in Paris was to link the whole climate agreement to a UN sustainable development agenda that in 2015 took as a core goal a minimum of 7 per cent growth rates for developing countries (Spash 2016).

Emerging movements (e.g. degrowth and environmental justice) highlight the importance of breaking the imaginary of "affluent materialist lifestyles for all" that has been pervasive in the Western world and spread globally. They call for a different system that rejects capital accumulation and hedonistic satisfaction based on consumerism as the primary guiding principles for humanity. Ideas of the morally "good life" for all, a meaningful life and Aristotle's virtue ethics contrast with the economic approach. While this might appear a utopian endeavour, it is no more, or less, so than the economic model that promotes sustained growth on a finite planet with finite resources and limited source and sink functions, or pretending all can benefit from a system based upon exploitation and cost shifting, or pretending there are miracle technologies that will solve all social, ecological and economic problems.

The ethics of compensation

A key assumption in mainstream economics is that everything can be made commensurate. This can take different forms. In the capital approach favoured by many statistical agencies commensurability means reducing everything down to forms of capital (e.g. natural, social, human) which can be traded-off one for the other. In the cost–benefit literature commensurability means that all impacts can be equated to all investment expenditures, which enables financial returns to be traded-off with a variety of losses from life to leisure. In the literature connecting growth to climate change, commensurability means increasing consumption can be used to compensate for the creation of harm.

The issue becomes especially apparent when looking at climate change impacts. For example, the small island states can expect to be submerged due to sea level rise. Under the mainstream economic approach this will involve estimating such things as the value of habitat for humans and non-humans, the loss of cultures, extinction of some fauna and flora, and the likely death of a significant number of people. The changes do not fit the industrial manufactured commodity framing, in which economics has developed its conceptualisation of the world of goods and services, where all things can be equated. Coral bleaching, for instance, threatens the existence of the Great Barrier Reef, the Earth's largest single structural compound of living organisms, and this is likely to occur at even low increases in temperatures (Stocker *et al.* 2013), which means it is not some far distant event. The attempts to value such changes in terms of hypothetical market preferences lack all theoretical foundation.

Even mainstream economists such as Stern (2014a) recognise there are problems here for mainstream economic analysis. His concern is for scale and the non-marginal character of the changes disturbing the theoretical validity of the economic approach embedded in integrated assessment models and welfare economics. That is, loss of major ecosystems is not a marginal change justifying economists in their assumptions of *ceteris paribus* and constant marginal utility of money as the measuring rod of all things. Yet, this has not prevented Stern from being fully prepared to claim rising future consumption can compensate for everything, and this (as mentioned earlier) is an underlying aspect of the justifications for his and others use of discounting (Baer and Spash 2008; Spash 2002a, 2007b). Nor did this, or any other of the long standing critiques in the literature, prevent global cost–benefit analysis from being central to the analysis and policy claims of the Stern Review.

Indeed, the Stern Review discusses picking a stabilisation target that is defended on grounds of welfare economics and a comparison of marginal costs and benefits. More specifically Stern (2006: 295) states:

> Our work with the PAGE model suggests that, allowing for uncertainty, if the world stabilises at 550 ppm CO_2e, climate change impacts could have an effect equivalent to reducing consumption today and forever by about 1.1 per cent. As Chapter 6 showed, this compares with around 11 per cent in the corresponding "business as usual" case – ten times as high. With stabilisation at 450 ppm CO2e, the percentage loss would be reduced to 0.6 per cent, so choosing the tougher goal "buys" about 0.5 per cent of consumption now and forever. Choosing 550 ppm instead of 650 ppm CO2e "buys" about 0.6 per cent.

There is no account of the involuntary imposition of physical harm and threat of harm to people spread across countries and generations. Framing the policy question as a trade-off between fewer commodities and greater risk of harm to the innocent is an ethical decision. The structure imposed by standard economic analysis makes inevitable the reduction of lost lives to their equivalent in lost consumption, a move that is in many contexts and to many people morally indefensible, and that is indeterminate even if it is accepted as necessary. In the end, the numbers produced by the Stern Review are only meaningful if one accepts that the prospective human deaths (plus extinction of species and other losses) due to human-induced climate change can be defensibly converted into equivalent amounts of consumption today (Baer and Spash 2008).

As noted by Spash (2007a), Stern makes much of the ethical basis for decisions on climate change being important, but there is no breadth or depth in argument or literature. Instead various moral theories are stated to collapse into concern for three objects of desire: health, environment and income/consumption (Stern 2006: 145). These objects are assumed commensurable (Stern 2006: 30–1). So, more consumption makes everything better, assuaging ethical concerns. For example, the displacement of people in developing countries is priced at three times per capita income (Stern 2006: 134). This means there is a price that can be paid and enough per capita income is a solution. The whole point of this approach is to place climate economics within a growth economy framing.

The rebalancing exercise that is implied concerns maintaining standards of living. A typical intergenerational statement along these lines is that "...future generations should have a right to a standard of living no lower than the current one" (Stern 2006: 42). The dubious ethics of the Paretian criteria and aggregating over generations is rarely recognised, i.e. being consistent with making the future rich richer while harming the future poor. Yet there is another issue that concerns a category mistake. That is, the approach conflates the use of resources for creating standards of living with compensation for harming innocent people, and these are not moral equivalents (Spash 2002a). Concerns that are variously termed opportunity maintenance, meeting needs, achieving capabilities, sustaining welfare and so on, are what has been termed basic distributional transfers as opposed to compensatory transfers (Spash 1993, 1994a).

Basic transfers are concerned with distributional justice. There is no particular reason to limit compensation for damages to calculations about distributional transfers of this or that resource. In contrast, compensation can be defined as making amends for loss or injury and implicitly involves an asymmetry of loss and gain. Environmental damages under the enhanced greenhouse effect entail an asymmetric distribution of loss and gain over space and time. Compensation is the attempt to counterbalance negative consequences by creating positive welfare in the same proportion (e.g. as measured by a common metric such as utility). This requires the use of transfer mechanisms, but all transfers need not be compensatory. The reference point for compensation is the level of damages caused to the victim (e.g. an individual, community). The reference point for basic transfers is the welfare level, difference in welfare or opportunity set of one group compared to another (see discussion in the context of intergenerational economics and ethics by Spash 2002a: 226–31). In simplified summary, generalised economic growth (even if it fulfils all its promises of utility and happiness creation) does not equate to discharging liability for creating harm to the innocent. Or to put the issue another way, equity under economic logic – commensurability and merging compensatory with basic transfers – can be achieved by evenly spreading social and environmental damages so all humanity suffers equally. The arrogance of economists is that they talk as if they could actually make such calculations about the future and, even more arrogantly, do so optimally.

Risk and uncertainty

Uncertainty is all pervasive in climate science, and the idea that it could be eradicated or limited through more research is a Cartesian dream applicable in a non-existent mechanical universe. Uncertainty will persist due to irreducible ignorance, social indeterminacy, non-linearity, irreversibility, surprise events, complexity and emergent properties. Human understanding is always and everywhere fallible. The problem is not one of establishing Humean cause–effect relationships, but rather of understanding the limits to human knowledge. Hence, the ramifications of a changing climate can only be outlined to leave us with "a rough sketch of many possible events rather than a detailed picture of the type and timing of exact impacts" (Spash 2002a: 90). The causal mechanisms that contribute to creating future climate are in competition and in themselves hard to discern in the open system reality within which humans operate and GHGs impact.

The closed system thinking of the scientific experiment is then often inapplicable and at best highly constrained in providing knowledge. For example, will the ice sheets melt, when and how fast? Even after they have melted, why they did so will remain uncertain because humans are always fallible. The pretence of science-policy that certainty can be provided, or, even more commonly, that risks can be specified in a deterministic sense, leads policy astray. The result has been to justify delaying action and funding more research, even though this itself is a dubious ethical stance. In fact, the rise of the precautionary principle was originally aimed against just such an approach.

Nevertheless, in the prevalent economic literature climate change is typically described as "a problem of risk management on an immense scale" (Stern 2014a: 398). This conveys the impression that the consequences of severe changes in atmospheric composition can be managed through managerial excellence, and sophisticated and sound risk management. The probabilistic and managerial approach to uncertainty has led to the creation by economists of numbers that appear precise, but are arbitrary and misleading for policy (Funtowicz and Ravetz 1994; Pindyck 2013: 860). The case against the Stern Review is a good example with its research claiming predictability using risk analysis to recommend a future 2°C to 3°C policy as the lowest option, based on economic efficiency, with higher temperatures justifiable (Spash 2007a). There was a later volte-face by Stern (Stewart and Elliott 2013), but this has not damaged his credibility nor his enthusiasm in continuing to push the same consequentialism and risk management under the more recently adopted 2°C target.

The ethical position of the consequentialist logic being employed is that outcomes must be made determinate. That is why this literature starts by identifying strong uncertainty, that relates to social indeterminacy and partial ignorance preventing knowledge of probabilities and consequences (Spash 2002b), but must then convert it into weak uncertainty, that relates to knowable outcomes and probabilities (Spash 2002c). Once again economics makes a major categorical blunder. Despite sometimes citing those, such as Keynes and Knight, who made the ontological distinction between strong and weak uncertainty, the climate economist goes on to contradict their writings with the imposition of risk management.

Conclusions

Work on human-induced climate change in economics tends to conceal more than it reveals and especially with regard to the underlying (moral, political and scientific) philosophy that it supports. The belief in the relevance of simplistic cause–effect relationships helps build an analytical approach that claims to be separated from ethics, because the facts can be observed (e.g. discount rates). The analysis frames the discussion as consequentialist and preference utilitarian with a philosophy of science that is in part an appeal to naïve empiricism. Yet, the role of deductive models remains in higher esteem with the commitment to orthodox theory coming prior to factual observation. Thus, for example, a world of economic growth must exist because that is in the model and the evidence for negative discounting must be ignored.

A prominent aspect of climate economics has been the focus on future generations. Intergenerational ethics is reduced to efficiency analysis where the systemic shifting of costs on to unborn generations is ethically unproblematic given some judicious assumptions that favour the status quo (e.g. Pareto efficiency, fixed time horizons, sustained consumption growth). Thus the red herring debates over the discount rate, and its high profile contestation in expert language and mathematics, merely serve to cloak ethical judgement in the guise of technicality and scientific objectivity. This also conceals the role of this expert discourse in the promotion of a capital accumulating, materially based, hedonistic growth economy.

As climate change not only extends over time, but also across space, intragenerational ethical considerations are central, although often sidelined by economists. A major ethical question is the attribution of responsibility and the implications for the mitigation measures deemed necessary and by whom action is required. The integration of historical responsibility is controversial, because today's wealthiest nations have built their wealth on fossil fuels and have already used more than their fair share of the total emissions possible without human-induced climate change. They have erected a military-industrial complex that maintains resource supplies and is itself dependent upon the fossil fuel economy. This creates ethical conflict and fundamentally relates to questions of power in the global economic order. The consequences of climate change create further ethical dilemmas because the distribution of impacts will be highly variable across space, and different nations have widely diverging abilities to respond to such changes, i.e. adaptation capabilities. Public policy in this area is highly problematic and involves ethical conflicts that cannot be dealt with by mainstream economic analysis, not least because it has a theory that has been deliberately divorced from considerations of power, politics and social structure as well as the biophysical reality upon which the economy depends. Human-induced climate change reveals all the inadequacies of mainstream economics and its inability to offer any meaningful insight into the complex of social, ecological and economic systems. At a time when major systemic change is on the agenda, the theoretical approach of orthodox economics is unable to grasp anything outside small deviations in the current system. Amongst other things, the economists reliance on marginal analysis is utterly useless and irrelevant for addressing global climate change.

Most economists ignore how humanity is embedded in biophysical reality and rely upon models that propagate the myth that economies can operate independently of both environmental and social systems. Climate change would seem to be a wake-up call in that regard. However, the drive for maintaining a growth economy remains unabated and a sustainable new era of growth is now being advocated as an ethically sound development model and the best response to climate change. The presumption is that economic growth must continue and cannot be questioned – a position supporting discounting. However, this fails to consider the ethical implications of imposing a model of hedonistic material affluence as the only goal for humanity and embedding this in a model of society as "freedom" to choose products in a market.

The ethics of economics on climate change must then be understood in the context of the economic commitment to growth. Climate economics builds on the assumption of a commensurable world, where environmental, social and economic meanings can be translated into a unidimensional framing in terms of capital and rates of return. Thus, economic models must produce numbers, and economic analysts arguments, that reduce the world to productivity and consumption. In this way the prospect of deliberately killing future humans and destroying ecosystems irreversibly can be "rationally" converted and made equivalent with the loss of goods and services from not doing so. Even better this can be discussed in terms of being optimal and the process conducted as an objective technical exercise. The underlying ideological and ethical commitment is to increasing material and energy consumption as the best thing for humanity. Justifying this in the context of climate change means arguing that growth will provide the answer to both poverty and environmental degradation. Fundamental ethical questions over burden sharing can then be sidelined. Meanwhile, the persistence of economics with some fundamental category mistakes – concerning both uncertainty and compensation – allows precaution to be ignored in favour of risk management and harm of the innocent to be justified by the promise of an increasing availability of consumer goods.

Note

1 The marginal utility of income is the additional gain in welfare (or utility) from having a small addition to income. The declining rate means the more income an individual has the lower the welfare gain (utility) from each additional unit of income. Economists also substitute consumption for income to give a declining marginal utility of consumption.

Bibliography

d'Arge, R. C. and Spash, C. L. (1991), "Economic strategies for mitigating the impacts of climate change on future generations", in R. Costanza (ed.), *Ecological Economics: The Science and Management of Sustainability*, New York: Columbia University Press, pp. 367–83.

d'Arge, R. C., Schulze, W. D. and Brookshire, D. S. (1982), "Carbon dioxide and intergenerational choice", *American Economic Association Papers and Proceedings*, vol. 2: 251–6.

Arrow, K. J., Cline, W. R., Mäler, K.-G., Munasinghe, M., Squitieri, R. and Stiglitz, J. E. (1996), "Intertemporal equity, discounting, and economic efficiency", in J. P. Bruce, L. Hoesung, and E. F. Haites (eds), *Economic and Social Dimensions of Climate Change*, Cambridge: Cambridge University Press, pp. 125–44.

Baer, P. and Spash, C. L. (2008), "Is cost–benefit analysis of climate change defensible: a critique of the *Stern Report*", in Â. Guimarães Pereira and S. Funtowicz (eds), *Science for Policy*, Oxford: Oxford University Press, pp. 167–92.

Brand, U. and Wissen, M. (2013), "Crisis and continuity of capitalist society-nature relationships: the imperial mode of living and the limits to environmental governance", *Review of International Political Economy*, vol. 20: 687–711.

Chang, H.-J. (2002), "Breaking the mould: an institutionalist political economy alternative to the neo-liberal theory of the market and the state", *Cambridge Journal of Economics*, vol. 26: 539–59.

Cline, W. R. (1992), *The Economics of Global Warming*. Harlow: Longman.

Fellner, W. and Spash, C. L. (2015), "The role of consumer sovereignty in sustaining the market economy", in L. A. Reisch, and J. Thøgersen (eds), *Handbook of Research on Sustainable Consumption*, Cheltenham: Edward Elgar, pp. 394–409.

Funtowicz, S. O. and Ravetz, J. R. (1994), "The worth of a songbird: ecological economics as a post-normal science", *Ecological Economics*, vol. 10: 197–207.

GCEC (2014), *Better Growth Better Climate: The New Climate Economy Report – The Synthesis Report*, Washington, DC: The Global Commission on the Economy and Climate.

Georgescu-Roegen, N. (1971), *The Entropy Law and the Economic Process*, Cambridge, MA: Harvard University Press.

Georgescu-Roegen, N. (2009 [1975]) "Energy and economic myths", in C. L. Spash (ed.), *Ecological Economics: Critical Concepts in the Environment*, 4 vols, Abingdon: Routledge, pp. 328–73.

Hoare, Q. and Smith, G. N. (eds) (1971), *Selections from the Prison Notebooks of Antonio Gramsci*, New York: International Publishers.

IPCC (2013), "Summary for policymakers", in IPCC, *Climate Change 2013: The Physical Science Basis. Contribution of Working Group I to the Fifth Assessment Report of the Intergovernmental Panel on Climate Change*, Cambridge: Cambridge University Press.

Jakob, M. and Edenhofer, O. (2014), "Green growth, degrowth, and the commons", *Oxford Review of Economic Policy*, vol. 30: 447–68.

Kapp, K. W. (1978), *The Social Costs of Business Enterprise*, Nottingham: Spokesman.

Kolstad, C., Urama, K., Broome, J., Bruvoll, A., Cariño Olvera, M., Fullerton, D., Gollier, C., Hanemann, W. M., Hassan, R., Jotzo, F., Khan, M. R., Meyer, L., and Mundaca, L. (2014), "Social, economic and ethical concepts and methods", in IPCC, *Climate Change 2014 Mitigation of Climate Change: Working Group III Contribution to the Fifth Assessment Report of the Intergovernmental Panel on Climate Change*, Cambridge: Cambridge University Press.

McGlade, C. and Ekins, P. (2015), "The geographical distribution of fossil fuels unused when limiting global warming to 2°C", *Nature*, vol. 517: 187–90.

Martinez-Alier, J. (1990), *Ecological Economics: Energy, Environment and Society*, Basil Blackwell, Oxford, England.

Nordhaus, W. D. (1977), "Economic growth and climate: the carbon dioxide problem", *American Economic Review*, vol. 67: 341–46.

Nordhaus, W. D. (2007), *The Challenge of Global Warming: Economic Models and Environmental Policy*, New Haven: Yale University Press.

OECD (2011), *Divided We Stand: Why Inequality Keeps Rising*, Paris: OECD Publishing.

Olivier, J. G. J., Janssens-Maenhout, G., Muntean, M., and Peters, J. A. H. W. (2015), "Trends in global CO_2 emissions: 2015 report", PBL Netherlands Environmental Assessment Agency; European Commission, Joint Research Centre (JRC); Institute for Environment and Sustainability (IES), Hague.

O'Neill, J. F. (1993), *Ecology, Policy and Politics: Human Well-Being and the Natural World*, London: Routledge.

Pindyck, R. S. (2013), "Climate change policy: what do the models tell us?", *Journal of Economic Literature*, vol. 51: 860–72.

Price, C. (1993), *Time, Discounting and Value*. Oxford: Basil Blackwell.

Raupach, M. R., Davis, S. J., Peters, G. P., Andrew, R. M., Canadell, J. G., Ciais, P., Friedlingstein, P., Jotzo, F., van Vuuren, D. P., and Le Quere, C. (2014), "Sharing a quota on cumulative carbon emissions", *Nature Climate Change*, vol. 4: 873–9.

Spash, C. L. (1993), "Economics, ethics, and long-term environmental damages", *Environmental Ethics*, vol. 15: 117–32.

Spash, C. L. (1994a), "Double CO_2 and beyond: benefits, costs and compensation", *Ecological Economics*, vol. 10: 27–36.

Spash, C. L. (1994b), "Trying to find the right approach to greenhouse economics: some reflections upon the role of cost–benefit analysis", *Analyse & Kritik: Zeitschrift fur Sozialwissenschafen*, vol. 16: 186–99.

Spash, C. L. (1996), "Human-induced climate change: the limits of models", *Environmental Politics*, vol. 5: 376–80.

Spash, C. L. (2002a), *Greenhouse Economics: Value and Ethics*, London: Routledge.

Spash, C. L. (2002b), "Strong uncertainty: ignorance and indeterminacy", in C. L. Spash (ed.), *Greenhouse Economics: Value and Ethics*, London: Routledge, pp. 120–52.

Spash, C. L. (2002c), "Weak uncertainty: risk and imperfect information", *Greenhouse Economics: Value and Ethics*, London: Routledge, pp. 97–119.

Spash, C. L. (2006), "The *Stern Report*: the continuing fallacy of global cost–benefit analysis", *European Society for Ecological Economics Newsletter*, November.

Spash, C. L. (2007a), "The economics of climate change impacts à la Stern: novel and nuanced or rhetorically restricted?", *Ecological Economics*, vol. 63: 706–13.

Spash, C. L. (2007b), "The economics of climate change: the *Stern Review*", *Environmental Values*, vol. 16: 532–5.

Spash, C. L. (2007c), "Fallacies of economic growth in addressing environmental losses: human induced climatic change", *Newsletter of the Australia New Zealand Society for Ecological Economics (ANZSEE)*, May: 2–4.

Spash, C. L. (2007d), "Problems in economic assessments of climate change with attention to the USA", in J. Erickson, and J. Gowdy, (eds), *Frontiers in Environmental Valuation and Policy*, Cheltenham and Northampton, MA: Edward Elgar Publishing Ltd.

Spash, C. L. (2007e), "Understanding climate change: need for new economic thought", *Economic and Political Weekly*, February: 483–90.

Spash, C. L. (2008), "The economics of avoiding action on climate change", *Adbusters*, vol. 16.

Spash, C. L. (2010), "The brave new world of carbon trading", *New Political Economy*, vol. 15: 169–95.

Spash, C. L. (2011), "Carbon trading: a critique", in J. S. Dryzek, R. B. Norgaard, and D. Schlosberg (eds), *The Oxford Handboook of Climate Change and Society*, Oxford: Oxford University Press, pp. 550–60.

Spash, C. L. (2014), "Better growth, helping the Paris cop-out? Fallacies and omissions of the new climate economy report", *Institute for Environment and Regional Development*, Vienna.

Spash, C. L. (2015), "Tackling climate change, breaking the frame of modernity", *Environmental Values*, vol. 24: 437–44.

Spash, C. L. (2016), "The Paris agreement to ignore reality", *Institute for Multilevel Governance and Development*, Vienna.

Spash, C. L. and d'Arge, R. C. (1989), "The greenhouse effect and intergenerational transfers", *Energy Policy*, April: 88–95.

Spash, C. L. and Clayton, A. M. H. (1997), "The maintenance of natural capital: motivations and methods", in A. Light and J. M. Smith (eds), *Space, Place and Environmental Ethics*, Lanham: Rowman & Littlefield Publishers, Inc., pp. 143–73.

Stern, N. H. (2006), *Stern Review on the Economics of Climate Change*, London: Government Economic Service.

Stern, N. H. (2014a), "Ethics, equity and the economics of climate change, paper 1: science and philosophy", *Economics and Philosophy*, vol. 30: 397–444.

Stern, N. H. (2014b), *Theories and Perspectives on Growth and Change: Guidance from the Economics Advisory Panel for the Report of the Commission*, Washington, DC: The Global Commission on the Economy and Climate, .

Stewart, H. and Elliott, L. (2013), "Nicholas Stern: 'I got it wrong on climate change: it's far, far worse'", *Guardian*, 26 January.

Stocker, T. F., Qin, D., Plattner, G.-K., Tignor, M., Allen, S. K., Boschung, J., Nauels, A., Xia, Y., Bex, V., and Midgley, M. (eds) (2013), "Climate change 2013: the physical science basis", in IPCC, *Contribution of Working Group I to the Fifth Assessment Report of the Intergovernmental Panel on Climate Change*, Cambridge: Cambridge University Press.

Watson, R. T., Zinyowera, M. C., Moss, R. H., and Dokken, D. J. (eds) (1997), "The regional impacts of climate change: an assessment of vulnerability", in IPCC, *Summary for Policymakers*, Geneva: IPCC.

World Bank (2016), CO_2 *Emissions (Metric Tons Per Capita)*, Washington, DC: World Bank.

11 A Lockean approach to greenhouse gas emission rights

Hans-Peter Weikard[1]

Introduction

Carbon dioxide (CO_2) was discovered by the Scottish chemist Joseph Black in 1754. A few years later, in 1769, James Watt introduced an improved version of the steam engine and coal became the primary source of energy for a wide range of industrial processes and for transport. At that time carbon dioxide was not considered a pollutant. It does not smell and it is not toxic. Today it is an established fact that CO_2 is the most important greenhouse gas with the potential to change the global climatic system. As a response the international community established the United Nations Framework Convention on Climate Change (UNFCCC) in 1992. With the ratification of the Kyoto Protocol in February 2005 international policies have been adopted aiming at a reduction of greenhouse gas emissions. A potentially efficient tool to implement reductions of greenhouse gases are tradable emission permits. In 2005 the European Union launched a system of tradable emission permits and thereby created new property rights. This system of property rights, however, does not cover emissions from all sectors of the economy and, more importantly, it is confined to European countries. The fundamental problem of implementing emission restrictions with limited global emission rights remains unresolved. Of the many reasons why a global agreement has proven to be difficult to obtain, one seems to be the most prominent: the unsettled question of who should receive the CO_2 emission permits.[2] While in practical political terms this may be a bargaining problem, it is certainly a problem of justice.

The emergence of property rights, and particularly the introduction of CO_2 emission permits, raises three different questions:

- The process of the emergence of property rights as a reaction to increasing scarcity. Increasing scarcity is a driver of institutional reform, including the regulation of access to resources (see e.g. Libecap 1989)
- The efficiency of a private property rights regime as compared to joint management of common pool resources is a debated issue; cf. e.g. Demsetz (1967) and Ostrom (1990) and Stevenson (1991); and
- The distributional aspects of an initial allocation of property rights.

This chapter is devoted almost entirely to the third question and will not discuss international political processes leading to institutions that would be better suited to address climate change. Also, for the purpose of this chapter, we will only consider private (property) rights to emit greenhouse gases and neglect the option of collective management.[3] The quest of this chapter is to identify guiding principles on which a distribution of property rights can be based.

While many facets of climate justice have been discussed in the recent literature (e.g. Gosseries 2001, 2004; Meyer and Roser 2010; Caney 2012) the Lockean perspective has remained underdeveloped. This is particularly striking because the Lockean theory of property rights offers a theory of just appropriation. It sets out in a state of nature where no private property rights are defined and then spells out conditions for justified private appropriation. Thus it seems to have an immediate bearing for the question how, if we introduce emission rights, these rights should be distributed within and between generations. Introduction of new property rights, rights to emit greenhouse gases, is an ideal case to explore the consequences of a Lockean theory of appropriation. Where, if not here, should a Lockean theory find an application, where it may help us judge the legitimacy of a property rights distribution? This chapter is not the first, however, that takes steps to develop a Lockean perspective on climate justice. Bovens (2011) discusses parallels and differences between the appropriation of land rights, Locke's paradigm case of private appropriation, and of carbon emission rights. In essence he defends the applicability of a Lockean theory of appropriation. Schüssler (2011) argues from a Lockean perspective that (mis)appropriation of emission rights in the early industrialisation does not imply an obligation to compensate for climate damages. In an earlier paper I argued that Locke's proviso for just appropriation can be interpreted in two ways: as an efficiency condition or as (resource) egalitarianism (Weikard 2004). Here we extend this discussion to shed light on the roles of time and knowledge for just appropriation.

This chapter contributes to the literature that develops a Lockean perspective on intergenerational justice and, in particular climate justice. We will first revisit the Lockean theory of property rights in the context of greenhouse gas emissions. Our starting point is the perspective of John Locke's (1967 [1690]) normative theory of property rights and Robert Nozick's (1974) development thereof. As admitted by Nozick this theory is in many ways incomplete and open to interpretation; cf. Waldron (1988). Steiner and Vallentyne (2009) distinguish what has been called *right-libertarian* and *left-libertarian* interpretations. In brief, according to the latter, legitimate appropriation requires the consent of all agents, while this is not required according to the former. Consequently right-libertarians have little concerns with the issue of intergenerational justice and I will not explore their position further.

In this chapter, the attempt to spell out a Lockean approach for greenhouse gas emission rights will serve a double function:

- it provides a line of argument that may support the process of climate policymaking; but

- it simultaneously provides interpretations and clarifications of the Lockean perspective on the justification of private property rights.

As will become clear below, an often overlooked feature of the Lockean perspective is that legitimate appropriation of resources, i.e. of private property rights, must make reference not only to natural rights but also to efficiency. Hence, we identify welfaristic traits in the Lockean approach. This suggests that a system of greenhouse gas emission rights must prove its efficiency in order to be legitimate.

The following section provides the starting point: my account of a Lockean theory of property rights. In section 3 I explore a Lockean justification of greenhouse gas emissions. While section 3 deals with the justification of momentary emissions, section 4 turns to the justification of enduring emission rights, i.e. rights produce a flow of future emissions. Section 5 closes with a brief summary of the argument.

The Lockean theory of property rights in a nutshell[4]

Locke's (1690) theory of individual rights is comprehensive and includes basic individual rights such as the right to life, generally referred to as *self-ownership*. Here we are concerned with a narrower set of rights, the rights of access to resources, simply referred to as property rights. Following Nozick (1974: 150ff.), a normative theory of property rights, called "entitlement theory", consists of three parts: (i) a theory of just appropriation, (ii) a theory of just transfers, and a (iii) theory of rectification.

(i) Appropriation

According to Nozick (1974) the idea of just appropriation can be developed along the lines of Locke's discussion of property (1690: chapter V). The first important thing to notice is that, according to Locke, private appropriation is *not* about appropriation of unowned goods. Appropriation is taking from the commons. Generally, in Locke's state of nature resources are the common property of mankind (§ 26). Second, private appropriation of resources, because it is taking from the commons, needs the consent of all others – in principle at least. Clearly, and this is important to notice, there is a contractarian element in Locke's theory. Since it is costly, time consuming and practically impossible to obtain the consent of all others before something is taken from the commons, Locke (§ 28) argues that the consent can be presupposed if two provisos hold:

> *First proviso:* a common good can be privately appropriated provided that nothing is spoiled.
>
> (§ 31)

> *Second proviso:* a common good can be privately appropriated provided that enough and as good is left for others.
>
> (§ 27, § 33)

Locke replaces an explicit consent of all others to the private appropriation of goods from the commons with the two provisos to account for transaction costs. Resources would be wasted to obtain consent and opportunities of use would be forgone while waiting for the consent. The First proviso is an efficiency condition. Who appropriates a resource must make the best of it. The Second proviso, in the literature often just dubbed "the Lockean proviso", poses a problem. On a literal interpretation "enough and as good left in common for others" (§ 27, and similarly § 33) implies a violation of the proviso whenever a resource is scarce. Locke develops his arguments from the presumption that there is no essential scarcity (§ 31, § 36). Resources are plenty and in combination with labour all needs can be satisfied. Now, if there is enough of equal quality for all, then a resource is not scarce and a justification of appropriation is, strictly speaking, not needed or at least not very interesting. Thus, if we were to assume satiable agents who do not want to acquire more than enough, there is no need to study the problem of the allocation of resources. A Lockean theory of appropriation is relevant where agents are not satiable. But then there is never enough. For our specific problem of the limited capacity of the atmosphere to absorb carbon and a human population whose welfare depends on cheap (fossil) energy we have to move to alternative interpretations of "enough and as good".

Nozick (1974: 174ff.) adopts a different interpretation of the Second proviso. According to Nozick the proviso is meant to ensure that a private appropriation of resources does not make others worse off. This is in line with Locke's argument that labour makes resources (land) more productive than in the state of nature (§ 36). The use of resources improves productive capacity and makes goods more readily available. This is to the advantage of all, including those who have not appropriated a similar share of resources. This Lockean argument has become prominent in libertarian thought and has been brought forward forcefully and more generally by von Mises (1993: 27), who argues that the productivity of a private property rights regime contributes to the benefit of all, even to the benefit of the poor who do not own any property. Hence we have the following version of the proviso:

> *Nozick's proviso:* a common good can be privately appropriated provided that, by putting it to productive use, no one's situation is worsened – compared to the situation where the good remains in the commons.
>
> (Nozick 1974: 176)

It is worth noting here that "appropriation" does not necessarily refer to full ownership. The formulation of Nozick's proviso is compatible with weaker forms of rights such as use rights (cf. Wolf 1995, Steiner and Vallentyne 2009).

A third interpretation of "enough and as good is left for others" has a strong egalitarian trait. Locke's discussion of private appropriation is largely built around the paradigm of appropriating land for agricultural use. For Locke "enough" is limited by the labour that the appropriator has available to make the resource productive (§ 31). At the time when Locke wrote, European settlers moving to North America found plenty of land. However, under conditions of scarcity, there will not be "enough" of a resource. What remains of the Second proviso is the "as good" which is naturally interpreted as egalitarian sharing of either the resource or the opportunities for welfare (Dworkin 1981, Arneson 1989, cf. Roemer 1998). This version of the proviso can be formulated as follows (cf. also Steiner and Vallentyne 2009: 60):

> *Resource egalitarian proviso:* a common good can be privately appropriated if an equally large share remains for everyone else. Hence, resources should be distributed equally across individuals.

(ii) Transfers

The second important element of an entitlement theory is justice in transfers (Nozick 1974). The main idea here is, again, a contractarian idea. The holder of a property right may with consent of others dispose of the property, exchange it for other property (trade), or give it away to others as a gift. The contractarian nature of justice in transfers implies the permissibility of constraints on disposal, market transactions and gift giving. For example, disposal of pollutants is not permitted, trade that undermines competition might be banned and bequests might be taxed; cf. Nozick (1974: 160ff.), Cohen (1995: 38ff.) and Weikard (1998: 369).

(iii) Rectification

In cases where an appropriation or a transfer was not justified, property rights must be rectified. Rectification would aim at reconstructing the situation that would have occurred in the absence of the unjust appropriation; Nozick (1974: 152). A stolen good, should be returned. If a good cannot be returned, then fair compensation is required. Given fair compensation the legitimate owner's position would not be worse than under legitimate ownership (Sher 1992). The challenge of rectification lies in the construction of an appropriate counterfactual (Lawford-Smith 2014).

Justifying greenhouse gas emissions

This section explores the implications of the Lockean theory of property rights for justification of greenhouse gas emissions.

To set the scene, let us take it for granted that greenhouse gases in the atmosphere cause global warming. Some limited global warming may even be considered a good thing such that nobody is harmed. We abstract from the many uncertainties due to our limited understanding of the climate system and the lack of reliable impact assessments and valuations. Let us assume that a threshold carbon concentration in the atmosphere has been identified above which the associated global warming causes harm to current and future people – more precisely, it causes harm that remains uncompensated by the benefits of fossil fuel use and land use change which cause the emissions. CO_2 is a stock pollutant in the atmosphere. It accumulates if emissions exceed decay. The atmospheric (and the oceans') absorption capacity for carbon is a scarce resource, although renewable. Greenhouse gas emissions exploit this resource.

We have to address two issues:

- Past emissions are appropriations from the common good "absorption capacity". To what extent can these be justified?
- If some threshold concentration must not be exceeded, current emission levels cannot be sustained, but rather must be cut considerably and rapidly. Here we arrive at the question, who has to cut emissions and by how much?

The Resource Egalitarian Proviso

The Resource Egalitarian Proviso is simple to apply if the resource is well-defined and the number of agents claiming a right is finite. Our problem is more complicated and we face two problems. We must consider an infinite sequence of generations, and the absorption capacity of the earth is not a well-defined concept. To address the latter issue first, assume that we can define a standard, i.e. a set of services that the atmosphere should provide but cannot provide if a threshold level of greenhouse gas concentrations is exceeded. We can always release more greenhouse gases, but only at higher costs associated with global warming. The optimal standard would be set such that benefits of the release of additional greenhouse gases just compensate for the associated damages. Since assessments of costs and benefits are notoriously difficult, one may resort to a politically negotiated standard. The target of limiting global warming to 2°K above preindustrial levels (negotiated in the Copenhagen Accords, 2009) is such a standard. We also assume that the remaining accumulated emissions compatible with this target can be calculated and we refer to this amount as the carbon budget.[5] If the carbon budget is exhausted, further emissions that exceed decay will be unjustified. The resource egalitarian argument can now be developed backwards. At the time when the threshold concentration is reached, all emission rights are limited by the amount of decay such that the atmospheric carbon concentration remain constant. At this future stage the task is allocating a flow, not a stock. The resource egalitarian distribution of emission rights would then simply equalise per capita emissions. There remains a problem, however. With a growing population and constant global emissions, per capita emissions must fall over time. With infinitely many generations and a growing population, resource egalitarianism must be violated (Weikard 2004). But, being a little pragmatic, we might dismiss this argument. Population growth rates are falling and when the global population stabilises, there is no conceptual problem to apply resource egalitarianism.

Going one step backward, turning to the stock, the distribution of the carbon budget is more difficult. If we are below the threshold, some emissions beyond decay can be justified. Then we need to distribute a finite stock equally among infinitely many generations. This is impossible. A pragmatic way out may be to refer to technological progress that increases the availability of alternatives to fossil fuels and reduces the need for carbon emissions. Such an argument, however, highlights the limits of resource egalitarianism and suggests replacing it by a welfaristic criterion. It is not the resource that is important, but what it can do for us (Arneson 1989, Beckerman and Pasek 1995, Steiner and Vallentyne 2009: 61). A resource that is more productive in the future, in the sense that the same service can be produced from less of the resource, can be distributed unequally. More specifically, if productivity is growing at a constant rate, resource use may decline at that rate and can be stretched out into an infinite future without reducing the service that the resource delivers (Solow 1974).

So far we have considered rights for future emissions without considering past emissions. Past per capita greenhouse gas emissions have been very unequally distributed between industrialised and developing countries. Unequal resource appropriation violates the resource egalitarian proviso. Pointing to the fact that CO_2 was not known to be a pollutant takes away moral blame but not responsibility. Resource egalitarianism, then, needs to provide principles for rectification, including answers to difficult questions of historical and collective responsibility. Who, if anyone, bears the responsibility for the emissions of the European steel industry of the 1930s? Resource egalitarianism might seek to identify each contemporary individual's responsibility. But such attempts can be regarded as utterly impractical, at the least. To ease the task, we might consider nation states (represented by their governments) as collective agents. Suppose it is true that industrialised countries have benefited from past emissions. Meyer and Roser (2010) and Baatz (2013) argue that being a beneficiary of a change may imply an obligation to compensate those who suffer from the same change, even if the beneficiary is neither causally nor morally responsible for the change. This argument shifts the focus away from responsibility for historical emissions and towards fair redistribution from the lucky beneficiaries of industrialisation to the unlucky victims of climate change. These arguments support compensation claims, but it is not obvious whether and how compensation claims should affect the distribution of future emission rights. Also we have assumed a small increase of temperature would not be harmful. Considering the stage where we have not yet passed the threshold, some emission rights can still be assigned. Who, in the light of history, is entitled to receive them?

Here is a simplified version of the resource egalitarian's problem. Consider Dave and Eve who have to survive in the forest for two days. They discover berries on a forest glade. Eve does not want any as she is not sure whether the berries are eatable. Dave finds them tasty and eats half of them leaving the remaining half for the next day. The next day Eve claims the remaining berries because Dave has had his share. Does Dave still have a claim? Assume Dave was justified to believe that Eve did not want the berries. Then he was justified to consume them as he liked. Effectively Eve has waived her claim to berries on the first day. On the second day she can only claim half of the remaining berries, that is one quarter. But what if Dave had taken two-thirds or only one-third on the first day? How does history matter? Here we can employ Baatz's (2013) argument that a beneficiary (of past consumption of berries) is obliged to compensate harm that is associated with the benefit even if the beneficiary is neither causally nor morally responsible for the harm. Tailored to this case, compensation is due until the beneficiary has delivered all her net-benefits or the harm is fully compensated (Baatz 2013: 99). Clearly Dave has benefitted from past consumption. But what harm has been done to Eve? In this case it is simply that Dave's consumption on the first day implies that less is left to be shared on the second day. To establish Eve's claim, we need to consider the counterfactual. If Dave had known that Eve would revoke the waiver of her claim on the second day, the total should be split in three pieces, one piece per person per day – enough and as good. Accordingly Dave should get two-thirds and Eve one-third of the total. Since Dave has benefitted from having more than a third on the first day, he owes compensation to Eve on the second day. This leaves Dave with a share of one-sixth on the second day. In this way historical resource consumption counts but it is acknowledged that past generations bear no moral responsibility.

Along this line of argument, with gross simplifications, one can distinguish two phases of greenhouse gas emissions. The first phase is the time of industrialisation before the greenhouse effect was noticed or taken as an established fact. Being pragmatic we could say that this phase ends in 1990 when the first IPCC Report was published. In the second phase, since 1990, the limited absorption capacity of the atmosphere (i.e. scarcity) is an established fact, but emissions have continued and even increased until today. According to estimates provided by the 5th IPCC Assessment Report (IPCC 2014) about half of the initial carbon budget has been consumed in the first phase and almost entirely by industrialised countries, accounting for one-third of the population. In the second phase (up to today) one-third of the remaining half has been consumed, again, mainly by industrialised countries, but China is rapidly catching up. Using the argument developed above we can say that developing countries do not have a claim to emission rights in the first phase. It was only industrialised countries that used the resource, not noticing that it would become scarce. Developing countries, not having developed coal-fired industries (a taste for berries) essentially waived their claim. Hence, developing countries' claim on the total carbon budget is limited to the second phase and, hence, is $2/3 \times 1/2$, assuming that they represent two-thirds of the population and half of the carbon budget accrues to each phase. Industrialised countries can have a claim of $1/3 \times 1/2$ in both phases. This gives equal claims to the total carbon budget. Industrialised countries have benefitted from previous consumption and have consumed their share already. The resource egalitarian argument, grossly simplified, implies that all remaining emission rights accrue to developing countries and they should be compensated for any additional emission rights taken by industrialised countries.[6] As developed thus far this argument ignores that some countries, some poorer countries in particular, are already suffering from climate change. Recall that we have assumed that emissions compatible with the target of limiting global warming to 2°K could be justified. But clearly, any damages that are caused by emissions will generate a compensation claim.

Nozick's proviso

Nozick's proviso is less strict. The private appropriation of a common resource is justified if no one's situation is worsened. Prior to industrialisation technological development was hampered by energy scarcity. The use of fossil fuels has triggered unprecedented technological development and growth of income, making people better off. But climate change causes damages. These damages are unevenly distributed between world regions and also between rich and poor people who differ in their adaptive capacities and, hence, in their vulnerability. Clearly, according to Nozick's proviso, further appropriations of the atmosphere as a carbon sink cannot be justified if they worsen the situation of some. Let us proceed in steps and first ignore the distributional consequences of carbon emissions and their associated climate damages. Considering, for the moment, only aggregate effects, we first need to ask, as with the resource egalitarian approach, what carbon emissions can be justified. Looking at aggregates, it is a necessary condition for the justification of emissions that benefits from emissions are large enough to compensate for all damages. If the benefits associated with a ton of CO_2 emissions are smaller than the associated damages, then necessarily someone must be worse off, compared to the situation where this ton of emissions had been avoided. Quite obviously then, Nozick's proviso implies that the justified carbon budget follows from the calculus of welfare maximisation, i.e. the amount of (maximally) justified emissions is determined by the marginal benefits and marginal costs of emissions, i.e. the extra costs and benefits that accrue to an extra ton of CO_2 emissions. Note that it is only a necessary condition for a justifiable appropriation that benefits are larger than cost. Whether it is sufficient depends on the distribution of benefits and costs to which we turn later. For simplicity assume, again, that a carbon stock compatible with 2°K global warming has been determined as the justified carbon budget. Then emissions may continue unregulated until that stock is reached. Everyone can take from the commons since no one is made worse off, compared to a situation where the commons remain untouched. There is one remaining issue now. As soon as the carbon budget is exhausted, emissions must be adjusted to the level of decay. Then the atmospheric capacity to store carbon is scarce and needs to be distributed. How can a Lockean theory of just appropriation help? Emissions below and up to the level of decay do not worsen anyone's position and are justified. But if collective (i.e. aggregate) emissions exceed the justified level, who is it who has to cut back? The Lockean who is not prepared to accept the resource egalitarian interpretation of the Second proviso can now refer to the First proviso, the "no waste" condition. The First proviso can be interpreted as an efficiency condition.[7] Its application would give priority to those emissions that provide the largest service per unit of emissions. Assuming that poor people benefit the most from the income generated by emissions, emission rights would be allocated more to developing countries. There is a countervailing force, however. With differences in technology the income generated per unit of emissions is larger in industrialised countries. Clearly an argument based on the "no waste" condition must employ a welfaristic weighing of the benefits of emissions. Moreover, if we consider a well-functioning carbon market, the users of emission rights need not be the beneficiaries. Rights could, for example, be assigned to developing countries who, let us assume, benefit the most from additional income and who would sell those rights to industries and firms that generate the highest value from a unit of emissions.

Thus far we did not address distributional issues associated with damages from emissions. We have simply assumed that no one is worse off through emissions that are covered by the carbon budget. Of course the assumption is *not* that there are no damages from climate change as the carbon budget gets depleted, but rather that benefits exceed damages. Implicitly then we have assumed that those who gain from emissions will compensate those who suffer losses. Compensation becomes an important issue. Only if appropriate compensation schemes are in place, the claim can be made that no one's position is worsened, the prerequisite for just appropriation.

We need to consider distributional concerns among contemporaries and between generations. The former is conceptually simple and could, for example, be addressed by a carbon tax coupled with a damage compensation scheme. Practically, however, it will be difficult to reach an international agreement on carbon taxation and to assess climate damages, since it is impossible to attribute a particular drought, flood or heat wave to climate change. This problem will return as we turn to the intertemporal distribution.

Carbon dioxide is a stock pollutant. Emissions are relevant only because they add to the stock in the atmosphere. The emission of a ton of CO_2 gives an immediate benefit, but the damages will stretch out into the future. Hence, again, we need to assess those damages. By their very nature damages are uncertain. We can neither forecast particular events like "a flood along River Rhine in the summer of 2027", nor assess the associated damages. Damage assessment will have to be probabilistic and can at best be based on a common understanding of "best guesses" about frequencies of certain types of event in different world regions. It remains then to intertemporally compare expected benefits and costs. This problem is not addressed here but it has been discussed extensively elsewhere; see e.g. Broome (1992), Portney and Weyant (1999), Gollier (2001), Stern (2008) and Hormio Chapter 7 this volume (2016).

Sustainable emission rights

Thus far we have mainly focused on the problem of taking from a limited *stock* of resources. In our case this is the problem of adding an extra ton of CO_2 to the atmosphere assuming a limited carbon budget compatible with, say, the 2°K target. Now let us include the *flow* of emissions compatible with maintaining the stock in consideration. In other words, this section considers the absorption capacity of the atmosphere as a renewable resource, which is more appropriate. The example of renewable resources motivates Roark's (2012) distinction between the appropriation of resources and the use of unappropriated resources; cf. also Wolf (1995). Our discussion so far has been dealing with the former; now we turn to the latter. To build intuition let us use an example.

Consider an unappropriated forest and a village with people collecting firewood from the forest. Initially there is enough and as good for everyone. The forest produces sufficient firewood for cooking and heating. As the population and the size of houses grow, more trees are cut. Eventually this reduces the availability of firewood in the future; it makes future people worse off. Use rights then must be restricted. There are two options:

- the forest remains in the commons and use rights are properly managed (Stevenson 1991); or
- individuals might appropriate the forest land as private property.

What conditions should be placed on introducing enduring property rights to forest land? The libertarian can, with reference to Locke, using Nozick's interpretation, point out that private appropriation is justified if no one's situation is worsened. This will be the case if the forest is well-managed leading to a better availability of firewood at lower cost for all households in the village.

Can we make a similar argument when it comes to the appropriation of enduring rights to CO_2 emissions? I think we can. The private appropriation of forest land implies that villagers without forest land are no longer free to collect firewood as they wish. Now, either firewood sold on the market is cheaper than individual collection would be. Then appropriation is justified. Or, if not, appropriation under Nozick's proviso must be accompanied by a compensation for those who lose the right to collect firewood and are worse off because of that. As Roark (2012) points out, there will sometimes be good reasons to leave the resources in the commons. Not all land is privatised: there are sites of cultural value and environmental resources. Even privatised forests are usually open to walkers or birdwatchers. In our example of the forest one possible response to overexploitation is the introduction of private property rights in forest land. The qualification is that the forest owner does indeed manage the forest better. The proviso must be satisfied also with respect to the future. Not only contemporary villagers, but also future users of firewood should not be made worse off by the appropriation. We can thus interpret the intertemporal application of the proviso as a sustainability condition. This applies as well to tradable CO_2 emission rights. Justifiable rights to emissions cannot exceed the carbon budget. Suppose a "grandfathering" scheme is adopted that distributes emission rights according to current emission levels. By the intertemporal proviso it is impossible that current emission levels are turned into enduring rights. At least emission rights must decline to the level of decay to stabilise atmospheric CO_2 concentrations. But what justifies grandfathering in the first place? Have those who are the first to use the atmosphere as a carbon sink established a right to emit? Locke argues that a property right in land can be established by "mixing" labour with land which is thereby removed from the state of nature (§ 27). Recent commentary has generally rejected Locke's argument (e.g. Nozick 1974, Waldron 1988, Steiner 1994) and there does not seem to be a good defence. Land tenure security, an enduring right to land, is often, in line with Locke, defended by associated productivity increases that stem from investments.[8] Can a similar claim be made for enduring emission rights? There are some common features. In the case of land, returns to investments to improve soil productivity can be privately appropriated if land tenure is secure. Secure emission rights can trigger, similarly, investments in cleaner production to improve the productivity of scarce emission rights. A firm improving its carbon efficiency can increase production or sell emission rights.

Still, security of enduring rights and the initial distribution of rights are different matters and mixing one's carbon with the atmosphere does not seem to generate a right to emit. Consider the forest once more. Suppose we have rich and poor villagers. The rich have big houses and collect large amounts of firewood. The poor have small houses and collect little. Does this support larger land claims by the rich when the forestland is privately appropriated? Or the reverse? The resource egalitarian proviso would offer an answer, while Nozick's proviso leaves this question open.

Conclusions

A Lockean programme can help us establish principles on which the distribution of emission rights can be based. However, in order to make sense of and satisfy the "enough and as good" clause, welfarist considerations creeps in. The "as good" introduces an egalitarian spirit in a libertarian philosophy and suggests either a resource egalitarian or a welfaristic interpretation. The latter flows almost directly from Nozick's interpretation that the Second proviso commands that no one's position should be worsened. We could then reformulate Nozick's proviso by saying that an appropriation must be a Pareto improvement, that is, no one is made worse off and someone is made better off by the appropriation. Arguing along these lines suggests that a cost–benefit analysis should be able to answer the moral concerns around climate policies, provided that beneficiaries (emitters) compensate those who suffer from the impacts. This line of argument boils down to an essentially welfaristic assessment of the legitimacy of property rights. Although, Nozick (1974: 177) explicitly rejects "a utilitarian justification of property", it remains unclear how welfaristic assessment can be avoided. When we try to spell out the necessary conditions for an appropriation of a scarce resource that builds on a "no worsening" we must resort to welfarist arguments. To guarantee the very possibility that no one is worse off through an appropriation, benefits and costs associated with that appropriation must be assessed. This is the case regardless of the baseline against which a worsening is assessed.

Finally, having another look at Locke's First proviso, the condition that nothing should be wasted, it seems impossible to avoid a welfarist interpretation. The no waste condition expresses the idea that resources should be used efficiently. The Lockean provisos foreshadow the welfare economic principles of efficient production and consumption (no waste) and Pareto improvements (no worsening).

Notes

1 I thank Alessandra Basso, Simo Kyllönen and the editors of this volume for critical comments that have helped to improve this chapter.
2 This phrase is borrowed from my earlier paper (Weikard 2004) on which some of the analysis in this paper draws.
3 For example, instead of assigning emission rights, a global carbon tax could incentivise emission reductions.
4 This section draws on my earlier summary of Nozick's (1974) account of a Lockean theory of property rights; see Weikard (2004).
5 In fact, the IPCC (2014: AR 5 Synthesis Report) reports an estimate that future accumulated emissions must not exceed 275 GtC if the 2°K target is adopted. For comparison, the total initial carbon budget prior to industrialisation was 800 GtC. Of these, roughly one-third was consumed in the period 1750–1970, one-third in 1970–2015 and one-third remains.
6 Allocating the remaining emission rights to developing countries need not cause inefficiencies if these rights are tradable, i.e. if an international climate agreement succeeded in establishing a global carbon market.
7 An alternative interpretation is that the appropriated resource must offer a direct benefit to the owner. Locke wants to rule out that resources are appropriated in order to withhold them from others for strategic reasons, i.e. to exert (market) power. Adopting this weaker interpretation would justify emission rights up to a business-as-usual emissions level and leaves open the question "Who has to cut emissions?"
8 But see Sjaastad and Bromley (1997) for a critical reflection.

Bibliography

Arneson, R. (1989), "Equality and equal opportunity for welfare", *Philosophical Studies*, vol. 56: 77–93.

Baatz, C. (2013), "Responsibility for the past? Some thoughts on compensating those vulnerable to climate change in developing countries", *Ethics, Policy & Environment*, vol. 16(1): 94–110.

Beckerman, W. and Pasek, J. (1995), "The equitable international allocation of tradable carbon emission permits", *Global Environmental Change*, vol. 5(5): 405–13.

Bovens, L. (2011), "A Lockean defense of grandfathering emission rights", in D. G. Arnold (ed.), *The Ethics of Global Climate Change*, Cambridge: Cambridge University Press, pp. 124–44.

Broome, John (1992), *Counting the Cost of Global Warming*, Cambridge: The White Horse Press.

Broome, J. (2010), "The most important thing about climate change", in J. Boston, A. Bradstock and D. Eng (eds), *Public Policy: Why Ethics Matters*, ANU E Press pp. 101–16.

Caney, S. (2012), "Just emissions", *Philosophy and Public Affairs*, vol. 40: 255–300.
Cohen, G. A. (1995), *Self-Ownership, Freedom, and Equality*, Cambridge: Cambridge University Press.
Demsetz, (1967), "Toward a theory of property rights", *American Economic Review*, vol. 57: 347–59.
Dworkin, R. (1981), "What is equality? Part 2: equality of resources", *Philosophy and Public Affairs*, vol. 10: 283–345.
Gollier, C. (2001), *The Economics of Time and Risk*, Cambridge, MA: MIT Press.
Gosseries, A. P. (2001), "What do we owe the next generation(s)?", *Loyola of Los Angeles Law Review*, vol. 35: 293. Available at: http://digitalcommons.lmu.edu/llr/vol35/iss1/8 (accessed 30 May 2016).
Gosseries, A. P. (2004), "Historical emissions and free-riding", *Ethical Perspectives*, vol. 11: 36–60.
Hormio, S. (2016), "Climate change mitigation, sustainability and non-substitutability", in A. Walsh, S. Hormio and D. Purves (eds), *The Ethical Underpinnings of Climate Economics*. London: Routledge. pp. 103–21.
IPCC (2014), *Climate Change 2014: Synthesis Report. Contribution of Working Groups I, II and III to the Fifth Assessment Report of the Intergovernmental Panel on Climate Change*, Geneva: IPCC.
Lawford-Smith, Holly (2014), "Benefiting from failures to address climate change", *Journal of Applied Philosophy*, vol. 31(4): 392–404.
Libecap, G. D. (1989), "Distributional issues in contracting for property rights", *Journal of Institutional and Theoretical Economics*, vol. 145: 6–24.
Locke, J. (1967 [1690]), *Two Treatises of Government*, ed. P. Laslett, 2nd edn, Cambridge: Cambridge University Press.
Meyer, L. H. and Roser, D. (2010), "Climate justice and historical emissions", *Critical Review of International Social and Political Philosophy*, vol. 13(1): 229–53.
Nozick, R. (1974), *Anarchy, State, and Utopia* (reprinted 1980), Oxford: Basil Blackwell.
Ostrom, E. (1990), *Governing the Commons*, New York: Cambridge University Press.
Portney, R. and Weyant, J. P. (eds) (1999), *Discounting and Intergenerational Equity*, Washington, DC: Resources for the Future.
Roark, E. (2012), "Applying Locke's Proviso to unappropriated natural resources", *Political Studies*, vol. 60: 687–702.
Roemer, J. E. (1998), *Equality of Opportunity*, Cambridge, MA: Harvard University Press.
Schüssler, R. (2011), "Climate justice: a question of historic responsibility?", *Journal of Global Ethics*, vol. 7: 261–78.
Sher, G. (1992), "Ancient wrongs and modern rights", in P. Laslett and J. Fishkin (eds), *Philosophy, Politics and Society: Series VI, Future Generations*, New Haven: Yale University Press, pp. 48–61.
Sjaastad, E. and Bromley, D. W. (1997), "Indigenous land rights in sub-Saharan Africa: appropriation, security and investment demand", *World Development*, vol. 25(4): 549–62.
Solow, R. M. (1974), "Intergenerational equity and exhaustible resources", *Review of Economic Studies*, vol. 41 (Symposium): 29–45.
Steiner, H. (1994), *An Essay on Rights*, Oxford: Blackwell.
Steiner, H. and Vallentyne, P. (2009), "Libertarian theories of international justice", in A. Gosseries and L. H. Meyer (eds), *Intergenerational Justice*, Oxford: Oxford University Press, pp. 50–76.

Stern, N. (2008), "The economics of climate change", *American Economic Review*, vol. 98(2): 1–37.

Stevenson, G. G. (1991), *Common Property Economics: A General Theory and Land Use Applications*, Cambridge: Cambridge University Press.

von Mises, L. (1993[1927]), "Liberalismus. Jena: Gustav Fischer", *Nachdruck mit einer Einführung von Hans-Hermann Hoppe*, Sankt Augustin: Academia Verlag.

Waldron, J. (1988), *The Right to Private Property*, Oxford: Clarendon Press.

Weikard, H.-P. (1998), "Contractarian approaches to intergenerational justice", *Archiv für Rechts- und Sozialphilosophie*, vol. 84(3): 383–91.

Weikard, H.-P. (2004), "Who should receive the CO_2 emission permits?", in R. Döring and M. Rühs (eds), *Ökonomische Rationalität und praktische Vernunft – Gerechtigkeit, Ökologische Ökonomie und Naturschutz: Festschrift für Ulrich Hampicke*, Würzburg: Königshausen & Neumann, pp. 71–82.

Wolf, C. (1995), "Contemporary property rights, Lockean provisos, and the interests of future generations", *Ethics*, vol. 105: 791–818.

12 Climate change policy, economic analysis and price-independent conceptions of ultimate value[1]

Adrian Walsh

> ...political economy has nothing to do with the comparative estimation of different uses in the judgement of a philosopher or moralist.
>
> (John Stuart Mill, *Principles of Political Economy* Book III, ch.i, §2)

Introduction – the dangers of conflating price and value in climate change policy

To what extent should the economic analysis of climate change be constrained by or evaluated against external ethical considerations? To what extent should it be subject to moral criticism? In determining appropriate responses to the challenges of climate change, governments and public policymakers have made great use of the tools of economics. Indeed, economic analysis and economic modelling have been central in such policy formation.[2] These economic evaluations of and approaches to the problems posed by climate change in the end rely for their efficacy on the pricing mechanism. The thought is that through the ascription of price – either via shadow pricing or the establishment of genuine markets – social goods will be allocated in such a way as to realise environmentally valuable outcomes; that is, outcomes in which the harms of climate change are mitigated. The success of such economic solutions is determined by the extent to which they realise environmental outcome that are better or more valuable than those that would have been realised by other strategies.

Within environmental circles, over the past twenty years, disquiet has been expressed by many about the use of economic analysis to capture or adequately represent environmental values. Thus, some critics have spoken of the commodification associated with the pricing mechanisms and the putative inappropriateness of attempting to price what they believe should properly be regarded as priceless. Herein I take a somewhat different approach and explore the relationship between price and *ultimate value*, which simply means intrinsic value in the moral philosopher's sense of the value upon which other values ultimately rest.[3] The idea of value in question is usefully captured by the philosopher Antony Flew when he says "[a] theory of value is a theory about what things in the world are good, desirable and important".[4]

It indicates a property or feature of a good that marks it as being worthy of some kind of respect. We need to be careful with our terminology here because of the ambiguities associated with "intrinsic value" and more generally "value" itself.[5] Intrinsic value, as John O'Neill notes, can mean the value that exists independently of there being any "valuers", or the value an object has solely in virtue of its "intrinsic properties" or it can function as a synonym for non-instrumental value.[6] Hence I shall use the term "ultimate value" in the hope of avoiding some of the potential confusions. This chapter suggests that fear of conflation of price and ultimate value lies at the heart of a great deal of that general anxiety by observers outside of economics about the role of this discipline in environmental policy and that such fears are well-founded.

Two central claims here are that:

- i we need to ensure that we do not conflate price and ultimate value; and
- ii we need to maintain this price independent conception of ultimate value to assess the pronouncements of climate economics.

However, there is significant *antagonism towards normativity* within economics and on the part of many – although not all – economists who are working on climate change policy. Indeed, one striking feature of the *public pronouncements* of some leading economists is that there is a reluctance to engage in grand ethical theorising. In fact, there is a strong tendency within economic thinking to reject grand scales of value. Consider the following quote from the climate economist Weitzman:

> relying mostly on a priori philosopher-king ethical judgements about the immorality of treating future generations differently from the current generation – instead of trying to back out what possibly more representative members of society ... might be revealing from their behavior is *their* implicit rate of pure time preference. An enormously important part of the 'discipline' of economics is supposed to be that economists understand the difference between their own personal preferences for apples over oranges and the preferences of others for apples over oranges. Inferring society's revealed-preference value of [the discount rate] is not an easy task ... but at least a good-faith effort at such an inference might have gone some way towards convincing the public that the economists doing the studies are not drawing conclusions primarily from imposing their own value judgements on the rest of the world.[7]

Broome, who discusses this very quote in his book *Climate Matters*, notes the antagonism to the very kind of analysis that is necessary for any adequate climate change policy. We also find the climate economist, Nicholas Stern, in a recent article, puzzling over why it is that so many economists recoil from the "recognition that an examination of ethics is unavoidable".[8]

In one sense this is all rather mystifying. What makes writers like Weitzman wish to avoid systematic analysis of ethics in this way? Why repudiate ethical theory? Stern is quite right to ponder why it is that economists have often gone to great lengths to dodge ethical discussion.

Closer analysis reveals that there is, in fact, a long history of this avoidance of the ethical within economics. This chapter claims that the history of the development of economics provides a *partial explanation* of this tendency. Further, when one explores that history one also finds discussions – albeit critical – of exactly the distinction and a mode of reasoning must be part of climate policy. In pursuing this task of explanation of the anti-normativity of much economics and of explicating the kind of evaluation or assessment that is critical to climate policy, I explore in some detail the so-called *Paradox of Value*.[9] This paradox, as discussed in its various forms by writers from Augustine through to Adam Smith, concerns cases where relative prices appear wildly variant from some putative ultimate scale of valuation. However, within economic circles it is largely rejected as having any intellectual merit or interest. Such a strong rejection of the Paradox of Value has many consequences for economic theory. One significant side-effect of this refusal to take the paradox seriously, in any shape or form, is a tendency within a great deal of economic meta-theorising to conflate price and value and thus not to maintain the possibility of an independent value framework for assessing price and economic assessments more generally.

This chapter claims, then, that the history of the development of economics (and more specifically how economics as a whole has responded to the Paradox of value) provides a partial explanation of the difficulties economics is facing with climate change. The examination of this history provides an explanation why it is that the discipline of economics finds it difficult to deal with normative issues, notwithstanding the willingness of some leading climate economists (and the IPCC) to acknowledge the need forms of ethical evaluation. Instead the focus is on prices and economic criteria. Notice, for instance, what the IPCC writes in a recent report:

> The first step in a practical economic valuation is to assign a monetary value to the costs and benefits that come to each person at each time from the change. This value may be either the amount of money the person is willing to pay for the change, or the amount they are willing to accept as compensation for it. If the change is a marginal increase or decrease in the person's consumption of a marketed commodity, it will be equal to the price of the commodity.[10]

So it would seem that at the heart of the economic approach to climate change are methods which assign monetary values to the changes of individual's well-being and which are limited to such monetary evaluations.

If the analysis in this chapter is correct, and economics itself, that is, its methods and results, need to be evaluated against some independent value scale, then this conclusion should give us a reason to change the mainstream current understanding of economics as giving a full normative evaluation of alternative policy choices; rather we (and the economists) should adopt a more humble attitude when they are giving policy advice. The thought is that economics provides some sophisticated methods for undertaking policy evaluation in a highly complex setting, but the sophistication itself does not mean that it can answer all the questions raised by climate change. Economics should not be accorded a privileged role in climate policy analysis – certainly it should play a role but not be regarded as the *sole* or *determining* factor in climate policy decisions.

Preliminaries

Before exploring some historical material on the background to the tendency to reject the distinction between price and ultimate value, it is important to note the following caveats:

- This chapter is not intended as – nor does it pretend to be – a thorough going critique of economic theory nor economic analysis as a whole. The discussion simply picks up on a tendency within economic theory that is harmful to the project of bringing ethics to bear on the economic analysis of climate change policy. It is a tendency that is a product of the history of economic theory and a natural error. Furthermore, as noted below, the price signal and the related intellectual apparatus is highly useful in public policy analysis.
- These criticisms differ from those that focus on the normativity embedded in economic theory. In recent years the economic approach to social policy formation has attracted a great deal of criticism amongst social scientists and political theorists. There are those who criticise it for trying to *price the priceless* and there are those who suggest that the *pricing violates the values inherent* in the goods that are commodified. The former involves a claim that the economist is attempting the impossible by imposing monetary values on things whose value cannot be quantified in monetary or financial terms.[11] The latter is a claim about the way that putting a price on a thing violates or is at odds with its central values.[12] In both cases, the criticisms are part of a more general critique of markets and commodification and the take-home message is that the application of economic values is inappropriate in at least some – if not all – spheres of social life. However, those *are not* the criticisms I wish to explore here – those criticisms are left to one side, because the focus here is not on the *effect* of economic analysis and economic practices on important human values, but with the importance of maintaining an external set of values against which economic evaluations, analyses and pronouncements are judged. The position defended herein is that economic analysis has a significant role to play in climate change policy, but any judgements and recommendations need to be assessed against fundamental normative criteria. Those engaged in employing

economic analysis to analyse the best ways of responding to climate change need to be mindful that economics analysis – be it understood in terms of price or welfare functions – is not the ultimate scale of value.

In this regard the approach is also markedly different from that of critics such as Mark Sagoff who hold that economic analysis has no proper role to play in climate policy. Sagoff claims – in works such as the article "The Poverty of Economic Analysis" and the book *Price, Principle and the Environment* – that economics fails to (and indeed cannot) capture the legitimate and pressing concerns associated with the challenges of climate change and hence should not be regarded as part of the solution to climate change problems.[13] Sagoff does not believe that this approach provides a useful way to think about the problems of climate change, claiming that, if we consider the intergenerational nature of the climate change problem, we soon see that economics cannot provide a "model, method or metaphor" for thinking through the issues. It is not that climate change creates a challenge for economic theory, but rather the problem is not one that it can adequately (or plausibly) frame.[14] This is not the place for a detailed response to Sagoff; briefly, however, Sagoff underestimates the utility of economic analysis in climate policy. Economic theory will be part of the solution but it requires, amongst other things, external normative criteria against which any economic proposal is assessed. So long as the analysis is not taken as the sole criterion for policy formation, then it will be part of the solution: the use of an external account of ultimate value allows us to assess the acceptability of any policy analysis or solutions in relationship to those values.

The third caveat here is that I am not championing any particular price independent scale of ultimate value. It could involve notions of well-being or expected utility or a capabilities approach. This chapter is not intended as a partisan defence of any particular scale of valuation. Whatever value theory is adopted, it needs inter alia to be able to provide grounds for preferring a low carbon economy and for defending the interests of future generations. These are essential *desiderata* for whatever price independent scale of value we choose. In this way our theory of ultimate value provides *the yardstick* against which to assess economic policy analysis and economic recommendations.

The fourth caveat is that this chapter is not an ambit claim for philosophy as the master discipline: it should not be interpreted in any sense as an imperialist grab for philosophy to be regarded as the master discipline. Philosophers have a lot to learn from economics and further public policy cannot do without input from economists.

Finally, it should be noted that the focus here will *primarily* be on the price mechanism – the assumption is that much of economics deals with issues of distribution and production through this mechanism and its success or failure rests on the capacity of the price mechanism to deal with the challenges of climate change in a public policy context. So much of the early discussion will assume that it is price that is central to analysis. However, welfare economists who are highly engaged with climate economics typically do not regard the price mechanism as fundamental and instead take aggregate states of welfare as being at the proper object of their analysis.[15] Hence rather than simply talking of maintaining a price-independent scale of value the claim here is the more general one that we need to maintain an assessment of economic analysis using a scale of ultimate value that is distinct from any form of economic analysis itself. The point of exploring the Paradox of Value is not so much for the intrinsic interest of the Paradox itself – although it is indeed interesting – but for what it tells us about the distinction between price and ultimate value.

Price and ultimate value: the illustrative case of the paradox of value

This chapter is, in part, a plea for the need, whilst engaged in the use of economic theory for public policy formation, of maintaining a distinction between price and ultimate value. In exploring this topic we need to distinguish two different uses of the term "value":

- The term has a characteristic *economic* employment that focuses on what causal factors determine prices. Typically in economic discussions of "value" the topic under discussion really is about what is *causally responsible* for the different prices one finds in the market. In this context the phrase "value theory" refers to theoretical explanations of variations in prices. Accordingly, Smith's so-called "labour theory of value" can be regarded as a systematic account that explains the different prices goods obtain on the market because of the different amounts of labour embodied in them.
- However, the term "value" also has a philosophical sense that concerns *ultimate ethical values*, where such values concern – as we noted earlier – the value upon which other values ultimately rest. It is the final or non-instrumental ground for action or evaluation.

In the context of economic analysis, employing the distinction between price and ultimate value involves:

a the use of a conception of value that is *independent of price* and is ultimate in the sense of being the final or non-instrumental ground or reason for action; and

b the use of a scale of ultimate value that can be used to assess proposed courses of action or *economic* recommendations for action when faced with a choice

Note also that herein we treat price and ultimate value as *conceptually distinct* – the idea here being that price and value are conceptually independent.

In order to illustrate this idea of the price–ultimate value distinction I shall begin by considering Adam Smith's discussion of what has come to be known as the "Paradox of Value" (or the "Water–Diamond Paradox"), and the subsequent interpretation of that paradox by many later economic theorists. Smith's Paradox is usefully illustrative because it involves a clear-cut case of a distinction being drawn between price and ultimate value and, further, because the reaction to it by many within the economics profession tells us something significant about their attitude to the idea of there being a genuine distinction between price and ultimate value. Let us consider the economics profession's relationship to the Paradox of Value as a way of teasing out the important claims about the importance of maintaining a price-independent scale of value.

Smith's Paradox of Value relates to what some might see as anomalous when we engage in the practice of comparing economic prices and an ultimate scale of value – whatever that scale may be.[16] The Paradox directs our attention to the bafflement that might arise when one considers the disconnection between the relative usefulness of some good and the relative worth on the market. Smith noted, with some bemusement, the strange relative prices of water and diamonds.[17] He was puzzled by the fact that, although water is necessary for sustaining life and has a high use-value, its exchange value was very low, while the exchange-value of a diamond was very high even though its use is much more limited. He puzzles about why the exchange value of a diamond is very high whilst water is very low. The thought here is that this is paradoxical in the sense of seeming an odd outcome when one has an expectation that the scale of prices *should* reflect the natural scale of value.

Smith's Paradox is, in fact, a modern variant of an earlier discussion by medieval writers who focused on cases where the proponents believed that the relative values of two or more goods were widely variant from some ultimate scale of value. In the medieval version of the Paradox the scale of ultimate value against which prices were compared was God's scale of natural perfection. The medieval version of the Paradox can be traced back at least as far as Augustine, and reflects the puzzlement one might feel when relative monetary scales are wildly variant from the "natural scale of perfection". Augustine noted with considerable bewilderment that a horse sometimes fetched a far higher price at the market than a slave. In the modern version of the Paradox, as discussed by classical economists, the comparative scale was utility. In both versions of the Paradox there is an underlying assumption of an ultimate scale of value against which the prices are judged "queer".

However, much modern economic theory tells us that Smith's Paradox – and by implication the idea of a distinction between price and ultimate value – is based on faulty premises, since the "measuring rod" of money does not measure the ultimate good-making features of commodities or of economic states of affairs. This seems correct when considering *causal accounts* of how prices are formed, but it does not entail the further claim that distinguishing between price and a scale of ultimate value when making judgements about the worth of a transaction is irrational.

If we follow what we might refer to as the "received history" of the development of economics, then the advent of Marginalism lead to a solution – as it were – of the classical paradox of value.[18] The *Marginalist Revolution* 1871 involved the innovative claim that it is not the total satisfaction or total utility to be derived from the possession and use of a commodity good that determines the price; rather it is the satisfaction from the last and least wanted addition (the "marginal" good) to one's consumption that "gives it value".[19] It is the supply of, and demand for, a good, not the overall utility, that Marginalists claim is the fundamental cause of the prices of any set of goods. According to marginal utility theory, the utility of a good diminishes, all other things being equal, with increasing availability, since it is the utility of the "last and least wanted good" – that is the utility of the marginal unit – that sets the price of all. The Marginalist approach differs from that of earlier economic theories in which relative prices were explained by some objective feature, attaching either to the good in itself, or to some aspect of the production process.[20] These objective features were thought to be unchanging qualities which were either inherent in the goods themselves or in the production process. Thus, following the latter reading, classical economists such as Ricardo and Marx concentrated on the labour embodied in the good, others (such as some medieval thinkers) on the cost of production to explain the relativity of prices. Marginalists by way of contrast argued that the economic value derives from the relationship of agents to particular goods, rather than from intrinsic features of the goods themselves.[21]

How might Marginalism be said to solve Smith's apparent dilemma? According to this received history, the problem of the Paradox of Value arose as a consequence of the classical theorists failing to understand the causes of price because they were focused on so-called use-values. This view is commonly propounded despite the fact, as we shall see, that it has little basis in historical fact. The well-known economist Richard Lipsey, who endorses this view of the history of utility theory, claims in *An Introduction to Positive Economics* that classical economists such as Smith and Ricardo believed that expensive goods should be ones with high total utilities and cheap goods those with low total utilities.[22] Lipsey claims that the paradox is solved by the discovery of marginal utility. According to writers like Lipsey it is because they fail to distinguish between marginal and total utility that relative prices appear paradoxical.[23] One remarkable feature of this received history is that it seems to have very little foundation in the actual history, since the classical economists held, as we noted above, a *labour* theory of value rather than one based on the total utility of a good.[24] Furthermore, the original Marginalists – and here I mean Jevons, Walras and Menger – did not think that their theory of value solved the Paradox of Value,[25] since they were all too well aware that the classical economists regarded labour as the fundamental determinant of price. Indeed for Smith the Paradox of Value was more of a curiosity than a serious concern for Smith: it certainly did not present itself to him as a causal paradox.[26] Smith introduces the Water–Diamond paradox so as to illustrate the distinction between *value in use* (i.e. total utility) and *value in exchange* and he was not attempting to *explain* the paradox.[27] What Smith would have found genuinely puzzling – and troublesome for his theory – were cases where relative prices stood in an inverse relation to the labour expended in the production of the commodity.

So what should we take from all of this? The Paradox of Value involves *in miniature* a form of reasoning in which we contrast the prices ascribed to goods against some scale of ultimate value. This seems to reflect an attitude about economic judgements and points to a form of reasoning that we need generally which involves not just a general account of ultimate value but one which is, significantly, price-independent. It is moreover, a form of reasoning that many economists, in their public meta-ethical pronouncements have often wished to repudiate, on the mistaken grounds that it involves some causal account of the formation of prices. One need not conflate the normative and the causal here in order to find certain pricing odd and even ethically perverse.

Denying a role for ultimate value – marginalism and the ethical subjectivism of much economic theory

In this section I shall consider the claims of those who, *on the basis of* results in economic theory itself, would deny a role for ultimate value, both in economic analysis and in the assessment of economic analysis within a public policy framework. In particular, I wish to respond to the claim:

> EV1: economic value is fully determining in a policy context because there are no relevant ultimate values or such values are identical with the prices determined in the market.

The take-home message from EV1 is that normative non-economic values are not of relevance to public policy. It is the idea expressed when economists such as Joan Robinson suggest that "[V]alue is just a word with no operational content".[28]

In response to EV1 I shall undertake a brief historical exploration of the reception of so-called Marginalism by writers in the field and particularly by economists. As we shall see, many writers in this area draw strong *ethical subjectivist* claims about value on the basis of developments in price theory itself. Ethical subjectivism is defined here as the view that there are no objective ethical values and thus any putative account of value must ultimately appeal to mere attitudes, feelings and tastes; that is, to the subjective standpoint. There is a tendency towards ethical subjectivism, as opposed to ethical objectivism, in a great deal of economic theory. Ethical subjectivism should be distinguished from *ultimate value neutrality*, which is another meta-ethical view one commonly encounters within economic discussions of method. When the economist and methodologist Lionel Robbins says that: "[E]conomics is neutral as between ends" and thus cannot pronounce on the validity of ultimate judgements of value, his view is best described here as defending the idea of ultimate value neutrality.[29] Instead of assuming that the ends of human action are subjective, Robbins is arguing that the economist *qua* economist should not make any judgements about ends.[30] This is quite different from the view that individuals subjectively determine values.

Some writers influenced by ethical subjectivism claim that there is no need for a price-external account of value because there is no distinction to be had between price and ultimate value. (We might refer to this, modelling the contours of the debate on debates in the philosophy of mind, as "price-value *identity* theory".) An early philosophical formulation of this idea that value is *identical* with price is to be found in the work of Thomas Hobbes, who writes in the *Leviathan*:

> The *Value*, or Worth of a man, is as of all other things, his Price; that is to say, so much as would be given for the use of his Power, and therefore is not absolute; but a thing dependent on the need and judgement of another.[31]

In addition to this "identity" theory of price and value, there is a more radical "eliminativist" view according to which talk of value is nonsense for there is only price. Consider the words of Pareto, who writes that all talk of value is "a jingle of words, which look like they mean something but other than that have no significance".[32]

If ultimate value is, in fact, as these writers suggest, nonsense or just another word for price, then assessing economic evaluations and analyses against normative ideals based on ultimate value is a foolhardy exercise.

What might lead economists, in particular, to such radical conclusions about the nature of ultimate value? One source of this attitude is an overly metaphysical interpretation of the implications of the Marginalist revolution in price theory. Recall that for the Marginalist the utility of a good diminishes with increasing availability, for it is the utility of the marginal unit that sets the price of all. This is in stark contrast to earlier theories of how prices are formed which focused on some objective feature of the good or the production prices. Marginalism rests upon the radical idea that objective features of the goods themselves do not determine the economic value (or price) of goods. The Marginalists' account of how prices are formed contains two significant elements for our purposes herein:

- i Economic values are relational and signify nothing whatsoever about the properties of goods in themselves; and
- ii Relative prices determined in a market do not represent a scale of ultimate values.

One conclusion then that we can legitimately draw on the basis of this – given that the Marginalists are correct – is that the "measuring rod of money" does not measure or gauge (at least directly) anything about the inherent properties nor inherent values. Indeed it is important that causal claims regarding how prices are formed and our normative evaluations of relative prices must be kept separate from one another. Price does not track ultimate value, unless of course one thinks ultimate value is some kind of subjective value. However, in the wake of the nineteenth-century Marginalist revolution amongst many economists and commentators on the history of economics it is common to find overstated metaphysical conclusions being drawn. This is probably a consequence – in part at least – of the fact that many commentators refer to Marginalism as the "subjective theory of value".[33] It is unsurprising that that some commentators might slide from this description to the assumption that Marginalism has more substantive meta-ethical implications.

One mistaken lesson to draw from the history of Marginalism and its reception within economic circles would be that it demonstrates that there is no such thing as ultimate value. A second closely related mistaken conclusion to draw from these events would be that the triumph of Marginalism demonstrates the truth of ethical subjectivism. The causal subjectivism of Marginalism is quite distinct from ethical subjectivism and the former provides no direct warrant for the latter.[34] While there might not be some objective value inherent in commodities that has a causal role in the formation of prices, it does not follow from this claim that no ultimate values exist. The crucial point is that the shift to a subjective theory of prices does not provide a warrant for *ethical* subjectivism.

There are three conclusions to be drawn from these discussions:

- The history of marginalism and its reception within the economics community provides a partial explanation for the tendency to reject the idea of ultimate value by many economists.
- The history of the development of economic theory – or at least this episode in the history – does not provide grounds for endorsing a form of meta-ethical subjectivism according to which objective value is nonsense. Of course this does not provide arguments in favour of ethical objectivism either. It simply says that the history of economic thought does not warrant adopting an ethical subjectivist approach to moral issues.
- Finally, the history of economic thought does not provide any grounds for rejecting the idea of assessing climate economics in terms of a scale of ultimate value.

Incorporating ultimate value into economic analysis?

There will also be those who argue that maintaining a price-independent scale of value against which one assesses the outcomes of economic analysis is entirely unnecessary because all relevant values can be captured within the price mechanism. External critique, according to such critics, is not required if it is possible to incorporate significant values fully and adequately into the economic analysis itself. The claim then would be:

> EV2: Economic value is fully determining in environmental policy and we do not need to refer to other normative values (or assess it against a set of distinct moral values) because those normative values, while significant, can be incorporated into the analysis.

Let us call those who defend the thesis that adequate values are embedded or represented within economic analysis "incorporationists". Most notably many welfare economists, who are, as a matter of fact, very active and hugely prominent in climate policy debates, hold *incorporationist* views.

There are two obvious ways to develop this view, the first relying on prices and the second on the idea of social welfare. On the first approach it is claimed that relevant ultimate values are embedded in economic analysis through the price mechanism. Underpinning this is a "democratic" view of the market. Roughly, the idea is that people vote with their dollars. Prices ascribed to goods and services reflect the aggregated and unstated and implicit values of the population with respect to those goods and services. The aggregated values of the population as a whole should be treated as the fundamental values against which any economic policy is assessed or evaluated. Since this is exactly what the market provides via the price mechanism there is no need for an external set of values to assess economic analysis or to assess the outcomes of market transactions. Indeed, it might even be claimed that the ultimate value and prices are identical and hence the kinds of contrast found in discussions of the Paradox of Value are simply wrong-headed.

This particular way of avoiding price independent accounts of value has not gone unnoticed. Nicholas Stern notes, *en passant*, that one common method economists use to dodge the ethical discussions surrounding climate policy is to suggest that all the requisite ethical parameters can be read off from markets.[35]

Space does not allow detailed examination of this position, but a brief glance shows that it is unlikely to demonstrate the truth of EV2. The democratic analogy breaks down when one realises that not everyone has an equal vote. Those with more financial resources obviously have more voice in the market and hence the prices do not fairly represent an aggregation of the social preferences of the society as a whole. Second, often the consumer choices made are restricted by what commodities are available on the market and do not genuinely reflect the preferences of the society as a whole, but rather the choices and preferences of those in control of the production and distribution of goods and services. This does not seem to provide a plausible way of defending EV2.

A more serious incorporationist challenge to the idea of the importance of maintaining a scale of ultimate value is to be found in the work of welfare economists who focus on the notion of overall social welfare. What follows is not a comprehensive account or detailed critique of social welfare economics and, indeed, there will be other authors in this collection who provide far more sophisticated analyses. For my purposes herein that is not required. All that I am focused upon is the question of whether social welfare economics implies that we do not require a scale of ultimate value against which economic analyses are assessed.

Welfare economics is, in short, the branch of economics that evaluates well-being (or welfare) at the aggregate social level.[36] It can be viewed primarily as an investigation of the methods for obtaining a social ordering over different possible states of the world in terms of well-being.[37] Such a social ordering enables one to compare all states of the world and rank each one as "better than", "worse than" or "equal to". Here a social state is typically understood as a particular allocation of resources. It involves ranking states of affairs in terms of specific economic characteristics. Welfare economics thus provides a framework within which the normative significance of economic events can be evaluated. In this context prices represent proxies for the "ultimate" value of welfare.

It is important to note that welfare economists are primarily interested in ranking states that differ in terms of their economic characteristics, for example outputs of commodities, supplies of factors to different uses, and distributions of commodities over households. Further, a large amount of welfare economics is grounded or based on the concept of economic efficiency. This idea is used to order social states on the basis of what is thought to be some minimal value judgement. There are also those who believe that simply focusing on efficiency is not enough for a complete study of welfare and hence develop a social welfare function. The welfare function is intended to go beyond the concept of economic efficiency. The work here involves designing some means of weighting the utilities of different consumer groups (usually households) and unsurprisingly entails that much stronger normative judgements are required. These judgements are codified into a social welfare function or ordering which is a central conceptual tool of welfare economics.[38]

Clearly all of this has built-in normative assumptions. Welfare economics also is underpinned by fundamental theorems all of which are normatively controversial. The fundamental theorems, however, are contested among welfare economics and different schools of thought champion remarkably different lists of what is fundamental, but all contain normative commitments. For instance, consider the three fundamental theorems as outlined in the *New Palgrave Dictionary of Economics*. The *New Palgrave* lists three basic tents of welfare economics. First, it is assumed that laissez-faire leads to the common good. Second, it is assumed that all individuals are self-interested price-takers. The *New Palgrave's* third tenet concerns Arrow's theorem and holds that there is is no Arrow social welfare function that satisfies the conditions of universality, Pareto consistency, independence, non-dictatorship.[39] All three are clearly normative. Our concern, however, is not with the existence of these normative assumptions within welfare economics, but rather with the question of whether they can completely capture the requisite values. Further, for my purposes, it also does not matter how one defines those fundamental theorems – what matters is whether or not welfare economics provides grounds for a defence of EV2. Does it therefore provide grounds for rejecting these claims of the need of external normative frameworks for assessing economic claims and economic analysis?

Before providing critical commentary on this, one comment is in order. It is striking that in those papers which attempt to modify welfare economics to accommodate important environmental concerns – such as a number of those within this volume – the success of the modification is typically assessed against external normative criteria. Indeed the success of the modification stands or falls on the extent to which it captures the normative values – such as a concern for future generations – that the authors consider to be significant. At the very least this demonstrates that, even if all values are captured within the welfare economic analysis, the analysis and the relevant normative criteria are nonetheless *conceptually* distinct.

But there are reasons for being sceptical that all values can be captured by economic analysis and, unsurprisingly, there are many welfare economists who regard the idea as implausible. If we consider the central economic categories that are employed in economic analysis of this kind, such as efficiency or outputs of commodities, it is hard to see how they could fully capture environmental goals, such as, for instance, the welfare of future generations. They might well be modified to take into account the needs of future generations, but that is not the same as providing a language that eliminates the need for external normative criteria. In order to ensure that relevant values are respected in whatever economic framework we adopt, we need to maintain those criteria. Further, many of those economic categories might well contain elements that are actually antagonistic to, for instance, future generations. The discounting of future preferences would be a case in point.

The upshot of this discussion is that we still require external normative criteria or, as described herein, a scale of ultimate value. Before leaving this discussion of welfare economics and EV2, I should note in passing the following point. Although it is doubtful welfare economics contains the intellectual resources required to defend EV2, nonetheless the project of incorporating normative ideals into economic analysis is highly admirable. Indeed the attempt to reconfigure welfare economics so as to incorporate important environmental values is at the heart of many of the chapters in this book. In no sense does this chapter repudiate those attempts, but simply maintains that an external normative theory is required to assess any economic analysis, no matter how much desirable normative material has been incorporated into the analysis.

Contemporary climate economics and ultimate value

Standard economic theory deals with policy in general and more specifically with climate policy in terms of market failure and conventional cost benefit analysis. As Nicholas Stern notes in "Ethics, Equity and the Economics of Climate Change", the criteria invoked in such theory "require us to examine how much welfare or utility of the individuals involved, directly or indirectly, rises or falls with utility increments usually added across individuals using a procedure for the social weightings of increments in utility or income".[40] Some economists and policymakers presumably hold that marginal economic analysis of this kind comprises the *whole* of what matters for climate policy; that is, that it is the *primary* determinant of climate policy.[41] But, on the contrary, the claim here is that we need to maintain an independent conception of value that we use to assess economic analysis.

But equally, at least, some economists working in climate economics – many of whom are highly influential figures – acknowledge the need for ethics to have a role to play in climate policy. Here it is not just that ethical considerations should be incorporated into economic analysis but that they have a role to play in policy formation itself. For instance, this more moderate view is clearly evident in the work of Nicholas Stern when he argues that science and ethics structure economic analysis.[42] He notes that the risks on the scale associated with the problem of climate change take us "far outside the familiar policy questions and standard, largely marginal, techniques commonly used by economists".[43] Instead they raise deep questions about ethical perspectives "beyond those traditionally captured in analyses of Pareto efficiency or standard social welfare functions".[44] He explicitly rejects ethics based narrowly on small Pareto improvements and social welfare functions.[45] According to Stern, a more thoughtful view of ethics is required than economists usually employ and he notes that the purpose of his writing is to combine economic and ethical analyses of the issues raised by the science of climate change and to do so in a way that will inform practical policy formation.[46] Stern concludes that economists are "badly under-performing in relation to their potential contributions" if they simply present their positive analysis without "thinking hard" about its relevance and relations to the issues, criteria, principles and political processes which might be brought to bear in taking decisions.[47]

One also finds the more moderate view that regards ethics as central to climate policy evident in the IPCC's Assessment Report entitled "Climate Change 2014: Mitigation of Climate Change". Here there is an acknowledgement of the role of ethics in policy analysis. The report is remarkable in many ways – not least for the extensive discussion of different theories of social justice – and makes claims one rarely finds within standard economic analysis. Consider the following elements of the report:

- There is a general acknowledgement that ethical assumptions underpin all public policy choice. The report then notes that ethical judgements of value lie beneath nearly every decision that is associated with climate change.[48]
- The authors claim that interpreting economic policy requires ethics; that is, they not only highlight the ethical assumptions that are implicitly being made where economic analysis is employed to inform a policy, but also claim that how society assesses any form of economic analysis is an ethical question:

  > Although economics is essential to evaluating the consequences and trade-offs associating with climate change, how society interprets and values them is an ethical question.[49]

- They observe that normative solutions involve *contestable* ethical assumptions.[50]

The authors of the report, then, maintain that both economics and ethics have a pivotal role to play in climate policy formation and they also view ethics as having a role to play with economic analysis itself. Early in the report they note that economic analysis is of help in the guidance of policy formation, so long as "appropriate, adequate and transparent ethical assumptions are built into economic methods".[51] Hence it is important that economists are aware of the ethical assumptions built into their work and also are cognizant of the substantive accounts of justice that have been developed over the past 100 years by moral and political philosophers. (The authors of the report do not attempt to answer ethical questions: their aim is simply to "provide policymakers with the tools (concepts, principles, arguments and methods) to make decisions".[52]

This is all to the good and most welcome. Clearly, many of the leading economists working on climate change are well aware of the significance of ethical analysis for public policy in the area. However, this does not in any sense render our earlier discussion redundant:

- Within the report itself there is a marked tendency to run together the project of incorporating ethical concerns into economic analysis with the project of maintaining external ethical evaluation of economic analysis. While it is vital that economic analysis takes into account ethical factors (such as an appropriate concern for future generations), there is a limit to how much ethics can be incorporated into such analysis. Indeed it is difficult to see how the kinds of issue raised in the IPCC report itself regarding different theories of justice could be incorporated into any contemporary economic analysis. Thus whilst the project of modifying economic analysis so as to make it more sensitive to the normative components is highly commended, we must also recognise the necessity of maintaining an external (and price-independent) system of value to be employed when assessing the acceptability and use of any economic analysis. The difference between these two roles in policy formation for ethical evaluation needs to be explicitly acknowledged by economists and policymakers.
- Although the concessions to ethical analysis made by Stern and the IPCC are clearly most welcome, it is doubtful that all contemporary economists are as sympathetic towards the idea of ethical evaluation having a role to play in policy. There will be those who hold "incorporationist" views and equally there will be those of a more positivist tendency who hold that marginalist methods are correct because there are no objective ethical values. In either case, such economists will not see the need for ethical evaluation of policy.
- Economic analysis itself still largely consist of cost–benefit analyses, shadow pricing and other marginalist elements and, even if one does not hold positivist views about the normative, it is quite easy for both economists and policymakers employing economic analysis to assume that the outcomes of well-thought out economic analysis are the only inputs required for policy formation. There is a simple slide from the use of these marginalist techniques to what seems to be the mistaken view that economic analysis is all that is required for good climate policy.

None of this is to reject the recommendations or the approach of the IPCC. We simply must be mindful of the need to maintain an independent ethical framework for the evaluation of climate economics. This needs to be explicitly stated and understood when developing all significant climate policy.

Concluding remarks

"...all talk of value is a jingle of words, which look like they mean something but other than that have no significance" (Vilfredo Pareto).[53]

We began our discussion with an exploration of the Paradox of Value. This paradox is significant because it illustrates and makes vivid a form of reasoning that is vital if economics is to play a positive role in Climate Policy. It picks out a distinction and a mode of economic reasoning that is often overlooked in economic discussions of public policy, yet which should be regarded as pivotal in the evaluation of any economic proposals. Moreover, the historical reception of the Paradox of Value within the mainstream economic circles provides a partial explanation of why economists themselves are unlikely to regard the distinction between price and ultimate value as being of any relevance to public policy. Indeed, the attitudes towards the idea of price-independent ultimate value expressed in historical discussions of that Paradox allow us to understand why there is likely to be some reluctance to see ultimate value assessment to be important in climate change policy.

Second, and perhaps more significantly, the discussion here outlines a *distinctive form* of normative critique that differs markedly from those commonly found in critical discussion of economics. There is a long tradition of political critique that questions the value-free status of economic analysis.[54] Within this tradition, the thought is that, by pretending to be value-free, economists are able to smuggle in substantive values. There is another critical tradition that attacks the instrumental attitude that economics allegedly encourages towards what should be regarded as intrinsically valuable entities.[55] The account developed here is noticeably distinct from both of those well-known lines of inquiry. It concerns the normative assessment of economics proposals rather than the normativity implicit within or encouraged by economic theory.

Finally, the discussion is important because there is also a strong proclivity within public policy circles to conflate economic analysis and good public policy. One might easily regard the course recommended by economic analysis to be the only consideration to be taken into account when formulating ways to combat climate change. It is important that the two be regarded as conceptually distinct and, in particular, that economic proposals be assessed against the moral goals that we wish to achieve in our public policy. The Paradox of Value reminds us that, just as price should not be regarded as the ultimate value, so too any economic analysis employed when exploring the best way to respond to climate change must ultimately be assessed against value criteria concerned with good human lives. The use of an external account of ultimate value allows us to assess the acceptability of any policy analysis or solutions in relationship to what we take to be price-independent values. What is required, then, in climate policy formation is precisely the kind of reasoning we find in the Paradox of Value.

Notes

1 I would like to thank Simo Kyllönen, Blake Francis, John O'Neill, Säde Hormio, Duncan Purves, Peter Forrest and Pekka Mäkelä for their very helpful comments on this chapter.

2 We can distinguish two quite distinct aspects relevant to economics and our response to climate change: (i) economic analysis of climate change and economic proposals for how to respond; (ii) free market solutions which rely on markets rather than government intervention.

3 O'Neill, 1992: 119–137.

4 Flew, 1979: 365.

5 Early versions of "value theory" did involve both senses in so far as prices were said to be determined by some aspect of their good-making features or other features thought to be intrinsic to the object. Some traditional pre-classical theories of the formation of prices attributed the source of a commodity's exchangeable value to one or more underlying value elements (in the normative sense), be it cost of production or the usefulness of the object. It is because of this ambiguity that throughout the rest of this chapter I shall use the term "ultimate value" to refer to the normative philosopher's sense of the word.

6 O'Neill, 1992: 119–20.

7 Weitzman, 2009: 1–19.

8 Broome, 2012: 106; Stern, 2014: 427. Stern suggests that one reason for the discomfort might be that allowing an ethical perspective to enter the argument might well provide justificatory reasons for government intervention in the market.

9 The historical reception of the Paradox of Value and the subtle indirect influence of that historical reception on the meta-ethical views of many within the economics profession are explored in far greater detail in Walsh and Lynch (2003).

10 IPCC, 2014: 227.

11 O'Neill, 1996: 98–103.

12 For a good example of this view, see Anderson, 1993.

13 See Sagoff, 2004, 2011.

14 Sagoff (2011) focuses on three ways in which economists might conceptualise the problem of climate change so as to provide solutions – (1) as a collective action problem, (2) as a market failure and (3) in terms of property rights – and then explains why he believes all fail as frameworks of understanding. In the first instance, they might conceive of climate change as a collective action problem; and, as a matter of fact, many critics have done so. Collective actions problems involve cases in which the pursuit of self-interest by individual agents in a group leads to the destruction of public goods and everyone is significantly worse-off. In such cases, the standard solution is the imposition of coercion that is mutually agreed upon and which is intended to preserve or provide a public good. However, he suggests this analysis does not fit the problem of climate change since there is no mutual advantage between the generations. Sagoff says that it is clear that present and future generations have no such common interest. Second, economists might characterise climate change as a market failure. Indeed, Nicholas Stern has described it as the "greatest and widest ranging market failure ever seen". A market fails when it generates externalities that the ordinary market operations will not correct. Sagoff makes the point in terms of unimplemented trades: a market fails when it does not implement gains that can be achieved through trade. However, this is not the case with future

generations since they are not in a position to trade with present ones. Since individuals not yet born cannot trade, it follows than an efficient market may ignore their interests. Thus, for Sagoff, the relationship between present and future generations is not a market relationship but an ethical, political or spiritual one. Third, economists might plausibly understand the problem of climate change in terms of the "allocation or distribution of property right" and solve conflicts of interests between competing parties via granting of such rights. However, such rights he suggests cannot be ascribed to hypothetical individuals who lack "existence, agency or identity". He suggest that future generations cannot any more assert their rights against us than we can against those who lived in earlier periods of time. In addition to these points regarding the inability of economic theory to conceptualise the problem adequately, Sagoff claims that the economist's notion of efficiency precludes sustainable policy since it depends on exhausting the benefits of trade. The thought here is that the idea of efficiency – which is an essential feature of economic analysis – necessarily impedes the formation of adequate environmental policy.

15 Feldman, 2008.

16 Of course, the analysis of economic-based policies is not simply concerned with individual prices, but it is the attitude towards the practice of comparing price and ultimate value that I wish to direct the readers' attention towards here.

17 Apparently the water–diamond paradox goes back to Plato. See Plato, *Euthydemus*, [304], in *The Dialogues of Plato*, trans Benjamin Jowett.

18 For discussions of the received history and the deep misconceptions contained within of it see Bowley, 1973 and White, 2002.

19 See Blaug, 1978: 324. For an insightful discussion of the central ideas and of the significance of the Marginalist revolution see Galbraith, 1987. It is also worth reading the original work of Jevons (1871), one of the three originators of Marginalism. The book is remarkably clear regarding the main ideas of his new analysis.

20 "The general notion appears to have been that value is absolute, and objective, and independent of price" (Haney, 1920: 90).

21 See Pribram, 1983: 14.

22 Lipsey, 1971: 162.

23 Samuelson in a section of his *Economics* entitled "The Paradox of Value" writes: "Adam Smith never did quite resolve the paradox.... Smith had not arrived at the point where he knew how to distinguish *marginal* utility from *total* utility!" Samuelson, 1976: 438.

24 In *The Wealth of Nations* Smith writes: "Labour, therefore, is the real measure of the exchangeable value of all commodities" (Smith, 1970 [1776]): 133).

25 White, 2002: 659–83.

26 See, for instance, Robbins, 1970: 17.

27 Bowley, 1973: 139.

28 Robinson, 1962.

29 Robbins, 1935: 147.

30 Robbins,1935: 25.

31 Cited in Laird, 1929: 9.

32 Pareto, 2004: 66. Pareto goes on to say: "Thus so many vague and occasionally evenly vaguely contradictory meanings have been given to the term *value* that it is better not to use it in the study of political economy."

33 Mark Blaug, a well-known and respected historian of economic thought refers to the three central Marginalists (Walras, Menger, and Jevons), as the "subjective value trio" without acknowledging in any way the connection of the term subjectivism to substantive claims in ethics. See Blaug, 1978: 324.

34 We might also distinguish ethical subjectivism from methodological subjectivism, which takes no stand on the real existence or otherwise of objective ethical values; instead it assumes the subjectivity to values as a heuristic for explanation. Hence, a

methodological subjectivist might claim that prices are ultimately determined by agglomerations of tastes without committing him- or herself to a sceptical position on ultimate values.

35 Stern, 2014: 428.
36 "Welfare economics attempts to define and measure the 'welfare' of society as a whole. It tries to identify which economic policies lead to optimal outcomes, and, where necessary, to choose among multiple optima.", Feldman, 2008.
37 Boadway and Bruce, 1984: 1.
38 See Boadway and Bruce, 1984: 2–4.
39 See Feldman, 2008.
40 Stern, 2014: 418.
41 This view is distinct from what I have labelled "incorporationism" since it concerns a strong claim about the primary role of economic analysis in policy itself rather that a claim about the ability of economic analysis to embody or capture all relevant moral values. Despite being distinct, incorporationism would provide one possible justificatory ground for the claim that we should regard economic analysis as providing all that is required for climate policy.
42 Stern, 2014: 418. He also speaks (p. 400) of how climate change policy has its foundations in ethical and economic analyses.
43 Stern, 2014: 398.
44 Stern, 2014: 398.
45 Stern, 2014: 409, 424.
46 Stern, 2014: 398.
47 Stern, 2014: 429.
48 IPCC: 11. There the authors write: "Indeed, ethical judgements of value underlie almost every decision that is connected with climate change, including decisions made by individuals, public and private organizations, governments and groupings of governments."
49 IPCC: 9.
50 IPCC: 10.
51 IPCC: 9.
52 IPCC: 10.
53 Pareto, 2004.
54 For instance, see Blaug 1978. Blaug argues that Paretian welfare economics is normative. He claims that there is no such thing as value-free welfare economics. See also Hausman and McPherson, 1996.
55 For an example of this line of reasoning see Anderson, 1993.

Bibliography

Anderson, E. (1993), *Value in Ethics and Economics*, Cambridge, MA: Harvard University Press.

Blaug, M. (1978), *Economic Theory in Retrospect*, 3rd edn, Cambridge, Cambridge University Press.

Boadway, R. and Bruce, N. (1984), *Welfare Economics*, Oxford: Basil Blackwell.

Bowley, M. (1973), *Studies in the History of Economic Theory before 1870*, London: Macmillan.

Broome, J. (2012), *Climate Matters: Ethics in a Warming World*, New York: W. W. Norton.

Feldman, A. M. (2008), "Welfare economics", in S. N. Durlauf and L. E. Blum (eds) *The New Palgrave Dictionary of Economics*, 2nd edn, Available at: www.dictionaryofeconomics.com/article?id=pde2008_W000050 (accessed 27 May 2016).

Flew, A. (1979), *A Dictionary of Philosophy*, London: Macmillan.

Galbraith, J. K. (1987), *Economics in Perspective: A Critical History*, Boston, MA: Houghton Mifflin.

Haney, L. H. (1920), *History of Economic Thought*, New York: Macmillan.

Hausman, D. M. and McPherson, M. S. (1996), *Economic Analysis and Moral Philosophy*, Cambridge: Cambridge University Press.

IPCC (2014), *Climate Change 2014: Mitigation of Climate Change*, available at: www.ipcc.ch/report/ar5/wg3/ (accessed 28 May 2016).

Jevons, W. S. (1871), *The Theory of Political Economy*, London: Macmillan.

Laird, J. (1929), *The Idea of Value*, New York: A. M. Kelley.

Lipsey, R. G. (1971), *An Introduction to Positive Economics*, 3rd edn, London: Weidenfeld & Nicolson.

Mill, J. S. (1878), *Principles of Political Economy*, London: Longmans, Green, Reader and Dyer.

Nordhaus, W. D. (2013), *The Climate Casino: Risk, Uncertainty, and Economics for a Warming World*, New Haven, CT: Yale University Press.

O'Neill, J. (1992), "The varieties of intrinsic value", *The Monist*, vol. 99, no. 2, April: 119–37.

O'Neill, J. (1996), "Cost–benefit analysis, rationality and the plurality of values", *The Ecologist*, 26: 98–103.

Pareto, V. (2004), "General notion of economic equilibrium", in R. Marchionatti (ed.), *Early Mathematical Economics, 1871–1915*, vol. 4, London: Routledge.

Plato (1892), *Euthydemus*, in *The Dialogues of Plato*, trans. Benjamin Jowett, Oxford: Oxford University Press.

Pribram, K. (1983), *A History of Economic Reasoning*, Baltimore, MD: Johns Hopkins University Press,.

Robbins, L. (1935), *An Essay on the Nature and Significance of Economic Science*, London: Macmillan.

Robbins, L. (1970), *The Evolution of Modern Economic Theory and Other Papers on the History of Economic Thought*, London: Macmillan.

Robinson, J. (1962), *Economic Philosophy*, London: C. A. Watts.

Sagoff, M. (2004), *Price, Principle, and the Environment*, New York: Cambridge University Press.

Sagoff, M. (2011), "The poverty of economic analysis", in D. Schlosberg, J. Dryzek, and R. Norgaard (eds), *Oxford Handbook of Climate Change and Society*, Oxford: Oxford University Press, pp. 55–66.

Samuelson, A. (1976), *Economics*, 10th edn, New York: McGraw-Hill.

Smith, A. (1970 [1776]), *The Wealth of Nations*, Harmondsworth: Penguin.

Stern, N. (2014), "Ethics, equity and the economics of climate change, paper 1: science and philosophy", *Economics and Philosophy*, vol. 30, no. 3: 397–444.

Walsh, A. J. and Lynch, T. (2003), "The development of price formation theory and subjectivism about ultimate values", *Journal of Applied Philosophy*, vol. 20, no. 3: 263–78.

Weitzman, M. L. (2009), "On modeling and interpreting the economics of catastrophic climate change", *Review of Economics and Statistics*, vol. 91: 1–19.

White, M. V. (2002), "Doctoring Adam Smith: the fable of the diamonds and water paradox", *History of Political Economy*, vol. 34(4): 659–83.

Index

Page numbers in *italics* denote tables, those in **bold** denote figures.

adverse possession, doctrine of 147
Aggressive Carbon Tax 145–8, 157n9
agricultural systems 51
Ames, James Barr 144
Arctic sea-ice cover 1
Arneson, Richard 67, 187
Arrow's theorem, of social welfare function 210

Bad Samaritan Laws 143
Barry, Brian 109, 114–16
Beckerman, Wilfred 30, 43, 108, 111–13
beneficence, moral duties of 9–10, 15–16
benefit argument, for deferring cost 58, 59
benefit, sense of 143; pure benefits 145
Bentham, Jeremy 23
best use argument, for zero pure time discount rate 44–5
biomass 10
Black, Joseph 183
blame-worthiness, concept of 93, 96, 100n14
Boyer, Joseph 44
Brennan, Geoffrey 104
BRICS nations, GHGs emission by 169
Bromley, Daniel W. 108, 112, 116
Broome, John 1, 31, 42, 55, 59
Brundtland Report (1987) 103, 107
burden-sharing, to deal with climate change 12, 19; bargaining about the distribution of 19; problem of distribution between nations 19

Calderón, Felipe 172
Caney, Simon 66, 77, 141, 152–3
capital, forms of 107
capital markets 26–8
capital stock and technology 109, 116
carbon: atmospheric capacity to store 191; social cost of 22
carbon budget, distribution of 188–93
carbon dioxide (CO_2) emissions 54, 103; due to burning of fossil fuels 172; impact on global climatic system 183; as stock pollutant 192; top six emitters 169; *see also* greenhouse gas (GHGs) emissions
carbon emissions: Aggressive Carbon Tax 145–8; business-as-usual emissions 147; compensation for 192; distributional consequences of 191; income generated per unit of 192; "no waste" condition 191; rights of 184; *see also* greenhouse gas (GHGs) emissions
carbon price 19–20, 22
carbon sinks 154, 191, 194
carbon stocks 191
carbon tax 19, 25, 145, 192; Aggressive Carbon Tax 145–8; effects of 146; legitimacy of 148; market regulation 148; revenue from 20
carbon-free energy 10
Casal, Paula 107
causal responsibility, concept of 88, 94
causal subjectivism, of Marginalism 208
charitable gifts 144
classical utilitarianism, theory of 28–9; criticisms of 29; people's rights and 29
clean technology 53, 56; investments in 113
climate change 1; burden-sharing among nations 12, 19; coastal impacts of 145–6; consequences of 14, 122; cost-shifting exercise 173; economic analyses of *see* economic evaluations, of climate

climate change *continued*
change; economic models of future impacts of 124; ethics of economics on 178; external cost of 12; harm benefit asymmetry in 145–8; human rights violation due to 32; human-induced 122, 152, 162, 164, 168, 177–8; impacts on life and well-being 122; imposition of damages 173; injustice caused by 14–15; injustice in dealing with 14–15; intergenerational dimensions of 43; intergenerational distribution related to 65; and maldistribution of well-being 15–18; and need for borrowing 18–20; Pareto improvement strategy for dealing with 12–14; policies to reduce risk related to 70; standard economics of 74–5; sufficientarianism and the economics of 70–5
climate damage: compensation for future generations 25, 33; liability for 33; zero consumption discount rate for 33
climate disadvantage: characterising and measuring well-being 127–30; dimensions of 134; identification of 125; justice within and across generations 135–7; mapping of 125–7, 132, **133**; multi-dimensional measures of 125, 132–5; social deprivation and 130; technological innovations and 136; vulnerability due to 130–2
climate economics 22, 177; cost–benefit analyses 104, 117; discount rate in 104–5, 168; discounting and acceptance of substitutability 104–6; ethical issues within 163–4 (*see also* climate ethics); intergenerational distribution in 71; methods of 66; mitigation strategies of 168; and ultimate value 211–14
climate ethics 105, 162; Aristotle's virtue ethics 173; of compensation 174–6; cost–benefit analysis 174; of economics on climate change 178; ethical decision-making 175; in growth economy 172–4; human-induced climate change, implications of 168; intergenerational 163, 164–8; interregional 168–72; of mainstream economics 172; Paretian criteria of 175; "person-affecting" view of 68; risk and uncertainty 176–7
climate inequality 125
climate injustice, dimensions of 123–5
Climate Matters 1, 199
climate mitigation 25, 43, 53, 68, 103; intergenerational justice in 106–11, 114; non-substitutability of 107
climate policies 103; dangers of conflating price and value in 198–201; economic evaluation of 80
climate sceptics 22
climate sufficientarian 70, 72, 75–7, 80, 82n7
climate-altering actions, effects of 99
coal, as source of energy 183
coastal impacts, of climate change 145–6; displacement of human settlements and forced migration 146; food production, impact on 146
combustion economy 170
compensation, ethics of 174–6, 192
consumer sovereignty and democracy: Marglin's plea for 27; principle of 26
consumption discount rate (CDR) 23, 25; changes in consumption against 26; market interest rate 26; prescriptive–descriptive debate on 26–8
consumption discounting 23–4, 26, 29–30, 33, 100n2, 100n6
consumption, notion of 23
cost–benefit analysis (CBA), of climate change 16–17, 32, 141, 148, 150, 152, 174; in climate economics 104, 117, 213; discounted utility model for 24, 28; of emissions-abatement policies 70; importance of 22; opportunity costs 23; reasonable man standard 33; Stern's and Nordhaus's model of 17–18
Cripps, Elisabeth 66, 70, 119n13
cultural capital 107

deferring cost 42, 50, 54–5, 57; benefit argument 58; Broome's views on 59; objection to growth 59–60; polluter pays principle 59–60
diminishing marginal utility, idea of 28–9, 55–6, 149
discount rates: in China 166–7; in climate economics 104–5, 168; consequences for action on climate change 167; definition of 165; economic (consumption) growth, effect of 165–6; and intergenerational ethics *167*; negative 29, 168; social *see* social rate of time preference (SRTP); social risk-free rate for consumption 166; in Zaire 167; zero pure time *see* zero pure time discount rate

discounted utilitarianism, theory of 29–31; justification of 30
discounted utility model, of consumption 24
distributive justice, issues of 48, 67
droughts 6, 103, 122, 125–6, 128, 130–1, 134, 136–7, 192

ecological economics 29
economic efficiency, concept of 3, 152, 164, 177, 210
economic employment 203
economic evaluations, of climate change 43–4; aggregating harms and benefits 148–52; asymmetry between harm and benefits 143–8; benefit, senses of 143; cost–benefit analysis 148, 152; Enforced Benevolence Argument 143; harm, account of 142–3; human rights and lexical priority 152–5; models of future impacts 124; qualification 155–6; and qualified defense of aggregation 152–6
economic growth, Ramsey's model of 4, 23–6; pure rate of time preference and 24; welfare function 24
economic risk management 162
economic welfare, theory of 74, 150–1, 156n2, 165
'efficiency without sacrifice,' idea of 55
emissions-abatement policies, cost–benefit analyses of 70
energy consumption 179
energy efficiency 146
environmental damage 33, 109–10, 115, 176
environmental degradation 33, 111, 179
environmental economics 78, 81, 107, 163
environmental justice 125, 163, 173
ethical evaluation, idea of 200, 213
ethical objectivism, definition of 206, 208
ethical subjectivism, definition of 206–8, 216n34
ethics in economics: on climate change 178; importance of 162

fact–value dichotomy 162, 166
Feinberg, Joel 142–4, 150–1
financial capital 107
Flew, Antony 198
flood disaster 23, 122; social displacement from 129
food production 79, 146
fossil fuels 56, 145, 151, 169–70, 188, 191; carbon dioxide emissions due to burning of 172; fossil fuel-driven economy 172
Fried, Barbara 150, 158n15
Friedman, Milton 148
Fund for Greenhouse Victims 25–6
future generation's consumption **17**; deontological and utilitarian approach 33; reasonable man standard 33; rightful claims of 27; rights and duties 32–3; zero consumption discount rate 33

Garnaut Review, The 43
global mean temperatures: increase in 1, 54; projections for 51
global warming 26, 188; due to greenhouse gas emissions 9, 187
God's scale of natural perfection 204
gratuitous benefit 143–5, 148–9
green investments, for reducing emissions 14, 19
greenhouse effect 169, 176, 190
greenhouse gas (GHGs) emissions 7, 9, 28, 54, 122, 141, 151, 154; appealing to self-interest 12–14; by BRICS nations 169; budget per capita 170; contribution to global warming 9; control costs of 48, 164; effects of 11; environmental damages under 176; external cost of 12; government morality and its limitations 11–12; historical accumulation of 169; income generated per unit of 192; justifiable rights to 193–4; justification of 187–92; Kyoto Protocol (1992) 183; Lockean approach to rights of 184–5; mitigation measures 168; Nozick's proviso on 191–2; on-going and irreversible damages caused by 170; permissible share of 170; plans for reducing 11; pollution problems due to 163; private morality and its limitations 9–10; regulations and taxation to control 11; Resource Egalitarian Proviso 188–91; responsibility for control of 168–9; sustainable emission rights 192–4
Griffin, James 153–4
growth discounting 41; concept of 48–50; deferring cost version of 50, 54–5; definition of 48; delaying action version of 50–2; idea of 49; implications of 50; proponents of 49; three arguments for 55–8
growth economy: climate ethics in 172–4; consequences of 172; link with poverty alleviation 173; trickle-down effect 172

halo effect 97
harm preventions 143; benefit asymmetry, in climate change 145–8; liberty limiting principle 151; moral significance of 144
Hayek, F. A. 148
health issues, pollution-related 147
heatwaves 122, 125–35, 137
Hepburn, Cameron 29–30, 43
Hobbes, Thomas 207
Holland, Alan 105
human capital 105, 107; importance of 115; substitutability of natural capital with 106
human rights: and lexical priority 152–5; threats to 152, 154; violation of 32, 92, 152
Hume, David 23, 30, 162
Humean cause–effect relationships 176
hurricanes 145–6, 150, 155–6

income taxes 20, 48
increments, social weightings of 211
industrial revolution 147
Integrated Assessment Models (IAMs) 25, 27, 51, 163, 174
intergenerational egalitarianism 59, 67
intergenerational equity, principle of 41–2, 47
intergenerational ethics: economic discount rates and *167*; notion of 163, 164–8
intergenerational justice 114, 116; components of 42–3; for maintenance of capital 109; principles of 53, 59; in protection of natural capital 106–11
intergenerational prioritarianism 4, 56, 59
intergenerational sufficientarianism 56–7, 59; appeal of 66–70; choosing the SDR on the basis of 76–8; in climate ethics 67; consumption-equivalent value 75; economic argument for equality 71–2; and economics of climate change 70–5; idea of 66; interpretation of 72–4; and intertemporal discounting 76–80; leveling-down objection 67; needs principle 82n7; priority view, problems related to 72–3; Ramsey's formula and its parameters 76; Repugnant Conclusion 68–9; standard economics of climate change, challenges to 74–5; strengths of 65; threshold, notion of 73
Intergovernmental Panel on Climate Change (IPCC) 10, 51, 79, 99, 117, 166, 200, 213; assessment of the science of climate change 22; "Climate Change 2014: Mitigation of Climate Change" Report 212; climate policy recommendations 103; *Fifth Assessment Report* of 53–4; report of Working Group III on mitigation (2014) 165; Working Group III 166
International Monetary Fund (IMF) 20
interregional ethics: human-induced climate change, implications of 168; notion of 168–72
isolation paradox 27

Jevons, W. S. 45
job creation 147
justice, moral duties of 9–10

knowledge capital 107
Kyoto Protocol (1992) 183

labour theory of value 203, 205
land rights, appropriation of 184
land tenure security 194
lay-offs 146–7
leveling-down objection 67
life-expectancy of people 114
Lind, Robert C. 26, 117
Lipsey, Richard 205
Locke, John 6–7, 147, 184–7, 191, 193

maldistribution, of well-being 4, 14, 15–18
man-made capital 5, 104, 108–9, 135
marginal rate of return on alternative investments (MRRI) 23, 25; discount climate damage against 25
marginal utility, of consumption 28–9
Marginalist Revolution (1871) 204–5, 207–8
Mazor, Joseph 109
Mendelsohn, Robert 53–4; opportunity cost argument, for delaying action 54
methane hydrates 54
Millenium Ecosystem Assessment 79
Moral Equality Argument 44, 46
moral equality argument, for zero pure time discount rate 44
moral responsibility, concept of 93–4, 100n12
moral thinking 1, 95

Nargis (Hurricane) 155
natural capital 106–7; features of 107; forms of 107; intergenerational justice

in protection of 106–11; non-substitutability of 107; substitutability of 104
natural resources, depletion of 29
negative discount rates 29, 168
Neumayer, Eric 105–6, 108, 114; Barry and Sen, criticism of 115; harm, concept of 115; Stern Review, criticism of 106; sustainability, definition of 116
New Palgrave Dictionary of Economics 210
non-identity, problem of 43, 68, 81n6, 119n13
Nordhaus, William 1, 16, 22, 26, 44, 48, 50, 165; dynamic optimisation economic growth model 105–6
Nordhaus's curve 17
Nozick, Robert 147, 184, 186; proviso on greenhouse gas emissions 191–2
Nussbaum, Martha 66, 130

opportunity cost discounting 4, 23, 41–2, 52–4, 60; opportunity–cost argument 54; reasons for caution 53

PAGE model 25, 175
Paradox of Value 200, 203, 209, 214; price and ultimate value 203–6; of price-independent values 215; role for ultimate value 206–8
Pareto efficiency, analysis of 172, 177, 212
Pareto improvements 12–14, 17–20, 164; implementation of 19
Parfit, Derek 31–2, 45–6
Paris Agreement 169–70
pay cuts 146–7
permafrost 54
"person-affecting" view of ethics 68
Pigou, A. C. 29, 45
polluter pays principle 59–60, 151
praiseworthiness, concept of 88, 93, 97
prescriptive–descriptive debate, on CDR 26–8
price and ultimate value: concept of 203–6; "identity" theory of 207
priority, notion of 73
private property rights 183–6, 193
probability discounting, in decision-making 100n2; additions and extensions of 98–9; Caney's objections to 88–92; casual responsibility and 94; climate-altering actions, effects of 99; conditions for 87; cost–benefit analyses of 87–9, 92; donation (low/high risk) 96–7; for evaluations of climate change 88; high risk subjective probability 94; low risk subjective probability 94; moral responsibility and 93–4; narrow-scope and wide-scope norms 101n14; positive argument for 92–8; and probability of rights-violations 89
probability weighting *see* probability discounting, in decision-making
property rights: allocation of 183; appropriation of 185–7; emergence of 183; entitlement theory of 185; to forest land 193; interpretation of 184; left-libertarian 184; Lockean theory of 184, 185–7; rectification of 187; right-libertarian 184; self-ownership of 185; transfer of 187
pure time discounting, concept of 41, 43–4, 47
pure time preference, concept of 34, 42–3, 76, 165, 199

quality-of-life, enhancement of 153

Ramsey, F. P. 28, 76, 106; choice of the SDR, formula for 76; discounting, formula for 106; model of economic growth 4, 23–6; optimal savings model 76; Ramsey equation 28, 35n4, 76–7, 137n2
Rawls's difference principle and sufficientarianism 31–2
Raz, Joseph 66
real capital 107
reasonable man standard 33
'recording machine' theory of government 27
Rendall, Matthew 50, 55
renewable sources of energy 10, 114, 145–6
Repugnant Conclusion 68–9, 81n5
resource distribution: decision-making 164; efficiency in 166; equity of 164; intergenerational 74
Resource Egalitarian Proviso 188–91, 194
resource egalitarianism: concept of 188; limits of 189; welfaristic criterion of 189
responsibility, principle of 59
risk management 112, 162–3, 177, 179
Robbins, Lionel 206
Robinson, Joan 206

Sagoff, Mark 202, 215n14, 216n14
same sex relationships 151
Sandy (Super Storm) 155
Scanlon, Thomas 150
sea-level, rise in 51, 145–6

Second Restatement of Torts (US common law) 33
self-ownership of property 185
Sen, Amartya 27, 66, 71–2, 114–15, 125, 127, 130
Shue, Henry 82n11
Sidgwick, Henry 28
Singer, Peter 29
Smith, Adam 200, 203–4
smog 12
social affiliation 136
social capital (social contacts) 107
social discount rate (SDR) *see* social rate of time preference (SRTP)
social networks 125, 127, 130–1
social rate of time preference (SRTP) 2, 34n2, 41, 70–1; on basis of sufficientarianism 76–8; choice of 76; dual-eta model of 78–80; dual-rate discounting model of 79–80; for public policy projects 165; Ramsey's formula and its parameters 76
social safety nets 146
social vulnerabilities 134
social weightings, of increments 211
social welfare function (SWF) 165, 210, 212
social welfare, idea of 209
solar power 113
Solow, Robert 107
squatters' rights 147
standard of living 2, 45–6, 48, 56–7, 60, 109, 118n5, 175
Stern, Nicholas 1, 16, 22, 26, 43, 81n1, 163, 165, 172, 174, 199–200, 209, 211–13
Stern Review (2006) 43, 49, 83n13, 105–6, 151, 177; Neumayer's criticism of 106
Stern's curve 17
suffering harm, notion of 142
sustainability of ecosystem: arguments about 114–16; climate change, risk of 103; definition of 103, 108, 116; laissez-faire policies on 113; normative 104, 111–13; strong 111–13; tenets of 108; weak 111–13
sustainable discounted utilitarianism 35n8

technological innovations 52, 113, 136, 148
Thomson, Judith 9

ultimate ethical values 203; contemporary climate economics and 211–14; distinction between price and 203; in economic analysis 208–11; formulation of 207; judgements of 206; neutrality of 206; Pareto efficiency, analysis of 212; price-independent scale 208; role for 206–8; social weightings of increments in 211; theory of 202
UN sustainable development agenda 173
United Nations Framework Convention on Climate Change (UNFCCC) 11–12, 169, 183; Conference of the Parties (COP) Paris Agreement 169
use-values 204–5
utilitarianism: discounted 29–31; problems of 68; sustainable discounted 35n8
utility: discounting 100n2; maximisation 164

value, labour theory of 203, 205

Warming the World 44
Water–Diamond Paradox *see* Paradox of Value
Watt, James 183
wealth, international redistribution of 29
Weitzman, Martin 26, 105, 166, 199–200
welfare economics 202, 209, 211; Arrow's theorem 210; concept of 210; development of 28; efficient production and consumption, principles of 195; framework of standard 4, 34; integrated assessment models 174; market prices and 117; normative assumptions within 210; Pareto improvements 171, 195; three basic tents of 210; on 'welfare' of society 217n36
well-being: average generation 74; discounting future 76; economic valuation of 73; equality of 16; global maldistribution of 14, 15–18; gratuitous benefit and 143; intergenerational 70; interpersonal comparisons of 28; notion of 202; social value of 72–3; social vulnerabilities and losses in 134; subjective 128
Wolf, Clark 82n7, 131, 193
World Bank 20, 170; development indicators 168
World Climate Bank 4, 20, 21n1
wrongful harm: concept of 142–3; difference with suffering harm 142; goal of reducing 142; nature of 142

zero pure time discount rate 43, 47–8, 61n8, 77; arguments for 44–6, 53; objections to 46–8

For Product Safety Concerns and Information please contact our EU representative GPSR@taylorandfrancis.com
Taylor & Francis Verlag GmbH, Kaufingerstraße 24, 80331 München, Germany

www.ingramcontent.com/pod-product-compliance
Ingram Content Group UK Ltd.
Pitfield, Milton Keynes, MK11 3LW, UK
UKHW021614240425
457818UK00018B/548

* 9 7 8 0 3 6 7 0 2 6 8 3 7 *